Praise for *Introduction to the Study of Religion*

'Students and teachers of religion in colleges and universities have needed a book like this for a long time – and never more urgently than today when religious discourses are growing in influence on a global scale and when a cultural ethos of politically correct toleration and a hardening religious insistence on religious rights and correctness work together to protect religion and the religions from hard-headed analysis and criticism in the public sphere. This protectionism also plagues the scholarly study of religion, where it is compounded with a historic tendency of religion scholars and teachers to play a caretaker role when it comes to religion.

One of the dearest prices paid for this tendency is a predilection for curricula and pedagogical practices that not only permit but encourage an *idiot savant* mode of approaching religion by relegating theoretical and conceptual thought on religion to a mere option or by introducing students to theories of and analytic approaches to religion as a final exit or capstone requirement. The great virtue of this book is that it refuses to agree to all this.

Without much ado the authors assume that students are members of the academy from day one and that from day one the study of religion is an exercise in thought for which an earlier rather than later or optional introduction to the intellectual lineages and theoretical discourses on religion is indispensable.

Accessibly, clearly, firmly, and kindly written, this book reliably introduces students to the history of the study of religion, focusing on its most defining approaches and controversies and highlighting the difference between "insider" knowledge of religion(s) and "outsider" study of religion. A substantial chapter that surveys the recent spate of popular books by detractors of religion and supporters of religion adds to the book's timeliness and clarity of argument. This book is a fine introduction to the study of religion that manages at the same time to be an important intervention in how that study is widely practiced.'

Willi Braun, *Director of the Interdisciplinary Program of Religious Studies, University of Alberta, Canada*

'Rodrigues and Harding give an overview of the study of religion that is at once inclusive and accessible. This book will help orient undergraduates to the field of Religious Studies, and will be a handy reference for graduate students and scholars of religion.'

E. Ann Matter, *University of Pennsylvania, USA*

'What exactly is "religious studies"? What is its relationship to theology? What about those pesky "new atheists"? Rodrigues and Harding provide a critical overview of various approaches to the study of religion, past and present, that is as insightful as it is accessible. This still largely undefined field would benefit greatly from its wide adoption in its undergraduate (and graduate) courses of study.'

Luther H. Martin, *Professor of Religion,. The University of Vermont, USA*

Introduction to the Study of Religion

Why do people study religion? How have they studied it in the past? How do we study religion today? Is the academic study of religion the same as religious education? These and many other questions are addressed in this engaging introduction to the discipline of religious studies, written by two experienced university teachers. The authors have crafted this book to familiarize novice students with key concepts and terminology in the study of religion. More advanced students will find a varied array of theoretical perspectives and methodological approaches to the field. Topics include:

- Definitions of religion
- Perspectives in the study and teaching of religion
- How religion began to be studied: traditional perspectives – philosophical and theological
- How people experience religion: perspectives in the study of religious consciousness and perception – phenomenological and psychological
- Studying religion within communities: social and cultural perspectives – anthropological, sociological, political and economic
- Judging religion: critical perspectives – feminist approaches, the interaction of popular literature and religion
- Contextual perspectives – historical and comparative

The book encourages students to think critically about the theories and methods presented. Students will find arguments for the strengths and limitations of these approaches, understand connections among religious studies and other intellectual movements, and develop their own ideas of how they might want to go about the study of religion. Summary boxes, a timeline, a glossary and other pedagogic aids help students grasp key concepts.

Hillary Rodrigues is chair of the Religious Studies department at the University of Lethbridge, and recipient of that institution's Distinguished Teaching Award (2000). He is a former chair of the Department of Anthropology.

John S. Harding is a member of the Religious Studies Department at the University of Lethbridge, Canada.

Introduction to the Study of Religion

Hillary Rodrigues and John S. Harding

Routledge
Taylor & Francis Group

LONDON AND NEW YORK

First published 2009 by Routledge
2 Park Square, Milton Park, Abingdon, Oxon, OX14 4RN

Simultaneously published in the USA and Canada
by Routledge
270 Madison Ave., New York, NY 100016

Routledge is an imprint of the Taylor & Francis Group, an informa business

Typeset in New Baskerville and Kabel by
Swales & Willis Ltd, Exeter, Devon
Printed and bound in Great Britain by
TJ International Ltd, Padstow, Cornwall

British Library Cataloguing in Publication Data
A catalogue record for this book is available from the British Library

Library of Congress Cataloging in Publication Data
Rodrigues, Hillary, 1953–
Introduction to the study of religion/Hillary Rodrigues and John S. Harding.
p. cm.
Includes index.
1. Religion.   I. Harding, John S., 1971–   II. Title.
BL48.R4725 2008
200.71—dc22
2008006986

ISBN10 0–415–40888–1 (hbk)
ISBN10 0–415–40889–X (pbk)
ISBN10 0–203–89172–4 (ebk)

ISBN13 978–0–415–40888–2 (hbk)
ISBN13 978–0–415–40889–9 (pbk)
ISBN13 978–0–203–89172–8 (ebk)

Dedicated to students of religious studies

Contents

x *Contents*

Preface

This book is an introductory guide to the study of religion. It is written from the perspective of the discipline of religious studies, and so is well suited for those engaged in first and second year courses on religious traditions at the post-secondary level, as well as those in upper level courses on theory and method in the discipline. In our experience, those who embark on the academic study of religion in senior high school or in their first years at college or university typically enroll in a course on World Religions or some specific major religious tradition, such as Christianity or Buddhism. More often than not, such courses deal primarily with the crucial essentials of those religions (e.g. their histories, doctrines, and practices), and students are left with little direction about the nature of religious studies itself. An often overlooked introductory chapter in a World Religions textbook or at most a couple of lectures on the religious studies approach are frequently the only teachings about the discipline provided in those early years. As a result, students are expected to pick up on the perspectives, methods, and terminology used in the academic study of religion through their teachers and textbooks, who and which are expected to exemplify these approaches. Unfortunately, in our experience, reality falls far short of expectations. Most students tend to focus on the content of the religions they are learning about, relegating disciplinary orientations to the margins, with detrimental effects on their understanding, performance, and progress. Such limitations can persist indefinitely, until students embark on their first formal course on theory and method in religious studies, which may often be at the late years of an undergraduate program, if ever.

This book is written to help rectify those shortcomings. It is designed to provide readers with a succinct and accessible inroad to the scholarly study of religion. It could serve as a handy and constant reference for religious studies students throughout their university years. Together with a source book of primary readings, it could serve as a text for an introductory course on concepts and methods in the study of religion. Alternately, it may be used in tandem with any introductory tradition-centered religious studies course texts, complementing the content-driven structure of such courses with pertinent information on the discipline of religious studies itself. Students might thus leave those courses armed with a functional toolbox for further studies on their own, while those who continue to upper level formal studies would have a solid foundational knowledge about the major thinkers, seminal writings, theoretical perspectives, and methodological approaches (and the jargon that accompanies these discussions), which have given shape to the discipline of religious studies.

Because it draws on a wide array of methods, many of which are characteristic of such disciplines in the humanities and social sciences as philosophy or anthropology, its interdisciplinary nature leads some scholars to refer to religious studies as a field of study, rather than a discipline. However, in this book the term "discipline" is used simply in one of its traditional meanings, as a branch of learning and knowledge.

Acknowledgments

We would like to express our appreciation for the contributions by students and colleagues at the University of Lethbridge who have participated in courses on theory and method in the study of religion, have asked for an introductory text to address an undergraduate audience, have reviewed our efforts to meet this demand, and have made useful suggestions along the way. In particular, we appreciate the insights of Tom Robinson and Jim Linville, with whom we have team-taught courses on methodology, and the careful reading and suggestions of some of our students majoring in religious studies, including Matthew Salmon, Erika Jahn, Nicole Hembroff, and Jason Stoltenberg. We owe a debt of thanks to various anonymous reviewers, who read an assortment of portions and drafts of the manuscript. Their encouragement and discerning comments have helped to improve this work markedly.

The development of religious studies, and our understanding of it, have benefited from seminal figures and schools of thought. We especially wish to thank faculty members with whom we did our graduate studies at McMaster University and the University of Pennsylvania. Although our PhD supervisors taught in different countries, each had studied under Eliade and his colleagues at the University of Chicago. However, as graduate students we were also mentored in theory and method by scholars from Harvard, Princeton, Yale, Münster, Columbia, Berkeley, and other institutions that have played key roles in shaping the discipline. We have had the good fortune of intellectually stimulating interactions with various figures, now deceased, whom we discuss in this text, including Clifford Geertz, Ninian Smart, and David Bohm. We want to acknowledge explicitly the aforementioned rich source of influences, and express our appreciation for the wide range of contributions these figures and schools have made to the discipline. We have tried to present accurately the diverse movements they represent, and modestly advance the legacy of earlier figures and schools without attempting to hold too closely to any one in particular.

This book might never have been written were it not for Lesley Riddle, the acquisitions editor, who immediately recognized the lacuna it would fill and offered enthusiastic support for our vision of the project. We extend our thanks to her and the production staff at Routledge, including Gemma Dunn and Amy Grant, as well as the editing guidance of Katy Carter and project manager Richard Willis.

It is our intention that this project will be ongoing in the form of a reader (forthcoming), and a website, www.sastor.com (Scholarly Approaches to the Study and Teaching of Religion). While we bear responsibility for the errors, omissions, or shortcomings of this introductory text, we plan to add further depth, breadth, and resources. We would like to thank, in advance, students and scholars who suggest improvements to this work and content, links, analysis, exercises, and applications to advance the study and teaching of religion through the sastor.com site.

1

Introduction

Defining religion

Religious studies scholars might certainly be delighted to have a definition of religion that everyone could agree on, but no such definition has yet emerged. Among the reasons for this lack of agreement is the tendency for people to define religion too narrowly, often from the perspective of their own backgrounds and culture. Imagine, for instance, persons raised in predominantly Christian or Muslim cultures, who would certainly note clear signs of religious beliefs and activities around them. If they belonged to those religions themselves, they would, of course, be active participants in the features of those traditions. But even as religious "outsiders" living within those societies influenced by the religious culture of Christianity or Islam, they would probably observe communal gatherings for preaching or prayer, the presence of religious edifices such as churches or mosques, the periodic celebration of festivals and rituals such as Christmas or Ramadan, and the presence of religious specialists such as priests, ministers, or imams. Thus, if asked, they would certainly agree that there was such a thing as "religion," and that it played a vital role in the lives of many of the people around them. However, when pressed to define just what religion is and what it entails, they would very likely provide explanations based on what they themselves believed or what they saw around them. So they might end up defining religion as requiring a belief in the one true god, in sin, in an afterlife, and so on. They might designate anything outside their own cultural tradition's notions of religion as not religion at all, but misguided beliefs and superstitious practices, or apply other such negative labels. Alternately, if attempting to be more inclusive, they might nevertheless define religion as a series of obligatory practices (such as praying regularly), with particular prohibitions (such as not eating certain foods, or refraining from certain acts such as murder or adultery), with particular beliefs (such as in a single high god, divinely revealed teachings, and in the concepts of judgment and punishment), and so on.

Although such descriptive definitions do encompass much of what is generally regarded as religion in many societies and cultures, they are still too narrow. For instance, they exclude aspects found in certain world religions that question the value of obligatory beliefs and practices entirely. So, while some religions promote an unquestioning faith in a particular set of teachings, in other traditions a healthy skepticism regarding religion is regarded as a vital element of being truly religious. This, for instance, is a crucial feature of Buddhist teachings, even though most Buddhists in actuality do adhere to an array of beliefs and practices. Indeed, not only among various religions, but even within the same tradition, one person's most deeply held religious convictions may be regarded by another as the height of delusion. Thus it has been challenging for scholars to agree on a definition that is sufficiently encompassing of humanity's wide variety of religious orientations.

The Christian theologian Paul Tillich (1886–1965) offered a broad definition of faith (or religion) as "being grasped by an ultimate concern." While to a Christian this ultimate concern might center on issues such as redemption, salvation, and being close to God for eternity, for a Buddhist it might be the state of freedom from all illusions through the attainment of *nirvana*. The notion of "being grasped" conveys the sense of some greater force or power that takes hold of persons, providing them with a perspective on what they deem to be most valuable and meaningful in existence. It is that collection of thoughts, beliefs, and values, which most shapes the character of their lives, upon which they base their most important decisions, and for which they may even be willing to give up their lives. This, then, would seem to be an effectively broad definition of religion, but it too is not without its problems; most notably for some scholars is the fact that it is too broad. It certainly circumscribes a Muslim's concern with Allah and his message conveyed through Muhammad, or a Hindu's concern with the attainment of *moksha*, a liberation from the cycles of rebirth, both of which most people would agree are clearly religious concerns. However, it would also define a woman's preoccupation with the attainment of wealth or power, if it was her central value, as her religion, or man's concern with personal beauty or the well-being of his children, were these his greatest preoccupations, as his religion. And it would include under the rubric of religion such things as political ideologies, sports, or artistic practices to which certain people find themselves thoroughly committed, and even willing to kill or die for. Although we might speak of a person "following Marxism with religious zeal," or say "money is his religion," we do tend to make distinctions between religion and, say, politics or art, which might elicit similar behaviors but strike many of us as somehow different.

The challenge in finding a suitable definition thus also lies in pinpointing just what constitutes that difference. However, if one looks at the entire question of definition anew, one notes that it is not really a concern for the average person, but is a concern for those of us who are engaged in the study of religion. On any given day, an individual may wake up, wash, adorn himself or herself, go to the temple, read from a religious scripture, sing a hymn, then go to work and try to earn money, avoid eating meat at lunch, play a game of football after work, attend a political rally, read a chapter of a detective novel, play electric guitar, say a prayer and go to bed. He or she is unlikely to be concerned with categorizing certain of these activities as religious, political, sportive, artistic, materialistic, and so on. Distinguishing between what is religious and what is not in those activities is more challenging than it might first appear. Even though one might be inclined to categorize this person's temple visit, hymn singing, or prayers as religious activities, the person's interior attitude during those activities may not have been grounded in a deeply felt "religious sentiment." They may have been acting out of habit, behaving in conformity with social expectations, and so on, while their real religious passion lay in the overlooked, seemingly non-religious acts, such as in personal hygiene, physical fitness, political activism, or musical composition. After all, the study of religion is not merely about what outwardly looks like or is simply designated as religion; it also attempts to explore the full terrain of what constitutes the religious impulse and character in human beings. A Christian may be acting out of far deeper rooted Christian sentiments when volunteering in a soup-kitchen than when attending a Sunday church service.

A defining feature of many religions, which separates them from other deeply absorbing and meaningful activities, is their concern with powers or agents that are regarded as mostly existing beyond the grasp of the five senses or instrumental apparatus. These spirits, gods, or energies are thus "super-natural," in that they transcend or are beyond the natural world. They are not merely unseen physical energies, such as certain frequencies of light or electro-magnetism, as studied by physicists. The religious individual conceives of reality as somehow larger than what is normally perceived or conventionally studied by the sciences. Furthermore, aspects of this larger-than-ordinary reality are often regarded as somehow set apart. Their special character is held to be sacred or holy, and thus to be approached or related to in appropriate ways that are generally differentiated from actions and attitudes appropriate for the non-sacred portions of reality. There are wide variations among people as to just what reality truly contains. For some it is populated with gods, angels, and demons. For others, these entities are precisely examples of the illusions that cloud one's perception of true reality. Equally varied are the features that groups regard as sacred or non-sacred (i.e. profane). An orthodox Jew or Muslim may consider it abhorrent to eat pork, while a Christian may enjoy eating a roast sucking pig on a religious holiday such as Christmas. Similarly, a particular piece of land may be regarded by certain believers as utterly sacred, a spot upon which a god was born or where a prophet received a visionary teaching. It is worth killing or dying for. To non-believers, it is just a piece of undesirable real estate.

However, the complexity inherent in defining religion adequately and satis-factorily is not ultimately a problem, even for scholars. It is common to most branches of learning. We routinely use words for a wide assortment of notions quite effectively without having to define them. The concept of "religion" is not particularly different in this regard. How does one define music or art? What exactly is the boundary between nuclear chemistry and nuclear physics, anthropology and sociology, history and literature, geography and environmental science, or quantum physics and mathematics? Confronting the challenge to find a suitable definition is just one of the venues through which one may actually learn more about one's object of study and one's own frame of reference. To ponder the question "What is religion?" is to have already embarked upon its study.

Assorted definitions of religion

Ambrose Bierce in *The Devil's Dictionary*: "Religion: a daughter of Hope and Fear, explaining to Ignorance the nature of the Unknowable."

Edie Brickell: "Religion is a smile on a dog."

Clifford Geertz: "Religion is (1) a system of symbols which acts to (2) establish powerful, pervasive, and long-lasting moods and motivations in men by (3) formulating conceptions of a general order of existence and (4) clothing these conceptions with such an aura of factuality that (5) the moods and motivations seem uniquely realistic."

William James: "Religion . . . shall mean for us the feelings, acts, and experiences of individual men in their solitude, so far as they apprehend themselves to stand in relation to whatever they may consider the divine. Since the relation may be either moral, physical, or ritual, it is evident that out of religion in the sense in which we take it, theologies, philosophies, and ecclesiastical organizations may secondarily grow."

The Oxford English Dictionary (1971): "Religion: 1) Action or conduct indicating a belief in, reverence for, and desire to please a divine ruling power; the exercise or practice of rites or observances implying this. 2) A particular system of faith and worship. 3) Recognition on the part of man of some higher unseen power as having control of his destiny, and as being entitled to obedience, reverence, and worship; the general mental and moral attitude resulting from this belief, with reference to its effect upon the individual or the community; personal or general acceptance of this feeling as a standard of spiritual and practical life. 4) Devotion to some principle; a strict fidelity or faithfulness; conscientiousness; pious affection or attachment."

Paul Tillich: "Religion is the state of being grasped by an ultimate concern, a concern which qualifies all other concerns as preliminary and which itself contains the answer to the question of the meaning of our life."

Adequate definitions of religion?

The HarperCollins Dictionary of Religion, edited by Jonathan Z. Smith (1995), addresses the lack of agreement on an adequate definition of religion and attempts to provide such a definition after discussing shortcomings of various inadequate definitions (pp. 893–4):

An Adequate Definition: One may clarify the term religion by defining it as a system of beliefs and practices that are relative to superhuman beings. This definition moves away from defining religion as some special kind of experience or worldview. It emphasizes that religions are systems or structures consisting of specific kinds of beliefs and practices: beliefs and practices that are related to superhuman beings. Superhuman being are beings who can do things ordinary mortals cannot do. They are known for their miraculous deeds and powers that set them apart from humans. They can be either male or female, or androgynous. They need not be gods or goddesses, but may take on the form of an ancestor who can affect lives. They may take the form of benevolent or malevolent spirits who cause good or harm to a person or community. Furthermore, the definition requires that such superhuman beings be specifically related to beliefs and practices, myths and rituals.

Defining religion as a system of beliefs and practices relative to superhuman beings excludes Nazism, Marxism, or secularism as religions. This definition also excludes varieties of nationalism and civil quasi-religious movements.

Other attempts

From *The Encyclopedia of Religion* (Winston King's entry "Religion" in the first edition):

In summary, it may be said that almost every known culture involves the religious in the above sense of a depth dimension in cultural experiences at all levels—a push, whether ill-defined or conscious, toward some sort of ultimacy and transcendence that will provide norms and power for the rest of life. When more or less distinct patterns of behaviour are built around this depth dimension in a culture, this structure constitutes religion in its historically recognizable form. Religion is the organization of life around the depth dimensions of experience— varied in form, completeness, and clarity in accordance with the environing culture.

From the *Columbia Encyclopedia*:

> Religion: a system of thought, feeling, and action that is shared by a group and that gives the members an object of devotion; a code of behavior by which individuals may judge the personal and social consequences of their actions; and a frame of reference by which individuals may relate to their group and their universe. Usually, religion concerns itself with that which transcends the known, the natural, or the expected; it is an acknowledgment of the extraordinary, the mysterious, and the supernatural. The religious consciousness generally recognizes a transcendent, sacred order and elaborates a technique to deal with the inexplicable or unpredictable elements of human experience in the world or beyond it.

Religious education and religious studies

People are motivated to teach about or to study religion for various reasons. However, there is a significant difference between the approaches taken by the discipline of religious studies and what may be broadly termed religious education. To some extent the difference hinges on distinctions between subjective and objective approaches to the study of religion.

Religious education can take a variety of forms. It generally derives from within a particular religious tradition for the purpose of teaching adherents of that tradition more about it. It is a mostly subjective experience. So a young Muslim boy may attend a school or classes where he learns to recite the Islamic sacred scripture, the Qur'an, and learn about Islamic moral values. Similarly, a Jewish boy may attend classes to learn how to read from the Torah before his Bar Mitzvah, a rite which grants him special privileges within his religious community. Certain Hindu boys may learn to chant the Vedas in a traditional school specializing in these ancient religious techniques, and in Thailand a young man may spend several months living the life of a novice Buddhist monk. In all these examples, instruction in the religion is often provided by an adherent of or specialist in that religion, such as a Muslim imam, a Jewish rabbi, a Hindu guru, or a Buddhist *bhikkhu*. Apart from dealing with the questions that derive from the curiosity, intrinsic skepticism, or doubt of the student, the teachers' task is to impart their religious tradition to their students in order to inculcate them more deeply into their own faith. It is education by believers for believers, with the purpose of solidifying in both teacher and student a foundation of understanding about their own religion.

Since belonging to a religious tradition has both inclusive and exclusive features, in that it provides a sense of allegiance to a particular group but also differentiates members of that group from others, religious education works to develop both of those aspects. Thus religious education always orients itself in some measure against other traditions. When a Jain is educated by Jains about Jainism, he or she is also learning how he or she is different from non-Jains. Even if one takes up the study of the major religions of the world, say, for instance, within a Catholic school, the rationale for such study is rarely to convey the teachings of those other traditions with a value-free orientation. This would undermine the intrinsic conviction of the institution that its own religious tradition is the most desirable of the lot. Of course, such courses or teachings may serve the purpose of informing the student about shared or similar values in other traditions, may help to nurture tolerance of the beliefs and practices of others, and may enable processes of interfaith dialogue so that people from differing religious traditions may connect meaningfully with each other. However, less sympathetic reasons for such teachings or studies might be to offer tacit critiques of other religions, to enable students to better defend their own faith in discussions with non-believers, or to help them to work as effective missionaries for their own religious message.

In contrast, students in the discipline of religious studies strive to examine all aspects of religion (or religions) with a value-free orientation. The discipline aims towards objectivity. It is the responsibility of religious studies scholars to try to position themselves outside all religious traditions and then examine each with a healthy measure of neutrality. However, in the last few decades we have been made amply aware that complete neutrality or objectivity is only an ideal, which is difficult, if not impossible, to achieve perfectly. We are each grounded in our own cultural, religious, or philosophical backgrounds and study the world from those situated perspectives. We are male or female, young or old, with experiences that shape and color the lenses through which we view the world. Nevertheless, religious studies scholars attempt to maintain a high level of awareness and a critical, self-reflexive stance in order to discern how those factors, some of which are constant (e.g. gender) and others shifting (e.g. experience), affect their investigations.

Beyond the realization that absolute neutrality or objectivity is nearly impossible to achieve is the recognition that such an orientation may not be completely beneficial for the most fulfilling understanding of the human religious experience. The experience of religion can be a profoundly emotional constellation of feelings for participants, spanning such sentiments as guilt, euphoria, love, or obedience. The worldviews in some religions include beliefs in angels, devils, genies, dangerous spirits, gods, goddesses, animal protectors, ancestral ghosts, and so on. There may be beliefs in realms such as heavens, hells, parallel world systems, underworlds, and so on, which are not necessarily part of the reality construct of the student. Although some might argue that attempts to enter into those realities are futile, it is crucial that religious studies scholars strive to pierce those realities, even if these are only regarded as realms of the imagination. Can it be done? Of course it can. Anyone who has listened to a story, read a novel, watched a play, or seen a movie has temporarily suspended certain levels of disbelief and entered into the world conjured up by the narrative before them. This is particularly true for works of fiction. It is imperative for religious studies students to try to understand as much as possible about the worldview of the religion they are studying and to enter into it through a temporary suspension of disbelief in order to resonate with the experience of some of the sentiments felt by adherents of that religion.

Some would argue that such an entry into the subjective dimensions of religion is undesirable, for it might color one's judgment, destroy one's own faith, and so on. While there are some valid cautions in such arguments, they are generally exaggerated. It is unlikely that someone entering the world of such fictive works as *The Lord of the Rings* or the Harry Potter novels would actually abide permanently in those imaginary worlds populated by sorcerers, elves, dragons, and so on. The German philosopher Goethe, promoting the value of learning other languages, commented that a person who knows only one language actually knows none. Indeed, in the same vein, the study of other religions may well enhance someone's understanding of his own religion (should he have one), or of religion itself, writ large. Just as learning another language does not necessarily impair one's facility with one's own mother tongue, so too the study of other religions does not necessarily handicap one's personal faith perspective. It may certainly cause one to reflect more profoundly on particular issues, but that is hardly a drawback.

The analogy of fictive works, however, has obvious limitations, even though for the student who is an outsider to a particular religion, that tradition's worldview and values may initially appear very much like works of fiction if not fantasy. However, for the Christian, the Muslim, the Jain, and the Siberian shaman, their religiously shaped worldviews are most certainly believed to be real. Thus the student of religion ought not to take a dismissive attitude to these varied religious realities, for it is a requirement of the discipline to take all features of the object of its study as worthy of attention and intellectual scrutiny. Aspects of these religions may represent the most cherished values and most profoundly regarded truths for their adherents, and it is incumbent on the student of religion to try to understand why that is so, without endorsing or embracing those beliefs. While the idea of ending up in a paradise in some uncertain upper realm, surrounded by angelic beings, fed with delectable food and drink, and so on, after this life ends, or suffering unimaginably horrible torments in some fiery hell located somewhere below, may seem like a childish fantasy to a skeptical outsider, such belief systems are widely held and are powerful enough to induce large numbers of people to die for the implications of those beliefs. Such beliefs may even induce them to kill others. Clearly, then, religious worldviews do not depict trivial realms as one might dismissively regard the worlds created in video games or sword and sorcery novels. Behaviors that religious worldviews elicit should not be taken lightly either. The exploration of these realities therefore requires the development of sensitivity and imagination in order to penetrate those worlds effectively. Most important, the student must work to develop a sense of critical judgment so as not to abide within those realms, for to study religion is to explore religious terrain but not set up one's home there. The student of religion should not be afraid to lay bare facts that contradict a religious tradition's claims (e.g. the historicity of events).

To study Buddhism does not require one to become a Buddhist, but it definitely helps if one understands the Buddhist conception of reality well enough to grasp why such a perspective is appealing to the millions who adhere to that tradition and pursue its goals. This is why arguments that promote a completely objective stance are not very compelling in the discipline of religious studies. Complete objectivity belongs to the mechanisms of computers, not human beings. To understand religion (as with art, music, or literature) requires a measure of appreciation, which is an emotional response. To appreciate why something appeals to another human being, to some degree one must experience those feelings which obviously resonate more deeply within the other. To understand love, jealousy, compassion, desire, or fear, it is imperative to have some subjective experience of those feelings. However, the religious studies perspective is not that of the religious seeker, and the scholars' quest is not primarily, remotely, or necessarily to find a suitable religion for themselves. The delicate balance between subjective involvement in a studied religion's world-view and the objective analysis of that reality construct needs to be scrupulously maintained. One ought not to plunge into embracing the belief systems that are being studied to such a degree that it would impede one's capacity to reflect critically upon those religions. And although they may have immersed themselves in the study of a particular religious tradition, investing substantial amounts of their time and intellectual energies on it, religious studies scholars do not wish to have those efforts undermine their ability to examine other religious traditions with the highest possible degree of neutrality. Ideally, one needs to be able to explore the unknown religious territory with a great degree of subjective involvement and report back on what one has discovered with a high measure of objectivity.

Of course, these ideals regarding profound subjective involvement and rigorous objective analysis are ultimately unrealistic to execute perfectly. If a musician who is schooled in the Western classical tradition begins to explore the blues, rock, hip-hop, or jazz, he or she may well carry certain stylistic influences from those explorations into subsequent compositions and performances. While the religious studies scholar is more like a music critic than a musician, the analogy of influence through exposure still holds true. The exploration of different religious worldviews inevitably expands and transforms one's own worldview. One gathers new terminology and varied perspectives on the human condition and the purpose of existence. In this regard, too, the discipline of religious studies differs from religious education, for while the latter strives to nurture and strengthen a particular worldview and its accompanying value system, the discipline of religious studies moves students towards broadening their understanding of religion and humanity.

Theology and religious studies

Theology (*theos*—god + *logos*—study) is a term typically applied to intellectual reflections on the nature of the divine. Theologians are generally deeply rooted within particular religious traditions and conduct their speculative thinking within the lines of their tradition's doctrines. Sometimes their efforts are directed towards providing justifications for their religious beliefs and practices. So Christian theologians might ponder the question "If God is just and loves humanity, why do seemingly good persons sometimes suffer terribly?" Note that there is already the assumption that there is a god (written with a capital G, as if there is definitely just one true god) who has certain characteristics (as per the doctrines of their faith), and so on.

If one reads definitions of theology written by theologians one might notice that many render *theos* as their vision of divinity, and often render the term *logos* as "science" to grant to their endeavor a sort of hallmark of rigorous method and systematic logic that we associate with the pure sciences, such as mathematics and physics. So they might set off by saying "theology is the science of God's plan for humanity as laid out in the Bible." Although sophisticated theology does try to apply the principles of logical argument when addressing questions, it typically compromises its logic in favor of the doctrinal or faith demands of the tradition. Thus a Muslim theologian may speculate on whether there are more gods than Allah but is unlikely to come to the conclusion that there are, or that there is no god at all. And a Christian theologian, nowadays, is unlikely to conclude that Jesus was fully human and not divine, although some did so in the past. Speculative philosophy is thus very much a part of theological thinking, but conclusions that contradict the fundamental beliefs of a religious tradition are generally not entertained, for this would put theologians into conflict with their tradition, sometimes with undesirable consequences, including excommunication or even death. Theological arguments that attempt to reaffirm, defend, or prove aspects of the doctrines of a tradition through the application of reason belong to the category of apologetics. And thus, in some measure, all theology is an exercise in apologetics.

This is what distinguishes theology from metaphysics (i.e. beyond physics), which is a branch of philosophy dedicated to a somewhat less bounded form of speculative thinking about the true nature of the whole of reality, especially that which exists beyond the grasp of the senses. When engaged in metaphysical thinking one might ask "Is there a god?" but not feel pressured to reach a positive conclusion. One might wonder, "Does the sense of an individual personality survive after death?" but not feel constrained to assume the existence of a soul, an afterlife, a heaven, hell, purgatory, and so on. One could thus suggest that theologies of any kind are a subset of metaphysics.

The discipline of religious studies, by contrast, is neither theology nor metaphysics. Religious studies has religion as its object of study, but does not attempt to promote or, for that matter, actually engage in the practice of religion. Thus scholars in the discipline may study theologies but should not engage in the act of theologizing (at least while engaged in their professional work). It is perhaps appropriate at this juncture to discuss the relationship between the personal and professional. Although Sir Isaac Newton was a Christian, he did not argue that the planetary bodies revolved around the sun because of God's plan for humanity, but strove to uncover physical laws of nature and the mathematical relationships among objects to describe his laws of motion. He applied and embodied the scientific method when engaged in science and left his personal religious beliefs out of his discussions on the mathematical principles underlying natural phenomena. Of course, Newton was one of the pioneers of the scientific method, and many of his contemporaries did not separate science from personal religious beliefs in their discussions. But in the centuries that followed, this has become the norm. Thus religious studies students or scholars (also sometimes known as "religionists," although the term "religionist" traditionally means someone deeply committed to a faith) are expected to set aside their own beliefs or disbeliefs when conducting their research, and most certainly in the presentation of their work.

It is therefore possible for both the devout theologian and the confirmed atheist (one who does not believe in the existence of any supernatural divine entity) to engage in religious studies, provided they are capable of "bracketing" their personal positions when researching and reporting on their work. When combined with the previous observations on the value of subjective involvement the task becomes even more challenging. For those with deep commitments to particular worldviews (i.e. believers or non-believers), the neutral, objective stance may be difficult enough to achieve when studying a "foreign" religion. However, these individuals should ideally strive to move beyond the neutral into a subjective involvement with the tradition studied, unless it is their own. As it has sometimes been put, one should attempt to be an outsider to one's own tradition (when studying it as a religious studies scholar), and an insider to other foreign traditions (those that one is studying). Thus, Christian or Muslim religious studies scholars should attempt to take up a stance outside Christianity or Islam and examine their own traditions with rigorous scientific scrutiny, for their personal involvement with their tradition, which has already given them the necessary advantage of subjective understanding, should now not act as an impediment to the objectivity demanded by the discipline of religious studies. And if studying Hinduism, the atheist (and Christian or Muslim) should attempt to do more than merely stand in some distant, seemingly neutral, location from the object of study. Here, one must strive to enter into a subjective experience of the tradition, so as not to be constrained in achieving a more thorough understanding of that religion by the seeming objectivity that the natural outsider status provides.

Are such changes in stance and bracketing of beliefs truly possible? Of course they are: imperfectly, perhaps, but they are definitely possible. Just as a scientist who may have personal convictions about the nature of something (e.g. that heavier objects fall faster than lighter ones), first steps back from those beliefs and then engages in experimentation to discover what is the truth, so too religious studies scholars must first step outside their personal belief systems in order to engage in their research. Just as a good actor puts on a costume and takes up the role of the fearless hero, the religious studies scholar takes up the role of an investigator of religious phenomena. Just as inept actors cannot stay in character, inept scholars let personal beliefs, biases, and such, tarnish the rigor with which they approach their research and reporting. Incidentally, the application of the scientific method to religious studies has led some scholars to call the discipline *Religionswissenschaft* (German for "the science of religion"). However, for other religious studies scholars, and for some of the reasons mentioned above, the "scientific method" is not the most appropriate approach to the subject, and so the term has had limited appeal. Indeed we shall see in this book that there has been, and continues to be, a wide assortment of perspectives and approaches with which to study human religiosity.

Admittedly, the discipline of religious studies has been shaped by some perspectives and approaches more than others. It is a relatively young academic discipline that arose primarily in Western universities. As a result, most of the seminal figures in the early stages of religious studies were European and North American, and their approaches, perspectives, methods, questions, concerns, theories, types of evidence, and arguments have been shaped by their own orientation and institutional setting—including the norms of related disciplines, such as anthropology, sociology, psychology, history, and to varying extents, theology. Religious studies has become increasingly global and inclusive. There is rich engagement with religious studies beyond Europe and North America as the home environment of scholars rather than just as sites of fieldwork. With this change there may be increasingly diverse perspectives, approaches, theories, and methods. In this book we are not trying to shape or predict this future so much as to provide a more modest overview of past developments as well as clarification of present practices, problems, approaches, and perspectives. As a result, most of the influential figures and seminal texts discussed in this book signal the Western origins of the discipline. We have attempted to ameliorate this in small ways, such as by the inclusion of Asian religious figures, concepts, examples, and perspectives. More could be done both in seeking out alternative modes of thinking about religion and testing the applicability of influential theories to Asian and other religious traditions. However, strides for greater balance and breadth in this regard are better directed toward future developments than toward a revisionist, or misleadingly selective, history.

Patterns in the study of religion

Religion has been and continues to be studied in a variety of ways. In this section we examine some of the most commonly encountered schemes and categories used to structure the study of religion. The divisions, categories, and themes employed to organize, compare, and understand religions sometimes reflect patterns found within religions themselves. They may also serve as patterns that give form to the study of religion. The religious studies scholar's choices may seem obvious, or may simply mirror a religion's own categories and divisions, which appear to be value-neutral. However, whenever we select an aspect to emphasize or a pattern to follow, we are actually shaping our object of study—religion—and influencing our analyses and conclusions.

Traditions

One of the most commonly encountered schemes used to approach the study of religion is to divide it into traditions. In a typical course on world religions, one is likely to find categories such as Hinduism, Buddhism, Daoism, Confucianism, Shinto, Judaism, Christianity, Islam, Jainism, and so on. This division into "-isms" is an expedient and convenient scheme with which to begin the study of the human religious experience, because these traditions are widely accepted labels and cut a wide swath through the religions of the people of the world. Of course, the true nature of religion is far more complex. For instance, in parts of East Asia, Confucianism, Daoism, and Buddhism can be deeply intertwined. Hinduism, Buddhism, and Jainism have certain similarities, sharing such ideas as the repeating cycles of time (creation and destruction of the cosmos) and the concept of rebirth. Thus scholars sometimes categorize religions by regions rather than traditions. They might prefer to talk about Japanese religions (which would then allow them to discuss the connections between Shinto, Confucianism, Daoism, and Buddhism), or East Asian religions, or South Asian religions.

It is quite common to find textbooks and courses on world religions divided into Eastern and Western religious traditions. The Western traditions typically include Judaism, Christianity, and Islam (which share common features), and the Eastern traditions generally include Hinduism, Buddhism, Jainism, Sikhism, Confucianism, Daoism, and Shinto. The East–West category is not without its problems. The vast majority of Muslims, for instance, are in Eastern countries (such as the Middle East, India, Malaysia, and Indonesia) although Islam is categorized as a Western tradition. Some scholars have also noted that the three major "Western religions" (Judaism, Christianity, and Islam) actually originated in the Middle East, so that one could argue that they too are actually "Eastern traditions."

Major religious traditions of the world

Buddhism: ethical and philosophical system developed from the teachings of Siddhartha Gautama, known as the Buddha (Awakened One); based on moral and contemplative practices.

Christianity: beliefs and practices of followers of Jesus of Nazareth, who hold him to be the sole son of God; grounded in the principle of love.

Confucianism: moral and ethical approach to life based on the teachings of the Chinese scholar Confucius; grounded in maintaining orderly relationships through the cultivation of human virtues.

Daoism: philosophy, beliefs, and rites grounded on a profound relationship to the mysterious workings of nature.

Hinduism: constellation of beliefs and practices that include acceptance of the scriptural authority of the Vedas and the class/caste system; religion of the majority of the populace in south Asia.

Islam: beliefs and practices based on the message transmitted by the prophet Muhammad and preserved in the Qur'an; characterized by strict monotheism.

Jainism: ethical and philosophical system grounded in the teachings of Vardhamana Mahavira, known as the Jina (Conqueror); based on moral and contemplative practices.

Judaism: beliefs and practices of the Jews, a people who follow the teachings contained in the Hebrew Bible (Tanakh); monotheistic; centred on maintaining a contractual agreement (covenant) with God.

Shinto: ritual-based tradition, with political overtones, indigenous to the islands of Japan, centered on the appeasement of spirits known as *kami*.

Sikhism: tradition primarily based on the moral and religious instructions of ten teachers (guru) and contained within a revered book, the *Guru Granth Sahib*.

Of course there is also the problem regarding what is included or excluded in these schemes. Clearly the major religious traditions of the world are not the only religions in existence. There is a rich assortment of aboriginal religions in North and South America, in Africa, Australia, and in the islands of the Pacific. Are they any less worthy of study? And what about the many religions of the past, such as the Roman, Greek, Egyptian, and Mesopotamian traditions, which have contributed much to the shape and form of contemporary religions? And when thinking about relationships and influences, is it really possible to understand Sikhism without knowledge of Islam and Hinduism, or Christianity without an understanding of Judaism, or Buddhism without Hinduism?

Furthermore, all these major traditions, when subjected to closer scrutiny, are actually composed of innumerable sects and subgroups. Among Muslims there are Sunnis and Shi'ites (and further subgroups). Among Christians, there are Catholics, Protestants, and Orthodox Christians. Among Jews, there are the Hasidim, Reform, and so on. Buddhism has its Mahayana and Theravada branches. And such divisions are themselves rather broad categories. Certain scholars have tried to emphasize and remind others that, in actuality, the degree of variation extends right down to the level of the individual, for the true constellation of beliefs and practices in any one person is unique to that person, and varies from every other, even those who profess the very same faith. No two Christians believe exactly the same thing, perform exactly the same religious activities, or share exactly the same interior disposition towards their religion. Although it is vital to keep this notion of individual variation in mind, it is not reasonable for the scholar of religion to attempt to study the individual beliefs of each of the world's billions of people. And it is for this reason that scholars seek broader categories through which to tackle what would otherwise be an unimaginably vast field of study.

Categories

Besides the classic divisions based on religious traditions or geo-political regions, scholars sometimes approach the study of religion through thematic categories. Many religions have high or sacred regard for a certain text or texts. This literature falls under the broad category of scripture. So scholars may focus on the study of particular Hindu scriptures, such as the Vedas or the Puranas. Scriptures that are officially sanctioned by the orthodox authorities in a religious tradition comprise the religious canon of a particular tradition. While insiders of a religious tradition are not encouraged to read or study material that is outside the officially sanctioned canonical material, it is common for religious studies scholars to examine that outside material as well, for as much can be learned by what was excluded as by what was included. Thus the discovery of a number of Christian gospels at the Egyptian site of Nag Hammadi, which were not included in the Christian scriptures collectively known as the New Testament, might reveal much more about the nature of early Christianity, particularly at the time when the canon was being compiled, than merely reading the material from the New Testament.

Just as scripture (both canonical and non-canonical writings) might form a category for investigation, so too might the stories that are told, either in writing or in other media, such as in oral narratives or visual art. These stories are generally called myths, particularly if they deal with supernatural beings or events. While the term "myth" is commonly used to mean a false belief, religious studies scholars use it to refer to narratives that are believed to be true by adherents of a particular tradition. One person's falsehood is another person's fact, and it is not generally in the religious studies scholar's agenda to evaluate the truth within myths. Certain Christians believe the story of Noah, who survived a great deluge by sailing in a giant boat or ark, to be historical truth, and some Hindus believe that the god Rama, the subject of the epic *Ramayana*, was an actual person, whose birthplace was marked by a now-destroyed temple. Although those beliefs seem dubious, there are, at times, actual historical strata within the body of myths, and certain scholars do work to ascertain what kernels of historical truth, if any, are embedded in such ancient myths. For instance, through clues provided in the *Ramayana*, Indian archeologists found ancient settlements at Sringaverapura, referred to in the myth. Similarly, work on the Greek epic, *The Iliad*, telling the myth of the battle that destroyed Ilium (Troy), enabled archaeologists to uncover the ruins of a city, Hissarlik, now fairly firmly identified as ancient Troy. This discovery does not prove that the myth was "true" in all of its features, but that in this case the narrative was built upon and around a nucleus of historical occurrences. Alternatively, in the Hindu tradition, the creator god Brahma emerges atop a lotus flower that grows from the navel of the preserver god Vishnu. It may be easy for Christians to regard this Hindu depiction of the origins of the cosmos as a myth (without any historical nucleus), but more difficult to hear their own tradition's creation story about the primal couple Adam and Eve, or of Jesus' birth from a virgin, classified as myths.

Religion is always expressed in action, and among the kinds of actions encountered within religious traditions one frequently finds rituals. Ritual is a complex category of human behavior, not found exclusively within what is clearly accepted as religious activity. It may be seen in most spheres of life, from politics to sport. Why is ritual often connected to religion? Do rituals have meaning? What functions do they serve? How have they changed or why have they remained unchanged? Can individual private prayer be regarded as ritual, or is ritual only public and collective? Tackling such questions enables the scholar to discover more about the nature of religion through focusing upon such an action-centered category as ritual.

There are other such categories through which religion may be usefully studied. These include core beliefs, ethical teachings, and religious specialists. Another rewarding category is the study of symbols and symbolism, sometimes known as semiotics. We typically associate certain religions with key signs and symbols, such as the Om/Aum sign of Hinduism, Islam's crescent moon and star, and of course, the Christian cross. Symbols can certainly be misinterpreted because the same symbol may carry a different meaning in different cultures, or meanings may have changed over time. The fearsome-looking goddess Kali, who is loved, feared, and venerated by many Hindus, who holds a severed human head and wears a garland of skulls, may appear like a demon to some non-Hindus. Similarly, others would find it difficult to imagine that the image of a tortured human being nailed to a cross and left to die is a symbol of divine love, forgiveness, and spiritual redemption. Merely looking at a symbol will not necessarily yield its meaning, and so the scholarly study of religion requires that one penetrates into the history, cultural contexts, and value systems of a religious tradition in order to extract the meanings within its symbols.

Founders of various religious traditions

Zarathustra (or Zoroaster) (c. 1100s BCE): Iranian prophet considered to be the founder of Zoroastrianism, to whom the composition of ancient hymns (*gatha*), contained within the *Avesta*, are attributed; Zoroastrianism was the dominant religion of ancient Persia, until the arrival of Islam in the seventh century, and now exists primarily among the Indian Parsi community in Mumbai (Bombay).

Laozi (or Lao-tzu) (c. 500s BCE): Mythic Chinese philosopher, credited with the formulation of Daoist (Taoist) teachings and attributed with the authorship of the *Daodejing* (*Tao Te Ching*).

Kongzi (also K'ung Fu-tzu or Confucius) (551–479 BCE): Enormously influential Chinese teacher of social and ethical values; teachings contained in the *Analects*.

Vardhamana (c. 549–477 BCE): Indian teacher; known as Mahavira; associated with conveying the teachings of the Jains; he is regarded as the last in a series of twenty-four great teachers known as Tirthankaras.

Siddhartha Gautama (c. 490–410 BCE): Indian teacher; known as the Buddha (Awakened One), and founder of the Buddhist tradition; associated with teachings for the ending of suffering and the attainment of spiritual liberation (*nirvana*).

Jesus of Nazareth (c. 7 BCE–26 CE): Jewish teacher (rabbi), designated by his followers as the Messiah or Christ; pivotal figure in Christian beliefs, in which he is regarded as God in human form.

Muhammad (570–632 CE): Arabian prophet and founder of Islam; believed by Muslims to have received the instructions of Allah (God), contained in the Qur'an.

Nanak (1469–1538 CE): founder of the Sikh religious tradition; he is the first of ten teachers (*guru*) whose writings are contained within the Sikh holy book, the *Guru Granth Sahib*.

Joseph Smith (1805–1844 CE): American preacher and prophet; founder of the Mormon religious tradition or the Church of Jesus Christ of Latter-day Saints (LDS); believed by his followers to have received teachings from the prophet Mormon, which are contained in the religion's scripture, *The Book of Mormon*.

Gerald B. Gardner (1884–1964): British civil servant, who together with **Doreen Valiente** (1922–1999), laid the foundation for the neo-Pagan movement, known as Wicca, which claims to have roots in pre-Christian spiritual traditions of nature worship.

2

How religion began to be studied

Traditional perspectives

Philosophical approaches

Philosophy (*philia*—love + *sophia*—wisdom) is the love or pursuit of wisdom. In the West, this pursuit has centered on the use of logical reasoning as its method, and the scholarly discipline of philosophy in many Western academic institutions still generally tends to favor rational thought as the most (and for some philosophers the only) acceptable technique for the acquisition of wisdom. However, in Eastern philosophical traditions, as well as in the past in the West, wisdom is and was generally regarded as deriving from the full compass of human abilities. Thus its methods, together with the application of logical thinking, include self-discipline, the cultivation of moral virtues, the use of the senses (i.e. empirical data), and the development of intuitive understanding. Some of these latter methods, such as attaining profound intuitive insights, are believed to grant superior access to wisdom than is granted by rational thought alone.

Nowadays, in the West, some of these non-logic-centered techniques are often considered to belong to a religious lifestyle. However, the separation of religion from philosophy is a phenomenon that gained momentum in the West during the period of the Enlightenment (eighteenth century). The Enlightenment was a post-Renaissance movement that promoted the use of reason and the scientific method to critique the large assortment of beliefs and practices that had dominated the Western world, in large measure through the dominance of Christianity and its worldview. People actually believed (and were pressured to believe) that the Earth was the center of the universe, which itself was created in six days by God, because such ideas were then forcefully promoted in the Christian worldview or articulated in its scriptures. The Renaissance (i.e. rebirth) brought about an intellectual and artistic awakening in Europe and the rest of Western culture. It began to free people from the bondage of obligatory beliefs and practices. New continents were discovered, and technologies developed through which one could observe, measure, and reason about the movement of the planets and stars, or the species of animal and plant life on Earth. The worldviews that were emerging through the application of reason and the scientific method differed dramatically from the vision that had been put forward by Christianity. Thus philosophy and the sciences broke sharply off from what was then designated as "religion," which was the previously held dominant worldview of people in the West. In some measure, "religion" came to represent all of the disproved, unproven, and unprovable assumptions and beliefs about reality that were left behind after science and rationality had extracted their understanding of the world. In other words, for many thinkers, religion was regarded pejoratively as the constellation of nonsensical beliefs and superstitions, which endured despite the advances of science and philosophy. Furthermore, in the West, it is still common for people (professional philosophers and scientists included) to mistakenly think of religion or the religious worldview as singular, namely, the Christian one, forgetting to take account of the plurality and diversity of religious worldviews in the West, and often completely ignoring the wide assortment of Eastern "religious" perspectives.

Eastern cultures, for the most part, avoided such a dramatic split. For instance, in Sanskrit, the ancient classical language that is central to many major Eastern religions including Hinduism, Buddhism, and Jainism, there are no distinct words for religion or philosophy. A term commonly used is *darshana*, which conjoins them. *Darshana* may most closely be translated as viewpoint, perspective, or worldview. A person's *darshana* is therefore his or her most comprehensive understanding of reality. It is also the way in which one approaches the acquisition of understanding and how one seeks to gain wisdom about oneself and the world. The term encompasses what, in the West, one might designate as a religious or philosophical approach. Thus major religious traditions, such as Buddhism and Jainism, are regarded as *darshanas*, but so are philosophical approaches such as logic and scientific speculation. So although the East may not have been officially engaging in "philosophy" as it is currently defined by the Western academic philosophical tradition, people in the East were just as passionately engaged in the acquisition of wisdom. For instance, it would not be incorrect to say that the core thrust of Buddhist teachings is the acquisition of wisdom.

It is instructive to recognize again that designations such as religion or philosophy are intellectual constructions created by scholars as an effective means of cordoning off their objects of study. It is also useful to note that people in the East and West have reflected on the nature of existence, who they are, and the meaning of life, certainly for as long as those capacities for wonder have been part of our species. Thus the philosophical approach to the study of religion, that is, the love and pursuit of wisdom, has been present in all human cultures throughout history. If this section emphasizes the history of Western approaches, it is primarily because there has been insufficient work on collating the history of Eastern reflections on the human religious impulse. And while in the modern West it seems reasonable for the "discipline" of philosophy to study the "phenomenon" of religion, it is a messier business for the perspective (*darshana*) of philosophy/religion to study the perspective (*darshana*) of philosophy/religion. Although messier, it has most certainly been done, for people in the East have abundantly ruminated on the nature of knowledge or truth, what obfuscates it, and how best to acquire it. It is akin to philosophy in the West turning its gaze on the discipline itself and on the act of philosophizing, on its assumptions, methods, and so on. This is indeed part of the Western philosophical tradition as well, for to pursue wisdom lovingly is to wonder about what wisdom truly is, how it may be acquired, and why we seek and desire it at all. Thus the story of philosophizing about religion in both the East and the West has ancient roots, a few traces of which we shall examine here.

Early Greek thinkers

In the great Western epics, the *Odyssey* and the *Iliad*, attributed to Homer (c. 700s BCE), we find enduring myths of gods and heroes, and indirect speculations on their nature and characters. In the works of the poet Hesiod (c. 700s BCE) one finds elaborations of the "five races or ages" of humanity, beginning with a golden age, in which the gods who dwell on Mount Olympus created a race of mortal men who lived in peace and harmony with their creators and without effort gained sustenance from the natural bounty from the earth. In Hesiod's scheme, there is a progressive decline in the subsequent created races/ages ending with what he terms the current iron age, marked by a degeneration of moral values and respect for the elderly, by warfare, strife within families, and so on. Interestingly, Eastern philosophers also articulated similar ideas in the concept of the *yugas*, cycles of time in which the quality of life and morals progressively deteriorate. We are currently regarded as dwelling within the Kali Yuga, the last and most degenerate of these eons. In *Theogony*, attributed to Hesiod, we find an attempt to systematize the then existing beliefs in the gods, their origins, relationships, and generations, and how they gained dominion over the cosmos. Thus Gaia, the Earth, developed after Chaos, and Gaia produced Ouranus/Uranus, the Heavens. In the more ancient Hindu Vedas, one finds hymns of wonder and praise to the gods, many of whom are personified powers of the natural world such as fire and wind. Some of the gods share names and attributes with their Greek counterparts, suggesting similar origins. For instance, the name of the Vedic god Varuna, who was also associated with the sky, is cognate with

Uranus. Contemporary scholars of comparative religions have found parallels between these Greek and Indian myths and the early myths recorded on stone tablets of the Babylonians and Hittites dating to about 1400 BCE.

The Greek philosopher Anaximander (c. 610–546 BCE) introduced the concept of a single, formless essence, known as the *apeiron*, the undifferentiated or limitless. From this ineffable source, which is beyond description and attributes, all things emerge as dualities or opposites, such as hot and cold, wet and dry, and so on, which interact with each other to generate the fullness of the creation. Ultimately these return to the ultimate, uncaused cause, the *apeiron*, which is equated with the Divine (i.e. God). In a similar vein, at around the same time, Indian philosophers in texts known as the Upanishads were articulating analogous ideas. They called the vast, expansive, and singular power from which all things emerged Brahman, and it too was thought of as beyond attributes and equated with ultimate divinity. Around the same time period, early Daoist philosophers in China were presenting the conception of the Dao, an ineffable mystery from which the all dualities (i.e. Yin and Yang) emerged and to which they returned.

The Greek philosopher Xenophanes (c. 580–490 BCE) was critical of the polytheistic ideas that abounded, also favoring the concept of a single overarching power. He pointed out how people make their gods in their own image, and so the gods of the Thracians had blue eyes and red hair, while those of the Ethiopians were black and snub-nosed. The Greek historian Herodotus described the religious beliefs of other cultures. Despite numerous errors and fabrications in his work, he noted how some Greek beliefs, deities, and rituals were derived from earlier Egyptian cults. These works of Xenophanes and Herodotus serve as early examples of speculations on the origins of myths and religion, and on the transformations of religious beliefs and practices over time as they spread to different regions and blended with local religious outlooks. Aristotle (384–322 BCE), the renowned student of Plato (c. 427–347 BCE), remarked how tyrants should pretend to be pious and uncommonly dedicated to religion, for in so doing they might treat their subjects poorly without them rebelling as quickly as they otherwise would. In such comments (humorous, cynical, or surprisingly discerning as they may sound to some), we note early theorizing on the relationship between religion and politics.

It is through Aristotle that we get the term metaphysics. The works which Aristotle designated as "first philosophy" accompanied his work *Physics* in the famous Library of Alexandria, and were thus filed and named metaphysics (i.e. after or beyond *Physics*). Aristotle's "first philosophy" or "metaphysics" included these components: ontology, which is the study of being or existence; theology, which is the study of God, the gods, or the divine; and universal science, which is the study of first principles, primary or axiomatic (i.e. assumed, presumed, and unproven) ideas about the world, or how we acquire knowledge or wisdom, such as the principle of non-contradiction. The principle of non-contradiction, for instance, would assert that a thing cannot be red and not-red at the same time, under the same conditions and contexts. We cannot prove this kind of assumption, but it underlies all of our thinking, for it is present in all of our efforts to think logically. Thus it is a first principle. Evidently, the study of being and divinity were of fundamental importance to Aristotle, as was an examination of our assumed truths and how we acquire truth. These days, metaphysics is generally used for ruminations on ultimate questions about existence or being (ontology), on the nature of reality/the universe (cosmology), and on the nature of the self, or god. It also includes reflection on the how one acquires truth (epistemology). Interest in metaphysics is sometimes gauged to be on the decline in departments of philosophy in Western universities.

Early Greek thinkers

Homer (c. 700s BCE): Greek poet to whom the major Western epics, the *Odyssey* and the *Iliad*, are attributed.

Hesiod (c. 700s BCE): Greek poet to whom the authorship of *Works and Days* and the *Theogony* are attributed. The *Theogony* deals with the origins of the cosmos and the genealogy of the deities, while *Works and Days* is concerned with living a moral and ethical lifestyle.

Anaximander (c. 610–546 BCE): Pre-Socratic philosopher known for his contributions in science and geometry; known also for his notion of the *apeiron*, a single, infinite, and boundless essence that is the source of all creation.

Xenophanes (c. 580–490 BCE): philosopher and poet known for his critique of polytheism; noted for his observation that human beings imagine their gods in forms that resemble themselves.

Heraclitus (c. 540–480 BCE): metaphysical philosopher known for his philosophy of constant change, summed up in the dictum, "one cannot step into the same river twice." His ideas are sometimes set in contrast with static notions of reality that emphasize "Being" over "Becoming," and he is thus considered one of the patriarchs of process philosophies.

Herodotus (c. 484–425 BCE): author of the *Histories*, an account of Greek struggles with the Persian invasions, and sometimes regarded as the father of history; his work laid a foundation for the discipline of history, narrative accounts of past events that strive for objectivity and point to their sources for verification.

Socrates (c. 469–399 BCE): philosopher known for his teaching method of questioning students; teacher of Plato; accused and convicted of corrupting the local youth, he chose a death sentence by drinking the poison hemlock, rather than give up his right to express his ideas freely.

Plato (c. 427–347 BCE): Tremendously influential philosopher; student of Socrates; thought contained in various texts known as dialogues, such as the *Republic* and the *Timaeus*; founder of a school for higher learning in Athens, known as the Academy, which is regarded as the first university.

Aristotle (384–322 BCE): Enormously influential and prolific philosopher; student of Plato and teacher of Alexander the Great; made contributions in numerous areas, particularly logic, psychology, natural science, ethics, and poetics.

Euclid (c. 325–270 BCE): mathematician, whose influential work *Elements* still forms the basis of classical (Euclidean) geometry.

Western philosophy through the Middle Ages

In the West, the heritage bequeathed by Plato, Aristotle, and the Greek philosophers in general, continued to co-exist, interact, and meld with the religious traditions of the Western world. The Western philosophical tradition had come under the sway of worldviews shaped by the Abrahamic religions (i.e. Judaism, Christianity, and Islam), traditions that claimed the prophet Abraham as a founding father. These traditions were grounded in a worldview shaped by the teachings of influential prophets after Abraham who claimed to receive further authoritative teachings from the same supreme power known variously as Yahweh, Allah, or simply, God. The prophets were elect individuals who were graced with these revelations from an otherwise hidden deity, to whose reality and message others did not have direct access. Thus, unquestioning faith in the claims by these prophets and the revealed teachings (i.e. scripture) formed the cornerstone of these traditions. Among the shared teachings of the scriptures of these traditions is that there is only one god. Hence if and when written, although there are restrictions on writing it, it is often rendered with a capital G, God. These religions are designated as theistic, because they include belief in a god, and they are monotheistic because of their belief in a single, supreme god. A unique feature of Christianity, which differentiates it from Judaism and Islam, is the belief that Jesus of Nazareth, the founder of the faith, is the son of God, an only son, and through a mysterious transfiguration, God himself. Christianity and Islam are missionary in nature, requiring their followers actively to spread their beliefs to unbelievers. The zeal to spread the teachings (i.e. to proselytize) is grounded in their belief that to join the community of the faithful saves one from eternal damnation in a painful, hellish condition at the end of time. Such teachings in various religions that deal with being saved are known as their soteriologies, while their teachings on the end-times are known as their eschatologies.

For more than a millennium and a half in the West, we encounter influential writings by thinkers striving to reconcile the demands of their faith-based religious traditions with the rational inquiring spirit of the Greek philosophical tradition embodied by Aristotle. Philo Judaeus (early first century CE) of Alexandria is a choice example of a thinker struggling to reconcile the teachings of his tradition with the Greek philosophical orientation. Philo is associated with the "allegorical method," an approach to reading scripture. In this method he points out that those contents of texts such as the Hebrew Bible (i.e. the Tanak, which is roughly the same as the Old Testament of the Christian Bible) that appeared to be unreasonable, should not be taken literally. In certain cases the language is symbolic, the tales allegorical, and thus efforts should be made to understand or interpret these portions in a manner that is congruent with common sense, natural law, and evident explanations about the world. Similarly, the Christian bishop Augustine of Hippo (354–430 CE) is also renowned for his efforts to discredit literal readings of the Bible in cases where certain assertions contradict the findings of natural law or the application of reason.

Although most modern believers in most religious traditions (East and West) use some sort of allegorical interpretive approach when engaging their religious litera-ture, there are substantial numbers who choose to read scripture literally, even today. These types of believers are often known as literalists. Religious fundamentalism is often built upon literalist readings of scriptures, as well as efforts to return to what are thought to be the original, core, or basic beliefs and practices (i.e. the funda-mentals). Literalists believe in such teachings as their scripture's cosmological explanations of the origins of the world, of heavenly and hellish realms populated by various divine and semi-divine beings such as angels and demons, of the miraculous deeds of their god(s) and prophets, of journeys to heaven, and of the dead returning to life. They are also offended by assertions that their scriptures are symbolic, allegorical, deriving from a culture with different values, or from a period in the past where there were evident human errors in our understanding of the world. Literalists might reject even more strongly the idea that the scriptures have been tampered with or composed by human authors, or that they are anything but absolute truth revealed by God and thus to be regarded as unimpeachable truth. Nevertheless, what the senses (i.e. empirical evidence) and reason tell us about the world often contrasts dramatically with the claims of scripture, and for more than a millennium and a half prior to the Enlightenment, the exploration of this tension formed the basis of most philosophy of religion in the West. However, as in the cases of Philo and Augustine mentioned above, most of it was from within the faith-based worldview and could thus be categorized as a sort of philosophical theology or apologetics.

Among the many intellectuals who made seminal contributions to philosophical theology we might include Moses Maimonides (also known as Rambam; 1135–1204), a prolific Jewish rabbi who authored the "Thirteen Principles" of faith, a Jewish creed. A creed is an officially sanctioned, succinct summation of the cardinal tenets of belief of a particular religious group, and it is often recited by the community in public gatherings or at initiation rites. In books such as the *Guide to the Perplexed*, Maimonides demonstrates the influence that Aristotle and various Muslim philosophers had on his thought. Among these Muslim scholars was the brilliant Ibn Sina or Avicenna (980–1037), credited with authoring over 450 treatises, mostly on philosophy and medicine. Maimonides' work influenced Christian theologians such as Thomas

Aquinas and John Duns Scotus (1266–1308). Thomas Aquinas (1225–1274) is arguably Catholicism's most influential theologian, particularly renowned for his *Summa Theologica*, a collection of rational reflections on virtually every issue in the Catholic faith. Aquinas exemplifies the scholastic tradition, a movement whose beginnings are placed as early as the ninth century, and which attempted to reconcile the Aristotelian philosophical tradition with theology. Although the term scholasticism primarily originates within a Christian context, Maimonides and Ibn Sina could also be regarded as Jewish and Muslim scholastics respectively. Scholasticism ended with the rise of modern Western philosophy.

Modern Western philosophy

Modern Western philosophy is often traced to the work of René Descartes (1596–1650), the French philosopher whose contributions include Cartesian or analytic geometry. Descartes is famously linked with his assertion *Cogito ergo sum* ("I think, therefore I am"), which places thought and thinking as the foundation of personal existence and the analysis of reality. Descartes asserted the proof of his own existence in the recognition that he was thinking, and then proceeded to use systematic thinking to describe and develop an understanding of the world. Among many other useful contributions, he eventually applied his method to offer (mostly unconvincing) proofs for the existence of God. This technique of utilizing rational thought as the primary instrument for uncovering Truth became a cornerstone of the modern Western philosophical tradition. However, it was not long before the tensions between faith and reason, which to Descartes were still not distinct contemplative approaches, came to a head. A cardinal voice for the limits of knowledge was the German philosopher Immanuel Kant (1724–1804). Kant argued that whatever reality may actually be, our understanding of it, even our perceptions of it, are shaped and restricted by our consciousness. The human mind filters all our sensory experiences of the world and thus limits our capacity to know what might actually be true. Although there is no evidence that Christian theologian-philosophers (i.e. scholastics) ever debated the question of how many angels could dance on the point of a needle, they did ponder questions about whether spiritual entities could occupy material space. This kind of philosophizing led Kant to point out that since metaphysical claims about spirits, god, and so on (that is, the claims of unquestionable, faith-based "truths" said to be revealed to others and often contained in scripture), are beyond an individual's personal experience, they cannot be grasped by human understanding. Thus, "god" or "angels," if such entities exist, cannot be meaningfully thought about or known. For certain Western philosophers after Kant, who accepted his arguments, this meant that all the metaphysical claims made by religions were not worth thinking about, because they could in no way lead to any firm and satisfactory knowledge. Furthermore, if one could not think reasonably about it, that is, grasp it intellectually, it might as well not exist. The concurrent development of the scientific method, with its foundational principles such as Occam's (or Ockham's) Razor, further marginalized religious and meta-physical claims. Occam's Razor is a principle in which, when choosing among various explanations for the same phenomenon, one favors the hypothesis or theory with the fewest assumptions behind it. When it came to understanding the universe, why postulate the existence of god or supernatural beings as causes, if simpler explanations were possible based on observable data, without recourse to such unseen, immeasurable, and perhaps non-existent factors? This heightened the rift between religion and philosophy.

Ludwig Wittgenstein (1889–1951) was one of several philosophers who tried to bridge this divide. Although he acknowledged that the ability to express human experience was bounded by our ability to communicate, he did not deny the possibility of religious experience. Wittgenstein drew attention to the "games of language," or the different uses to which language was put. Parables and myth were as different from each other as the languages of liturgy or theology or historical report. In resonance with the allegorical method articulated by Philo nearly two millennia earlier, Wittgenstein's position would be that even a statement such as "God exists" in a religious context is not like the same statement made in a philo-sophical argument. Wittgenstein pointed out how when someone kisses a photo-graph of a loved one in private, this act is not based on a belief that they are actually kissing the person, and although it is a gesture of love it is different from actually kissing the person, or even saying "I love you." Each of these actions may express similar attitudes but have different contexts and purposes. Religious actions and religious language may belong to different categories of human behavior than philosophical discourse, and may serve different purposes. It is foolish to hold one kind of language to the formal constraints of the other.

This brief historical survey of the relationship between religion and philosophy in the West demonstrates the non-distinction between them among the early Greeks at the time of Plato and Aristotle, although the Socratic approach of free inquiry and metaphysical speculation was the hallmark of their thinking. As Jewish and Christian (and later Islamic) worldviews grew dominant in the Middle East and the West, philosophy was primarily a form of apologetics for religious doctrines grounded in rational arguments. One of its greatest exemplars was the Catholic theologian, Thomas Aquinas, and such philosophical approaches still form the essence of what is known as theology. By the period of the Enlightenment, a rift developed between philosophy and theology, and metaphysical speculation was one of the casualties. Philosophy aligned itself with the pure and natural sciences, and metaphysics was subsumed into scientific hypotheses and theorization. Theology continued in its apologetic vein, struggling to reconcile the scriptural teachings of particular faiths with a worldview progressively shaped by the findings of science. What was lost in this divide was a means of satisfactorily addressing the kinds of questions about the mystery of existence that were not entertained seriously by science or convincingly by conventional religions. Is there a purpose to our existence? What does it mean to live meaningfully? What is beauty, evil, love, or truth? Is there a god or some power(s) higher than human consciousness?

Religion and modern science

By the middle of the twentieth century, observations had damaged science's own previously constructed worldview, its paradigm, which had conceived of the universe as a giant machine operating according to laws of nature such as those discerned and mathematically described by Sir Isaac Newton. This Newtonian worldview has begun to yield to a newer but as yet unclear paradigm shaped, in part, by relativity and quantum theories. The primary building blocks of matter, namely atoms, are apparently made up of a dazzling array of sub-atomic particles far smaller than the previously known protons, neutrons, and electrons. The observed behaviors of these particles, and light energy, which acts both like a particle and an energy wave, are puzzling. They seem to suggest that each particle exerts instantaneous influences on every other particle across the cosmos, that even within material things there is very little matter and mostly space, and that particles might shift locations without actually moving through space. The Heisenberg Uncertainty Principle highlights our inability to know, with certainty, certain minute features of the things we attempt to observe, such as both the speed and location of an electron, because we affect "the observed" through the very act of observation. So, the scientific stance of absolute objectivity is jeopardized, because even in the seemingly neutral act of observing and measuring some phenomenon, the subject (i.e. the scientist) may be affecting the object and the observation.

The new, emerging, but incomplete scientific paradigm has provided fertile ground for the human imagination. Since the descriptions of the observations themselves, their implications, and the corresponding scientific hypotheses and theories are conceptually difficult to grasp, they are often misunderstood. While many high-school graduates know Newton's laws of thermodynamics, and can solve equations for the trajectories of a snowball in flight, only a small fraction of the world's population can honestly claim to understand the theory of quantum mechanics. Even fewer can articulate its implications for the nature of the world. None can reconcile the differences between relativity and quantum theory. Science's inability to articulate a convincing worldview for the masses has led to a revival among those religious faithful who feel that the teachings of their scriptures are just as viable a description of reality as that produced by science. The scientist's speculations on the nature of quarks, a kind of subatomic particle, are no less remote to the average person than the medieval theologian's purported debates about the nature of angels. They are quite different, of course, because science is grounded in experimentation and the testing of hypotheses. Nevertheless, science's capacity to demystify the nature of existence is currently under severe duress. Impressive scientific speculations, such as string theory, find themselves removed from the scientific method's crucial anchor of validation, namely, through experimentation.

The crumbling Newtonian (i.e. mechanistic) paradigm has also spawned a number of quasi-religious movements that invoke the jargon of the new science. We thus have "quantum" weight-loss, fitness, healing, and life-extension programs. More problematically, the intellectually challenging subtleties within the theories of modern science have led to a resurrection of disputes that were thought to have been mostly resolved. For instance, despite its inability to answer all questions about the formation and variation of species, evolutionary theory in biology has been corroborated and fine-tuned for over a century through the application of the scientific method, involving the painstaking gathering and examination of evidence of life forms in existence and in the fossil record. However, various segments of the population, who are disposed to give primacy to their belief in scriptural truths rather than what science has to offer, have been lobbying to have their particular religiously grounded visions of the origins of human life (e.g. various formulations of God's plan for humanity), which are cloaked in the language of science, taught to children within or alongside the science curriculum. While this may seem as unusual as arguing that one should teach a scientific cosmology within or alongside religious ones during religious gatherings, the efforts to conflate the two often derive from misunderstanding the nature of science and the scientific method, while believing that the religious explanations (often misrepresented as complying with the parameters of science) are equally valid.

However, there is also a revival of metaphysical speculation in the classical sense, which is built upon a solid grasp of the observations and theories of science. This breed of philosophy is not grounded on an outright rejection of the scientific method and what benefits it has to offer. It is an effort to secure a worldview that is holistic, more encompassing than the narrow concerns of science, and thus, it is hoped, embracing of the fullness of the human condition. An early example is found in the thought of Alfred North Whitehead (1861–1947), a British philosopher of science and logic, whose approach is often known as process philosophy. Aware of the shifting paradigm in the scientific worldview brought about through new observations and theorizing, Whitehead offered a view of the world that was not grounded in substance but in process. One might say there are no "things" in existence, only "events" or "happenings." Whitehead rejected what he termed scientific materialism, that the universe is made out of bits of material, and that mind or consciousness is derived from these static bits of matter. The worldview he postulated, aspects of which are aligned with the observations and theories of many contemporary scientists, is that there is a fundamental interconnectedness between everything in existence, and that all these are in a condition of change. For Whitehead, the ultimate purpose of the creation, that is, its teleology, is towards the production of Beauty. Features in Whitehead's philosophy resonate surprisingly well with more ancient ideas found in Eastern religions such as Buddhism and Hinduism, to which we shall turn shortly.

Whitehead's process philosophy has led to the rise of process theology, a novel re-envisioning of the nature of God and the creation, which has received mild support from some liberal Christians and Jews. In the work of the theoretical physicist David Bohm (1917–1992) we see an example of a scientist striving for a holistic understanding of the full compass of reality. For instance, Bohm had hypothesized that the explicit events, objects, and such that we perceive around us are derived from a vaster, although mostly hidden, implicit structural order to the universe, which in essence is a singular unbroken whole. The foregoing approaches point to a movement towards the reconvergence of philosophy, theology, and science. Although there are cogent criticisms of this brand of exploratory holistic thinking, it also often receives denigration from those who are determinedly situated within the compartmentalized disciplines of philosophy, theology, and science, because it breaches each of these discipline's respective restraining parameters.

Philosophy in the East

As early as the fifth century BCE, Eastern thinkers had also philosophized on the relationship between mind and matter, the nature of particles, and the limits of rational thought. Philosophers of the Vaishesika school in India had speculated on the nature of the fundamental building blocks of matter, the atoms, and how, if identical, they were different from each other. They also wondered if atoms, like the Greek geometer Euclid's "point," had any dimensions, and if not, then how dimensions such as length, width, or height could emerge. And if atoms had some fixed dimensions, just how small were they? We note how these questions continue to challenge physicists today. Around the same time Siddhartha Gautama (a.k.a. the Buddha) had pointed to the inability of thought to deal adequately with transcendent entities, and grounded his perspective of reality on the transient or impermanent nature of existence. This moment is different from the one that just passed, and while the past is no longer here it has somehow contributed to shaping or conditioning the present. The "things" we perceive and label with our thoughts are like a candle flame as it burns from beginning to end, appearing as one thing but in fact always changing, neither the same as when it was first lit, yet somehow not different when it is about to die out. To cling to permanence in the face of this continual process of change is an error that leads us to suffer.

Certain of Gautama's ideas were more thoroughly developed by the Buddhist philosopher Nagarjuna (c. second century CE) who also attempted to demonstrate through logical argumentation that nothing arises or exists independently, and that "things" as we conceive them are thus conditioned or influenced by our thoughts. The Hindu philosopher Shankara (c. eighth century CE) elaborated on the concept of one overarching power or reality, known to the fifth century BCE philosophers of the Upanishads as Brahman. Shankara offered up the concept of Brahman (the Great, or Absolute Reality) as beyond all description by the mind. It was beyond predication (i.e. nothing could be attributed to it or said about it that would not be a distortion or reducing of its true nature). In part, this is because human beings and thinking itself derive from Brahman, and are but portions of what Brahman truly is. Thus rational thought is fundamentally handicapped in its capacity to know Absolute Reality. The notion of the interconnectedness between all reality, including mind or consciousness and the objects of thought, became the basis of the Hua Yen (Flower Garland) school of Chinese Buddhism. A symbolic image used in Hua Yen is the Jeweled Net of Indra. In myth, Indra is a Vedic god whose net consists of jewels at each of its knots. Each jewel thus reflects every other jewel in the net, and each such reflection contains reflections of all others, and so on. Thus each jewel, which symbolizes each bit, piece, or fragment of reality, is somehow connected to, interpenetrates, and/or is dependent upon every other bit of the whole. One might even suggest that the part somehow encompasses the whole. Each perception, each thought, or each action is fundamentally linked to everything else in existence, across both space and time.

In this short excursus into a few Eastern conceptions about mind, thought, and reality, one can see ideas that resonate well with certain perspectives in modern Western philosophy, as well as in some modern metaphysical conceptions of reality. Whitehead himself acknowledged the similarities between his ideas and aspects of certain Eastern philosophies. Just as a shard of a mirror may reveal as much as the whole mirror, and a piece of a hologram may still produce the complete image when laser light is passed through it, David Bohm's notion of the universe as a holo-movement (akin to a flowing hologram) suggests that in some measure every bit of time and space (i.e. every bit of manifest reality) somehow encodes the whole. Such imagery from a respected contemporary theoretical physicist resonates surprisingly with the ancient symbol of the Jeweled Net of Indra discussed above. Efforts to show such similarities between the findings of modern physics and Eastern philosophies are also evident in books written for popular consumption, such as Fritjof Capra's *The Tao of Physics*. Whatever the shortcomings of such attempts might be, they point out that the modern Western philosophical tradition had, for many centuries after Descartes, focused its attention and critiques on theistic (i.e. god-centered) religions, as if these alone were "religion." They had ignored Eastern religious philosophies, some of which espoused ideas that were not too remote from the classical concerns of the Western philosophical and scientific traditions.

Influential Western philosophers and scientists

René Descartes (1596–1650): French thinker; regarded as the father of modern Western philosophy; known for the dictum, *cogito ergo sum* ("I think, therefore I am"); developed coordinate or Cartesian geometry.

Isaac Newton (1643–1727): English physicist; known for his laws of motion and gravitation, presented in *Philosophiae Naturalis Principia Mathematica* (1687), one of the most influential scientific treatises ever written.

David Hume (1711–1776): Scottish philosopher; known for his criticism of the argument for the existence of God based on the notion of intelligent design.

Immanuel Kant (1724–1804): German philosopher; known for metaphysics and epistemology.

Charles Darwin (1809–1882): English naturalist known for his theory of biological evolution through natural selection, presented in his landmark book, *On the Origin of Species* (1859).

Herbert Spencer (1820–1903): English philosopher; coined the term "survival of the fittest" to explain Charles Darwin's theory of evolution; promoted the notion of the evolution of societies.

Friedrich Nietzsche (1844–1900): German philosopher known for his critique of religious morality; remembered for his statement "God is dead."

Alfred N. Whitehead (1861–1947): English mathematician and philosopher; associated with the development of process philosophy.

Bertrand Russell (1872–1970): British mathematician and philosopher; major contributor to the development of analytic philosophy.

Albert Einstein (1879–1955): German-born theoretical physicist and winner of the Nobel Prize in 1921; known for his theory of relativity with its famous equation, $e=mc^2$, and his contributions to quantum theory (e.g. photoelectric effect).

Ludwig Wittgenstein (1889–1951): Austrian philosopher; known for his contributions on the philosophy of language and on mind.

Werner Heisenberg (1901–1976): German physicist; known for the Heisenberg Uncertainty Principle; awarded the Nobel Prize in 1932.

David Bohm (1917–1992): American physicist and philosopher associated with concepts such as the "implicate order" of reality, which is seen as a "holomovement."

Stephen Hawking (b. 1942): British scientist, one of the world's leading theoretical physicists renowned for his work on black holes; published the popular *A Brief History of Time* (1988), which made conceptually challenging notions in theoretical physics accessible to the public.

Philosophy of religion

It would be misleading to leave this discussion without some description of the current sub-discipline known as the philosophy of religion. Of course, this approach derives from the distinction made between philosophy and religion, and is the Western, reason-centered philosophical scrutiny of religious notions. Since this approach developed in the West, it has tended to be preoccupied with theistic religious questions. As such it might analyze rational arguments put forward to justify the existence of god, or what god and god's attributes might be. For instance, the

Christian theologian, Anselm of Canterbury (1033–1109), put forward the argument that by God we mean something beyond which nothing greater can be thought. Because we can imagine this concept, God must exist. But Kant refuted this line of reasoning by pointing out that just because something, such as "a chair," is said (or thought) to exist, does not make it exist, nor does such an assertion add to the concept of "chair." To conceive of something like "god" does not make god exist, and does not add to the understanding of what "god" might be. Kant pointed out that ultimately such arguments go nowhere because they deal with categories that are beyond human experience and attempt to utilize tools and judgments (i.e. rational thought) which are actually only suited to deal with the content of experience.

Another such argument for the existence of God is commonly known as the "argument from design." In this it is postulated that the seemingly orderly workings of the cosmos, the planetary movements, the seasonal changes, and so on, appear to be the result of some conscious power, akin in nature to human consciousness but vastly superior. These orderly workings could not emerge purely by chance, and thus we can infer the hand of some great designer in the everyday workings of the cosmos. The orderly creation is empirical evidence for the existence of God. The classic refutation of this argument belongs to the philosopher David Hume (1711–1776) who convincingly demonstrates that the cosmic order that we observe can as easily be explained by laws of nature, without recourse to a divine agent that is different from the creation. It would be interesting to explore the application of Hume's argument to certain Eastern religious notions in which God/Brahman is and is beyond the natural world, as in Hindu panentheistic formulations, or where no static Absolute is affirmed, as in Buddhist metaphysics. These Eastern perspectives differ from the Western one, because the conscious agent (i.e. god or awakened consciousness) is not separate from the creation, but inextricably within it, within the very consciousness (i.e. the scientist and philosopher) that explores it.

Hume also demonstrated some of the inconsistencies in typical theistic formulations. For instance, theists typically claim that God is all-powerful (i.e. omnipotent). They may further claim that God is all-good. However, they also agree that there is evil in the creation. Hume argued that if God is able to prevent evil but is not willing to do so, then he is not all good, but malevolent. If God is willing to prevent evil, but cannot, then he is not omnipotent. And if he is both able (i.e. omnipotent) and willing (i.e. good), then evil cannot exist. In response to this kind of argument, theologians have offered counterarguments for the existence of evil in the face of God's omnipotence and goodness which forms a branch of theology known as theodicy (*theos*—God + *dike*—justice). Typically, these arguments might postulate that evil only appears to exist from the limited perspective of our consciousness, but if viewed from God's perspective what appears to be evil is actually good. Alternately, arguments might revolve around the notion of free will, in which God grants freedom to human beings to make certain choices. However, this concession compromises the absolute omnipotence of God.

Philosophy of religion will be progressively enriched as it begins to tackle more thoroughly the formulations of Eastern religions. In the non-dualistic formulations of Kashmir Shaivism, a medieval Indian religious philosophy, for instance, God (i.e. Shiva) is omnipotent, but chooses to limit himself precisely as an expression of that omnipotence. This limitation is the creation, and, although God is more than it, he is present within all of it. Thus the direct experience of God is available to everyone. Goodness and evil are relative and related categories whose seeming tension is resolved when one obtains a complete realization about one's true nature. This is known as *moksha* or liberation. We can see here the interplay among a number of ideas that form the basis of Western religious thought, such as the relationships between omnipotence and limitation, self and God, goodness and evil, and so on. Kant suggested that the philosopher's task was not to promote or add to the substance of religious beliefs, but to analyze their structures and lay bare their presuppositions, judgments, and inconsistencies. This is generally the approach taken by philosophy of religion courses taught in philosophy departments in most Western universities. Nevertheless, there have been philosophers who have not simply taken a neutral analytic approach to religious traditions. Friedrich Nietzsche (1844–1900) launched an all-out assault on Christianity in his work *The Antichrist*, and is remembered for his dictum "God is dead." In this Nietzsche is pointing to the impotence of conventional concepts of God to provide any basis for morality or meaning for people in the modern world. A more sober summary of philosophical arguments against some Christian beliefs is found in Bertrand Russell's (1872–1970) lecture "Why I am not a Christian."

There is also another type of philosophy of religion that is primarily theological in orientation. It is perhaps more correctly called philosophical theology, and although still ultimately a form of apologetics, is less rigorously bound to the strict canons of belief in the religious traditions it examines. An exemplar of this approach is John Hick (b. 1922), whose intellectual struggles with issues of theodicy and God's love have moved him into studies of religious pluralism, so that he now challenges fundamental Christian doctrines, such as belief in the divinity of Jesus of Nazareth. Nevertheless, this brand of philosophy of religion is still theology, because it does not content itself with analysis, but attempts to put forward its own formulations. It is engaged in the process of adding to or subtracting from the actual content of certain religious traditions.

One of the more influential of modern metaphysical philosophers of religion is Alvin Plantinga (b. 1932), who may be classified as a Christian apologist. Among Plantinga's contributions is his intellectual attack on the foundations of knowledge. For instance, he questions many atheistic arguments that claim theism (i.e. a belief in god) is irrational. Plantinga points out that such a notion of irrationality implies that the believer is somehow mentally dysfunctional or flawed. However, he argues that a thing might be regarded as functioning properly if it fulfils the reason for its creation. A theist might then argue that our cognitive faculties function properly if we are fulfilling God's reason for having created us, and that belief in God is one intrinsic indicator of a properly functioning mind. The atheist, by contrast, is somewhat hard pressed to provide a rationale for why belief in God is a cognitive malfunction. After all, such belief does not necessarily prevent believers from satisfactorily achieving their goals, or diminish their capacity for survival. Do saintly figures such as Mother Teresa need to be criticized for not adequately applying their rational thinking skills, which would make belief in God seem unreasonable?

Theological approaches

In the introduction to this text, we briefly differentiated religious studies from religious education in general and theology in particular. The differences are important and often misunderstood. However, the relationship between the two is more complex than strict opposition. In fact, theological approaches have been the most influential mode of studying and transmitting religion for most of history. Theology is no longer the overarching "Queen of the Sciences" as it was once known in European universities, nor is it the dominant mode for studying religion in the secular university setting. In fact, many scholars pursuing the "scientific" study of religion explicitly distance themselves from theological approaches. However, they use the term "scientific" in keeping with social scientific ideals of objectivity and theories responsive to observation, repeatable experimentation, and analysis of data, which is in turn modeled on the systematic testing and modification of hypotheses characteristic of the scientific method in the physical sciences. The earlier assertion of theology as "Queen of the Sciences"—admittedly not the only discipline to make this claim—concerned a broader conception of science as a wide-ranging body of knowledge that employed reason to systematically pursue wisdom about nature, human beings, and the divine.

This theological approach has not disappeared, and it continues to shape religious understanding about doctrinal issues, ethics, interpretation of sacred texts, guidance for lay people and religious officiants, and answers or reflections on a variety of philosophical and spiritual questions. There are times when this approach crosses paths with other approaches in religious studies, but it is often separate in its questions, answers, and sources of authority, which are from within the faith tradition. We will return to the complex relationship between religious studies and theology, including different institutional configurations, in the second half of this section. First, we will briefly describe theological approaches through an eclectic survey of select religious thinkers who exemplify aspects of this approach in different eras and traditions. The term theology is typically used to discuss systematic Western formulations of thinking about God and religious belief in the Christian tradition. Its use at times extends to similar activities in closely related traditions, such as Judaism and Islam. It is less often used for Asian religious traditions, such as Buddhism and Hinduism, and many scholars of religion have rightly criticized misrepresentations and the ensuing misunderstandings that can arise when religious language developed in and for one tradition is used to describe or analyze something similar in another religion.

For example, soteriology is a technical term in the study of religion that refers to the doctrine of salvation. It is most at home in Christian theology, but at times it is applied to other traditions, such as Buddhism, that have highly developed texts, practices, and ideas related to religious salvation. However, the use of the term soteriology has fallen out of favor in much of the recent Buddhist scholarship for fear that it brings too much baggage specific to Christian ideas of salvation. Problems of language and the trade-offs that arise in borrowing a term from another tradition— both the advantages for comparison or clarification of unfamiliar traditions by means of a familiar term and the disadvantages of misrepresentations and conflation of meaning—are age old. Buddhism entered China from India in the first century CE, and for centuries translators and Chinese literati used Chinese characters and terms associated with Daoism, which they believed most closely approximated the concepts from this culturally and linguistically foreign Indian religion. Only near the middle of the first millennium were many of these terms dropped or clarified as translations were improved, Buddhism was better known in China, and Buddhists more forcefully differentiated their tradition from Daoism in recognition that the Daoist terms had brought with them Daoist lenses through which Buddhism had been misread. The view of Buddhism was thus distorted by the concepts, categories, and context of Chinese culture and the Daoist religious and philosophical worldview. Often the misreading was not intentional, and the Daoist terms served as a bridge between cultures until their distorting disadvantages outweighed their initial service of making the foreign tradition relatively accessible and meaningful.

These examples are a roundabout way of explaining why we are including examples from other traditions, such as Buddhism, in this section. Christian theologians might object to the inclusion of figures from these other traditions or to the limited coverage of the giants in their own tradition, and scholars of these other traditions might object to placing writings from Asian religions under this "theological" heading. However, our review of theological approaches concerns an orientation toward studying, reflecting on, systematizing, disseminating, defending, and promoting one's religion from within that tradition. This is a mode that can be employed in any tradition, and it is a mode that often comes into conflict with the ideals of the academic study of religion in the secular university. Just as Buddhists in China reached beyond the limitations of Daoist terms 1,500 years ago and scholars of Buddhism have questioned the usefulness of Christian terms, such as soteriology, for their studies in more recent years, a student of religious studies reading this text may come to challenge the fit between these examples and the category "theological approaches." However, exposure to these examples beyond the Western study of Christianity can familiarize students with core issues and concerns in the increasingly broad study of religion.

Early Christian theology

Although we will not limit our survey to Christian theologians, it makes sense to begin with Christianity. Theology certainly has not disappeared due to the arrival of many other approaches to the study of religion, and studying Christianity through theological and other approaches remains vibrant even as attention devoted to non-Christian traditions in Western universities has exploded in the last forty years. This recent past includes a diverse array of theologians, but the history of Christian theology remains rooted in much earlier seminal figures, such as Augustine of Hippo (354–430 CE). Augustine became Bishop of Hippo, a wealthy Roman port city in North Africa, at the end of the fourth century. His theological assertions therefore carried the authority of his high office. In his *Christian Doctrine*, Augustine formulates biblical interpretation and theological assumptions that remain influential today. He demonstrates a blend of argument based on reason with the more ultimate and authoritative basis of divine revelation. Augustine built on the foundation of theological assertions that had been formulated, contested, and clarified at the councils of Nicea in 325 and of Constantinople in 381. These councils addressed key theological issues, such as the nature of the Trinity (i.e. God the Father, Jesus Christ the Son, and the Holy Spirit), and established an authoritative creedal statement about core Christian beliefs, which is still recited today by hundreds of millions of Christians. This Nicene Creed begins, "We believe in one God, the Father Almighty, maker of heaven and earth, and of all things visible and invisible. And in one Lord Jesus Christ, the only begotten Son of God, . . . consubstantial to the Father, . . . Who for us men and for our salvation came down from heaven. And was incarnate of the Holy Ghost and of the Virgin Mary and was made man; was crucified also for us under Pontius Pilate, suffered and was buried; and the third day rose again according to the Scriptures."

These excerpts from the Nicene Creed illustrate the importance of orthodoxy, or correct belief, in Christianity and the continuity and enduring influence of theological formulations of belief from Augustine's time to the present. Similarly, later theologians built on Augustine's *Christian Doctrine* as well as his other major works, such as *Confessions* and *City of God*, by means of insights and analysis derived from both reason and faith. The quantity and quality of Augustine's output were impressive, and medieval and contemporary theologians return to his writings in their own assertions about doctrinal issues and theological responses to personal, institutional, and political questions. For example, Augustine's writings are still used in discussions about "just war theory"—the conjecture of philosophers and theologians regarding when and how war can be waged within permissible limitations and ethical guidelines.

The scholastic period

Thomas Aquinas (1225–1274) is frequently invoked in these same discussions, and his influential thought owes much to earlier theologians, including Saint Augustine, but also to earlier philosophers, especially Aristotle. Aquinas is a towering figure in the histories of theology and philosophy. Augustine and other Church Fathers—early Christian theologians writing in Greek and Latin during the Patristic era, which lasted for five or six hundred years following the composition of the New Testament around 100 CE—often presented faith as prior to and supportive of reason. Aquinas, instead, epitomized the medieval scholastic era of Christian theology, which is characterized by more systematic elevation of reason as separate from but ultimately equal to and aligned with faith. Aquinas and others used reason, once it was deemed not to be in conflict with faith, to prove and defend faith. Aquinas's writings, including his reflections on the nature of God, ethics, and Christ in the *Summa Theologica*, became central to the medieval European university setting in which scholasticism thrived.

Influential theologians in the centuries before Aquinas's time also attempted to work out this relationship between faith and reason. For example, Peter the Lombard's treatise, *Sentences*, provided a seminal contribution to Christian theology in the twelfth century CE. Some theologians, within and beyond Christianity, promoted the value and capacity of reason to understand and support religious truth, while others doubted that reason could access the mysterious depths of religion, which they felt were better plumbed by intuition, revelation, and religious— rather than philosophical—reflection and contemplation. Muslim and Jewish thinkers were among the influential religious and philosophical figures who addressed these issues. In fact, the resurgence of Aristotle's thought and other aspects of Greek culture owe a great debt to Muslim thinkers and Islamic civilization more generally for keeping alive and contributing to texts and ideas that had been lost to Europe.

Averroes (1126–1198), also known as Ibn Rushd, was just such an influential Muslim philosopher and theologian. He was born in southern Spain in the city of Cordoba and his extensive commentaries on Aristotle helped to reintegrate Aristotle more fully into Western theology and philosophy. In fact, his commentary provided a model for the style and Aristotelian leanings of Aquinas. Ibn Sina (980–1037), known in Europe as Avicenna, can in turn be understood as a model for Averroes, whose contributions also ranged from theology to medicine. Ibn Sina was a multi-talented Persian physician and philosopher. His genius was both broad and deep. His breadth is evident in volumes of writings ranging from medicine to theology, physics to metaphysics, logic to poetry. The depth of his insight and influence is particularly clear in the field of medicine, where his *Canon* remained the standard work in European medical schools, as well as throughout the Islamic world, for centuries. He, too, wrote commentaries on Aristotle, which influenced Muslim theologians and Christian scholastics. The influence of these great medieval thinkers on one another was not simply a matter of adopting the theological systems of a predecessor as a whole. Averroes criticized aspects of Ibn Sina's commentaries and Aquinas disagreed with some of Averroes' interpretation of Aristotle. The shared interest in Aristotle across cultures and religious traditions during this medieval period demonstrates shared concerns about the roles of reason and faith and illustrates how theological approaches, far from being confined to Christianity, were influenced by Muslim thinkers at that time. The examples of these eminent medieval men of letters also illustrate that theology was one sphere of inquiry that overlapped with interests in medicine, natural sciences, metaphysics, philosophy, law, etc.

Two more examples of great religious thinkers from this theologically rich era illustrate influential theological contributions in Islam and Judaism. Al-Ghazali (1058–1111), also known as Algazel by the European scholastics, remains one of the most influential Muslim theologians in history. His unique academic and religious life oscillated between the extremes of academic training and philosophy on the one hand and personal religious questing and contemplation as a Sufi mystic on the other. His insights and writings integrated, systematized, and moderated extremes of philosophical reason, Sufi mysticism, and Sunni orthodoxy. He employed his mastery of Greek philosophy, which had earlier caused him to doubt his faith and leave his professorship on a religious quest, to use the logic of Aristotle and methods of the Neoplatonists to demonstrate the limitations of reason as well as its value. In particular, he asserted that reason and philosophy are not capable of reaching beyond finite boundaries and experiencing the infinite, absolute, divine. His identity, practices, and perspective as a Sufi were crucial to his religious under-standing, but he sought to rein in what he perceived as excesses of Sufism as well. His integrative and systematizing genius harmonized Sufism and Sunni orthodoxy with close attention to ethics, beliefs, and practices—including detailed daily guidance. His writings exemplify many aspects of theology, from studying and interpreting authoritative scriptures and precedents to determining norms and standards, speculating about metaphysical and spiritual understandings of the divine Absolute, and giving detailed guidance for how a believer should live his life.

The final Western medieval theologian in our survey is Moses Maimonides (1135–1204), also known as Rambam. Like his contemporary, Averroes, he was born in Cordoba, Spain, and was a tremendously influential physician and philosopher. Unlike Averroes, he was a Jewish rabbi and thinker. His early education benefited from the cultural and intellectual flowering of Islamic southern Spain, but he and his family had to leave Cordoba when he was thirteen, and he eventually fled Spain in his twenties due to persecution of non-Muslims. After brief stays in Morocco and Israel, he moved to Egypt and spent most of his life as a leader of Cairo's Jewish community. His life story illustrates both the cross-cultural and inter-religious dimensions of knowledge exchange, including theology, as well as the ways religion can divide. In this case, his leaving Spain was forced by political orders backed by religious authority demanding that he convert to Islam or go into exile.

Moses Maimonides, like the other medieval theologians, took up the issue of faith and reason. He, too, read Aristotle, including commentaries by Ibn Sina, and he determined that religious people need not be embarrassed by apparent con-tradictions between philosophy and the Torah because ultimately there is no contradiction. God revealed the truths in the Torah and God endowed humans to come to complementary truths through reason, science, and philosophy. Moses Maimonides used reason to argue proofs for God's existence and unity. He was a great Talmudic scholar, whose commentaries on Mishnah offered interpretations, systemization, and guidance on the religious and social duties outlined by Jewish law. Along with setting norms for Jewish practices, he also formulated the "Thirteen Principles" of faith, which served as a Jewish creed where adherence to these fundamental principles establishes membership in the "Community of Israel." His *Mishneh Torah*, along with the more philosophical *Guide for the Perplexed*, which masterfully harmonized faith with reason as developed in philosophy and science, provided lasting contributions to Jewish thought and marked the apex of medieval Jewish theology and philosophy.

As already noted, these medieval Western theologians were also philosophers and often physicians, scientists, and more. The category of "theological approaches" under which we have grouped them does not exhaust their contributions, but it is fundamental to their thought and influences. Each resolved potential tensions between reason and faith by firmly establishing the legitimacy and importance of faith and using reason to further bolster the position of faith. Certainly, they started with the importance of faith as a given, and they might not have been placed in this category if their ultimate conclusion dismissed faith and other core aspects of their religious identity. Al-Ghazali, for example, left his professorship when he felt his faith was threatened because he decided that the benefits of his status paled in comparison with the religious stakes of eternal reward or punishment. In other words, the religious commitment of these thinkers was primary and their brilliant philosophical and other contributions were linked and at times determined by or in the service of this religious commitment.

Post-Enlightenment theology in the West

Many theologians in these and other faiths have also contributed religious insights and guidance in more recent eras marked by tensions between science and religious faith. Apologetics in Christian theology took various forms to defend divine revelation against scientific truths found in nature, to defend Catholic or Protestant positions against each other, and to defend Christianity against a host of perceived religious and secular challenges. Various movements loosely labeled "liberal theology" incorporated reason, skepticism about dogmatic claims concerning revelation and miracles, biblical criticism that investigated the age, authorship, and variant readings of the Bible, and increased openness to the role of humans and specific historical and cultural contexts in shaping religion. Karl Barth (1886–1986), an eminent Protestant theologian born in Switzerland, was educated in this liberal theological mode, but broke away from its direction and from natural theology in a return to a more dogmatic position centered on biblical revelation as the only way to know God. Unlike various attempts to harmonize theology with philosophy or various sciences, Barth asserted a theology that depends only on the "word of God." Human beings' investigation of God will always fall short just as their too-human images of God do not appreciate God's transcendence.

Barth's example is useful to illustrate the fact that theological approaches, and other approaches to the study of religion, do not simply move in one direction. Assuming that theology would necessarily continue moving in a liberal direction might be akin to the mistaken assumptions about the impending disappearance of religion altogether in what theorists assumed to be an increasingly secular world. At the same time, even the work of an influential theologian of Barth's stature does not lead to the demise of liberal theology or to a divorce between theological approaches and contemporary currents in philosophy. There are many influential liberal theologians today, and well-known contemporaries of Barth, such as Rudolf Bultmann (1884–1976), shared some of Barth's concerns but also sought to demythologize the New Testament for a clearer and more immediate existential encounter that might provoke the believer to lead a life of authentic meaning. Existentialism refers to a philosophical approach that emphasizes the individual's choices and responsibility to forge a meaningful existence through encounters with a world that has no set meaning. Many existentialists are atheists; however, there are other important existentialist theologians as well. Martin Buber (1878–1965) and Paul Tillich (1886–1965) are two more examples of influential, existentialist philosopher-theologians from Judaism and Protestant Christianity respectively.

An earlier forefather of existentialism and modernism, the great Danish philosopher Søren Kierkegaard (1813–1855), laid a foundation for "a leap of faith" characterized by passionately embracing faith and participating in religion as a focused and subjective commitment beyond a sense of merely following one's duty as dictated by philosophy, ethics, or dogma. These eminent thinkers' identities as philosophers and theologians blur distinctions between these categories in ways that recall what we saw with medieval Christian, Jewish, and Muslim philosopher-theologians. However, Kierkegaard and many other subsequent philosophical and religious thinkers differ from their medieval predecessors in acknowledging insurmountable contradictions between reason and faith; and proclaiming their own choice of faith over reason for reasons of existential rather than logical necessity when confronted with such gaping discontinuity.

Some influential Christian theologians

Augustine of Hippo (354–430 CE): Influential Christian Church father; known for his doctrine of original sin; author of *City of God*, *On Christian Doctrine*, and the *Confessions*.

Anselm of Canterbury (1033–1109): Italian; influential early scholastic known for his ontological argument for the existence of God; served as Archbishop of Canterbury.

Peter Lombard (c. 1100–1160): Italian-born, French scholastic; renowned for his *Four Books of Sentences* (c. 1150), a systematic summary of Church doctrine, which functioned as the standard Christian theological text of the Middle Ages.

Thomas Aquinas (1225–1274): Italian Dominican friar; possibly the most influential of Catholic theologians; attempted to reconcile rational philosophy in the style of Aristotle with Church doctrine in his *Summa Theologica* (1265–74).

John Duns Scotus (1266–1308): Influential Scottish theologian, supporter of the Catholic doctrine of the immaculate conception (i.e. born without original sin) of Mary, mother of Jesus.

William of Ockham (c. 1288–1347): English scholastic philosopher, critic of the papacy, known for the doctrine of parsimony in the formulation of explanations and theories (Occam's Razor).

Friedrich Schleiermacher (1768–1834): German thinker; arguably the most influential Protestant theologian of the nineteenth century; conceived of religion as founded upon inner sentiments, such as the feeling of utter dependence.

Søren Kierkegaard (1813–1855): Danish philosopher/theologian; known for his contributions to the notion of faith, laying the foundations of the philosophy of existentialism, and criticizing systematic rational perspectives for inadequately depicting the reality of the human condition.

Rudolf Bultmann (1884–1976): German Lutheran theologian; associated with efforts to "demythologize" scripture by uncovering personally useful theological messages within scriptural narratives, rather than affirming their literal meanings.

Paul Tillich (1886–1965): German-American Protestant theologian, known for his emphasis on religion and theology as founded upon a human being's ultimate concern; wrote his *Systematic Theology* (in three volumes) over a period from 1951 to 1963.

Karl Barth (1886–1968): Influential Swiss-born Protestant Reformed theologian, who studied in Germany; a pacifist who opposed the Nazi regime, he was deported to Switzerland; his *magnum opus* (great work) is the thirteen-volume *Church Dogmatics*, written between 1932 and 1968.

John Hick (b. 1922): American theologian and philosopher of religion, known for reflections on theodicy and support of pluralism, i.e. the view that salvation may also be available through other faiths.

Alvin Plantinga (b. 1932): American philosopher/theologian; Christian apologist, associated with the idea that faith in the existence of God needs no proof, and some features of intelligent design.

Some Eastern "theologies"

Although examples of theological approaches have focused on religious thinkers and dynamics in the three Abrahamic traditions, there are many thinkers from Asian traditions who could be brought into this discussion of theological approaches broadly conceived. As with their Western counterparts, they do not neatly fall into just one category, and several who immediately come to mind could also be categorized as philosophers. The following examples from China, Tibet, and Japan have been chosen because they exemplify the normative interpretation or systemization of a religious tradition, or types of apologetics, where the religious thinker is defending or promoting his tradition over other religious traditions. Generalizations about East Asian religions' harmonious coexistence, and even complementary relationship, are relatively accurate and helpful up to a point. However, there are conflicts and polemical writings in Asian religions too. Polemical writings are common in most theological and philosophical traditions, and consist of arguments attempting to disagree with or refute the opinions of others. Despite Beat Zen and similar Western notions of Buddhism that ignore its institutional forms and history, Buddhism has its own tradition of textual interpretation and missionary activity. The category of "theological approaches" for the following examples may not fit perfectly, but has some explanatory power.

The interaction between Buddhism and other religious traditions in East Asia stimulated new formulations to define and justify each tradition in light of the others. For example, just as Daoist terms were used in early Chinese translations of Buddhist texts, Buddhist apologists used arguments from Confucian classics to define and defend their "foreign" tradition in Chinese culture. This approach is analogous to the use of reason and philosophy to support religious faith at times when there were tensions between those spheres. In the case of Buddhism entering China, there were tensions between Chinese cultural sensibilities, as articulated by Confucian values, and the foreign Buddhist notions of monastic life, which threatened traditional modes and the importance of having children to serve their living parents and venerate their deceased ancestors. The Buddhist apologetic tract, "The Disposition of Error," appears to have been written in the middle of the first millennium CE in response to anti-Buddhist polemical writings. The author of this work quotes Confucius, Laozi (Lao Tzu), and other venerated Chinese philosophers from 1,000 years earlier to rebuff challenges that Buddhism should not be followed because it is not Chinese, and to answer a series of questions about Buddhist beliefs regarding death, rebirth, the lack of a recipe for immortality, and Buddhist foreign practices—namely, celibacy, harming one's own body, and renouncing worldly pleasure.

Around this same time, the sixth-century CE Chinese monk Zhiyi (Chih-i) founded the Tiantai (T'ien-T'ai) School of Buddhism and systematized the vast corpus of Buddhist *sutras* (i.e. summaries of doctrines) and commentaries that had arrived from India. His monumental task included sorting out and harmonizing apparent doctrinal discrepancies found in the religious writings from India. The resulting synthesis respects philosophy and practice while promoting a unified vehicle of Buddhism with the *Lotus Sutra* as the dominant text. During the following 1,400 years, East Asian religious thinkers have interpreted from this *sutra* the meaning, order, and structure of the Buddha's teachings, as well as guidance for daily life, and more lofty promises of protection, enlightenment, and world transformation. Nichiren, a thirteenth-century Japanese Buddhist monk, went beyond defensive apologetics to denounce Buddhists of other schools and rulers who did not show sufficient reverence for the *Lotus Sutra* and failed to invoke it through the practice of reciting its title. The polemical passion of Nichiren's assertions of orthodoxy and orthopraxy, right belief and right practice, is not the norm for Buddhism. Nonetheless, the example is useful to demonstrate that even the divisive connotations of theology have counterparts in Asian traditions.

Tsong Khapa (1357–1419) provides a powerful example of a Tibetan Buddhist systematizer, reformer, and theologian who instituted rigorous standards of virtue, practice, textual study, interpretation, and debate. The influential Gelugpa sect, of which the Dalai Lama is the head, arose out of his reforms and systemization. He presided over a monastic university with thousands of monks and is credited as the teacher of the first Dalai Lama, although the title came about centuries later and was assigned to Tsong Khapa's student retroactively. The title Dalai Lama means "Teacher [who is an] Ocean [of wisdom and compassion]." Tsong Khapa's *Great Exposition of the Path* typifies a theological *magnum opus* (i.e. great work) capable of integrating diverse teachings and offering guidance for Buddhists' daily life, philosophical perspective, and ultimate religious aims.

Finally, for more recent examples from Asia, we will briefly mention two Japanese Buddhists. Shaku Sōen (1859–1919), a Zen monk and abbot, is the most famous of the Japanese Buddhist representatives who attended the 1893 World's Parliament of Religions in Chicago. This widely publicized event was part of the Columbian Exposition, which was a particularly influential and well attended World's Fair. The very concept of holding such a forum of religious representatives from around the world stemmed from liberal theological optimism of shared brotherhood in diverse traditions as well as impulses to improve or solidify the standing of individual religious traditions through the process of comparison and to bolster the position of religion as a whole. Religion was facing considerable challenge from the surging authority of science and the perceived disconnect between Charles Darwin's theory of evolution, as well as subsequent forms of social Darwinism, and religious doctrine including biblical explanations of creation. Shaku Sōen's presentation, "The Law of Cause and Effect as Taught by Buddha," is noteworthy for how it explains a fundamental Buddhist teaching while emphatically asserting that this is a "law of nature, independent of the will of Buddha, and still more of the will of human beings." He and his fellow Buddhist delegates emphasized rational dimensions of Buddhism for their own strategic, apologetic reasons of promoting Buddhism as a universal religion particularly well suited to modernity. The final figure, Abe Masao (1915–2006), continued this work of representing Zen Buddhism in the West; however, his training in Japanese and Western philosophy as well as theology equipped him for in-depth forms of interfaith dialogue. This dialogue has attempted to provide a bridge of understanding between traditions through discussion and debate of shared and differing practices and philosophical and theological perspectives.

Theology vis-à-vis religious studies

The preceding eclectic examples of theologians from various times and traditions illustrate certain theological concerns as well as the overlap between theology, philosophy, and other disciplines. This section will attempt to situate these theological approaches in relation to religious studies in academic settings today. Secular religious studies departments and academic programs at universities only came onto the scene in the second half of the twentieth century. Although some of the seminal thinkers, texts, and approaches to the secular, academic study of religion were earlier products of the nineteenth century, religious studies as a discipline is much younger than the millennia-old traditional perspectives in the study of religion—philosophy and theology.

Theology is typically the domain of religious "insiders" who are actively promoting, defending, transmitting, and shaping their tradition. Of course, theologians reflect on issues that are important beyond the boundaries of their tradition, such as the nature of the divine, of humanity, of existence, and of a meaningful life. This mode of inquiry is highly valued in many traditions and by many people. The questions and answers are shaped by a particular tradition and are typically directed toward members of that same tradition—to deepen faith, convey wisdom, inspire or curtail certain actions or beliefs. They may offer guidance in understanding the tradition, leading a life according to the tradition, and formulating positions on a range of new or timeless issues often by extrapolating from traditional, authoritative sources. Whereas apologetics can include theological arguments that defend or explain the insider's tradition to an outsider, theology more typically denotes an authoritative voice from within a particular tradition speaking to other members of the same religious community about their shared tradition, values, and concerns.

The discipline of religious studies in the secular university differs on each of these main points. The scholar studying religion in this academic setting need not be an insider in any tradition. She can be religious, but might direct her academic research to a religious tradition other than her own and in any case should self-consciously attempt to avoid privileging her tradition or restricting questions and analysis to views sanctioned by her religious tradition. Just as the scholar need not be an insider, the scholarship is generally not conducted for or targeted to a specific religious audience. Religion is considered to be one of many subjects of study for which the scholars, students, questions, concerns, and approaches resemble what one finds in other disciplines in the humanities and social sciences, such as in history and anthropology. Some of the same questions of ultimate meaning arise, but for religious studies there is often a sense that it is not the scholar's role to sit in judgment of religious or metaphysical claims of ultimate truth or divinity so much as to analyze these claims, along with a wide variety of practices, beliefs, texts, and perspectives, for what they reveal about society, history, culture, and people and their religions. In short, the religious studies scholar should avoid the normative role of determining what the norms or standards of a religion should be and what its followers should believe, whereas the theologian's role can go beyond these boundaries by actively shaping and defining norms as well as defending and promoting a tradition.

As you may have noticed, this last sentence, which asserts that religious studies scholars *should* not play a normative role in dictating what a religion should be, is itself a normative statement. However, it is a normative statement about what the *academic study of religion* in the secular university should be, not an attempt to regulate the members, beliefs, and practices of a religious tradition. This is intentional. By means of this introductory text, we aspire to introduce students to the academic study of religion, including a sense of the norms and standards for this pursuit in a university setting. Students and scholars, both within and beyond religious studies, often confuse and conflate religion, the study of religion, and being religious. When kept separate, there is no contradiction in asserting that a norm for the academic study of religion should be to avoid determining norms for how a religious tradition should be practiced. However, these categories are not always understood to be separate. Sometimes this is simply a matter of mistaken assumptions. For example, an acquaintance at university might automatically assume that a student majoring in religious studies is especially religious. That may or may not be true, just as another student who is majoring in biology may or may not be religious.

Even other university professors can make this mistaken assumption. One of our colleagues in religious studies noticed that a professor of biology had just finished giving an exam in the room where he was about to teach. He jokingly invited that professor to stay and teach his religious studies class and received the earnest reply that the biology professor could not possibly teach that course *because he is not religious.* Our colleague jokingly replied, "Do you have to be a frog to teach biology?" This humorous exchange is not meant to suggest that someone who is religious cannot do religious studies—unlike the frog, which would presumably be hard pressed to lecture on biology. Instead, it reinforces the fact that *religion* signifies the *object of study* for religious studies, and *not the required disposition* for religious studies scholars and students. The example highlights the distinction between religion, religious studies, and being religious. The other professor mistakenly declined because he is not religious, whereas he would have been perfectly justified to refuse because he did not have training in religious studies, or was not an anthropologist, historian, or sociologist who focused his attention on religion as an object of study.

This attempt to separate and clarify the distinctions between religion, the study of religion, and being religious, runs into difficulty with the theological approach. In this approach, there is often an intentional conflation of these categories. Or, from the perspective of this approach, the theologian might argue that it is the secular religious studies attempt to separate these categories that is mistaken and confused.

This is a fundamental difference. Consequently, we are pursuing two purposes in this section on the theological approach, which are partially in tension with each other. In addition to offering a preliminary and general idea of what this approach entails, we are simultaneously attempting to differentiate it from the other approaches in the academic study of religion in order to clarify the boundaries and norms of our discipline for the secular university setting. Clarification of a complex relationship risks oversimplification, but remains worth pursuing in an introductory text precisely because confusion within and about religious studies often centers on these dichotomies of insider/outsider, subjective/objective, descriptive/normative, and religious studies/theology.

Interaction at university

However, to define religious studies simply as apart from theology ignores how centuries of theology influenced the relatively recent discipline of religious studies, as well as how theological approaches continue to interact with other modes of religious studies. This interaction is part of a complicated relationship with a spectrum of attitudes and institutional dynamics. There are religious studies scholars who are adamant that theology has no place in the academic study of religion and even perceive theological thinking as a principal threat that religious studies must guard itself against. Conversely, there are theologians who see no value in secular modes of inquiring about religion and see menacing attempts to limit, reduce, and "explain away" religion in everything from the scholars' use of the category of "religion" as one of many facets of human culture and activity, to the social scientific modes used to describe, understand, and explain religious practices and beliefs. There are many positions in between these extremes that acknowledge more or less value in either theology or religious studies as a mode that can supplement or at least provide material for their own mode of studying, analyzing and interpreting religion.

Institutionally, the relationship between theology and religious studies has varied at universities depending on the country, era, and history of each institution. For example, there are many religious seminaries, colleges, and universities in Canada and the United States. In these institutions, religious education is often theological and is characterized by believers of one faith teaching, interpreting, and shaping their tradition for believers of that same faith. Public universities and secular private colleges and universities in North America often seek clear separation between theology and religious studies. Here the era and history of each post-secondary institution plays a role as some are now only nominally attached to religious identities that were more important when they were founded. In other words, they may have had religious education requirements emphasizing a single tradition early in their history, but have since moved to a secular religious studies model. Well-known universities, such as Harvard and Yale, have a divinity school as well as a much younger program of religious studies. At these schools of divinity, theology and the training of ministers continued to be central to their role even after the addition of programs for the study of various religions using secular, academic approaches. On the other hand, their fellow Ivy League institution, the University of Pennsylvania, never had a school of divinity. As a result, the secular academic mode of religious studies did not contend with or separate from theological approaches.

Admittedly, Harvard promotes the interrelatedness of its Divinity School, various departments in the Faculty of Arts and Sciences, and centers and committees focused on the study of religion. However, models of institutional separation between theology and religious studies, or the presence of only one or the other, are more the norm in North America. Universities in Great Britain, on the other hand, often integrate the two more fully. The theological approach has been an especially influential mode of reflecting on religion at major German universities. Of course, each institution has its own history and all are constantly changing from era to era. Change, alongside continuity, is evident in the study of religion from new Buddhist-oriented universities in western North America to some of the most respected and tradition-conscious European centers of learning. For example, "D Society" seminars at the University of Cambridge's Faculty of Divinity continue to draw brilliant scholars and theologians to fortnightly lectures followed by debates that are both spirited and thoughtful. However, there are important differences between past and present. The professors and lecturers are no longer all Anglicans. Not all focus exclusively, or even primarily, on Christianity. Moreover, participants read widely beyond theology and incorporate theories and data from other approaches of religious studies and beyond.

In short, the relationship between religious studies and theology is complex, varied, and still developing in each era, place, and institution. Theology, generally conceived, has been central to teaching, learning, interpreting, and shaping religious understanding in most places for most of history. However, it is at times marginal or oppositional to the secular academic study of religion. That is to say, depending on the time, place, institution, and scholar, a theological approach may or may not be perceived to be part of religious studies. In fact, some scholarship that is not explicitly theological may be characterized as a sort of crypto-theology, or hidden theology, due to its normative claims about what religion or certain religious traditions, practices, or beliefs should be, or how a sacred essence of religion can only be understood or interpreted from within a religious perspective or a privileged religious experience. Some phenomenological approaches, which we address in a later section, are accused of being too theological or insufficiently scientific in their quest for the essence of religion or the real meaning or ultimate importance of religious experiences, beliefs, or practices. Not only is the relationship between theology and religious studies complex and controversial, it is not always clear where the boundary should be drawn between the two or which side of that contested boundary certain scholars, essays, or approaches inhabit. In fact, theologians can do academic religious studies and can make use of any of the approaches surveyed in this text. Religious studies scholars *can* ask theological questions and engage in theological reflection on a religious tradition. However, confusion arises when scholars slip into a theological mode without being clear about what they are doing—

either because they do not realize that they have crossed this tenuous boundary or because they do not acknowledge to their audience which hat they are wearing from one essay to the next or even in the middle of a given essay or lecture.

We have devoted quite a bit of space to this issue of the relationship between theology and religious studies precisely because it has been and will almost certainly continue to be a tension in the study of religion and a point of confusion and controversy for students pursuing religious studies in a university setting. Of course, scholars of religious studies can help clarify the muddied waters by being more aware, forthcoming, and consistent about which hat they are wearing in their writing, lectures, and class discussion. Moreover, students' understanding of religion and religious studies can benefit from greater sensitivity to the distinction between the two and awareness of the perspectives, objectives, and possible biases of each voice they encounter. This benefit is not restricted to greater scrutiny of what students encounter at university—in their textbooks, films, lectures, research, and discussions with professors and fellow students—but extends out into the rest of their life and society from interaction with neighbors, relatives, and acquaintances to more savvy analysis of portrayals of religion in news media and popular culture.

3

Studying religion within communities

Social and cultural perspectives

Anthropological approaches

As noted in the previous sections, certainly by the time of the early Greek philosophers, people in the Western world were speculating on the origins of religion, and doing so through comparison with other cultures. Xenophanes had speculated on how people imagine gods in their own image and appearance, and Herodotus had noted how deities from a foreign culture had migrated to and been adopted by people in his own culture. To some extent these philosophers/historians were engaged in a sort of rudimentary anthropology of religion. However, the discipline of anthropology, as it is currently conceived, is a relatively recent phenomenon rooted in the spirit of the eighteenth-century Western Enlightenment. As its name suggests anthropology (*anthropos*—human being + *logos*—study) is the study of human beings, persons, or humanity (or as encountered in older, now inappropriate, non-gender-inclusive language, the "study of man"). In telling ways the discipline of anthropology is also rooted in the age of discovery and colonial expansion, which began in the fifteenth century. The European contact with New World cultures, as well as with people from societies in Africa and the East, led to a fascination with the appearance, behaviors, and artifacts of these "others." When conjoined with the emerging theory of evolution—for Charles Darwin had published his influential *The Origin of Species* in 1858—early anthropologists began to see their studies as contributing to the understanding of human evolution. Thinkers such as Herbert Spencer (1820–1903) had extrapolated the theory of the evolution of species to the evolution of societies in what is sometimes referred to as social Darwinism. Eurocentric attitudes concocted the notion that European societies (and Western monotheistic religion) represented the apex of an evolutionary process in which non-European societies and people could be seen as lower on the evolutionary ladder. Many early anthropologists were thus measuring skulls and other body parts of so-called primitive tribes to demonstrate how these meshed with the archaeological discoveries of prehistoric hominids. It was thought that people who lived in technologically simple societies, in a close interrelationship with nature (i.e. hunter-gatherers, or small scale agriculturalists), were physically, mentally, socially, and religiously closer to some ancient extinct hominids such as Neanderthals. Much of this kind of anthropology has mostly been abandoned, as the study of human biological evolution has been ceded to physical anthropologists, archaeologists, and biologists. From the late nineteenth century, anthropology began a shift in emphasis toward the study of human culture, and this is its defining characteristic today. The notion of social and cultural evolution is still promoted in various forms but is in tension with the prevailing theories that regard particular societies and cultures as developing according to their distinctive historical and environmental circumstances, and not as situated along some imaginary path in which high technology or large cities are necessary features of the evolutionary frontline.

Culture, society, and religion

Franz Boas (1858–1952) is often regarded as the father of American cultural anthropology. Trained as a scientist and geographer (Boas had a doctorate in physics), he naturally did not repudiate the value of scientific observation and data collection, which he held to be the cornerstone of cultural studies. Boas, nevertheless, understood culture as a malleable and dynamic category, and its study as not an exact science, and thus one in which humanistic features, such as the study of historical processes, should play a part. At the same time, in England, Bronislaw Malinowski (1884–1942) was promoting the indispensable value of fieldwork—that is, of living for extended periods of time within a foreign society, learning the language of its people, and participating in its ways of life. His approach has come to be known as participant observation, for participation needs to be blended with scientific distance, observation, and data collection. When conducting fieldwork, anthropologists should not remain distant from the people they are studying, but should, as much as is reasonably possible, interact with them and share in their culture, striving to be able to understand it from the cultural native's own point of view. However, unlike the native of a particular culture, the anthropologist must attempt to reflect on the gathered pieces of cultural information and endeavor to uncover larger or underlying patterns, interpreting and theorizing on the human condition. This heritage of Boas and Malinowski is still vibrantly alive in anthropology, which seeks to understand what it is to be human, primarily through the study of others whose societies and cultures seem markedly different from our own. British anthropologists have been associated with emphasizing the social scientific dimensions of the discipline, while the American heritage has emphasized, particularly recently, the interpretation of culture. However, the distinction between British social anthropology and American cultural anthropology can be misleading, for although the styles of individual anthropologists may lean in one or the other direction, the discipline of anthropology strives for holism in understanding others and requires the study of the dynamics of both social configurations and culture. Such studies are known as ethnographies.

While the term society may be somewhat less problematically defined simply as any group of people who share some cohesive element, "culture" is as elusive a term to define as religion. Anthropologists do not use the term culture to mean "having an elite set of behaviors" as in the expression, "They are uncultured boors!" All societies have culture. Culture is the full corpus of the collectively shared beliefs and activities of any social group. Culture plays an important role in binding social groups together, and those who do not share crucial aspects of culture are regarded as outsiders. Culture is transmitted through the generations, and among members of a social group, and many of its features may be so deeply rooted as to be simply assumed by members to be the way things are. This is why studying one's own culture is not preferred in anthropology, because the contrast offered by another society's cultural practices enables one to discern deeply embedded structures in one's own cultural behaviors. So while simply reaching out to shake someone's hand as a gesture of greeting, or belching in public after a good meal, may appear to be normal etiquette in certain cultures, they are not so in others. Such rules of etiquette are obvious markers of difference and may be relatively trivial in their implications, but people may also be particularly attached to certain powerful cultural symbols in non-trivial ways. A public gesture of irreverence, such as defacing a political symbol (e.g. burning the American flag), or despoiling a religious icon (e.g. tearing up a photo of the Catholic Pope, making satirical depictions of the Muslim prophet Muhammad, destroying Buddha images or a Hindu temple) can cause outrage, and even induce some people to acts of violence, including murder. Religious beliefs are not trivial factors in a person's existence, and the study of religion therefore requires that one develops an awareness of the weight of its influence on individuals and their societies.

The anthropological study of religion thus brings the two nebulously defined categories of religion and culture into relationship with each other. Since culture is such a broad category, religion may be regarded as a cultural system that is a subset of it, since religious history, beliefs, and practices form a distinctive set of cohesive cultural elements for particular social groups. For instance, when one begins to study the society and culture of the nation of India (bound by a political cultural system), one discovers that there are large numbers of smaller social groups that one might examine (which cohere due to other cultural factors), most of which overlap and intersect with each other. There are political divisions (e.g. states, cities, villages), geographical regions (e.g. Himalayan, coastal, desert), kinship relations (e.g. caste, tribal), and religious groups (e.g. Hindu, Muslim, Jain, Buddhist, Sikh, Christian, Parsi, etc.) among others. One might more narrowly study the culture of any of these subgroups. Thus Hinduism or Hindu culture appears to be a simple subset (in the category of religion) of Indian culture. When examining Hindu religious culture one would further discover that there are sectarian subdivisions focused on particular deities—e.g. Shaivas, Vaishnavas, or Shaktas, who worship Shiva, Vishnu, and the Goddess, respectively—or followers of particular charismatic religious leaders—e.g. Sai Baba, Bhagwan Rajneesh (Osho)—or sub-categories based on religious approaches—e.g. ascetic renouncers, or householders who prefer devotional worship—and so on. So the idea of religion being a subset of the larger culture seems to be clear, as does the notion that there are subsets within the culture of any particular religion, such as Hinduism. However, when actually attempting to study a particular Hindu householder, one may discover that he hopes to be an ascetic renouncer on retirement, listens to the talks of both Sai Baba and Osho, performs devotional worship to Shiva, Vishnu, and the Goddess, and has a wife who has embraced Buddhism and who influences him with its religious philosophy. He may be a businessman, but with Marxist political leanings, who belongs to a caste that has large numbers in a desert state of Rajasthan near the Pakistan border although he now lives in Bangalore, a big city in the country's interior. On satellite television channels, he and his children watch music videos and evangelical Christian broadcasts that originate in the West. Through internet outsourcing of jobs, he works part-time calculating the annual income tax returns for American householders. Is he really a Hindu? Of course he is, within any reasonable parameter of the category. Do his religious beliefs affect his business practices and influence his political leanings? Of course they do.

It is instructive to be reminded that categories such as religion, culture, Indian, Hindu, householder, Marxist, devotional worshipper, Shaiva, or urban dweller are intellectual categories created for our convenience, to enable us to think about the world and better understand it and ourselves. However, the individual human being is not the smallest unit within such categories, who, like an odd, even, or prime number, can be placed (or pigeonholed) into the appropriately described mathematical set. It might actually be more correct to say, if only to elicit some attention to the point, that all those intellectual sets could be placed within the individual, for the human mind is the creator of such categories, including religion. It is at least true to suggest that individuals belong to multiple categories and through their personas (i.e. their actual shifting beliefs and behaviors) attempt to sustain, yet constantly transform, the very categories into which they seek to place themselves and others. It is thus naïve to think of religion as a monochromatic cultural subcategory bounded by firm lines, and separated from other spheres of life. Religion, as embodied in any individual, to some degree permeates virtually every aspect of that person's social reality, and is a dynamic, ever-changing thing. A person's religion is no more static than the person herself. Thus the category of religion, within the framework of the discipline of anthropology (i.e. the study of human beings) needs to be examined with as much attention to its complexity, subtlety, and shifting features as one would expect to grant to the study of any other feature of human culture.

Approaches and themes in the anthropology of religion

Early theorists

A pioneer in the discipline of anthropology and in the anthropological study of religion was Edward Burnett Tylor (1832–1917), whose two-volume *Primitive Culture* presents many of his ideas. Tylor is associated with promoting the concept of animism, through which he hoped to explain the origins of religion and its evolutionary development, and develop a science of culture studies. Tylor argued that when our ancestors wondered about differences among such states as sleep, dreams, and wakefulness, and between life and death, they applied their rational faculties to these observed phenomena, but were impeded by a lack of correct supporting information. They thus surmised that spirits or souls animated or gave life to things. Tylor regarded this belief in supernatural beings, which are thought to reside in humans, animals, and the natural world, as the earliest form of religious thinking. The separation of spirits, and their independent existence apart from the living beings and other natural phenomena that they were believed to inhabit, subsequently led to the development of polytheistic beliefs, since certain individual spirits were raised to the status of deities. Eventually, this assortment of disparate deities was coalesced into the concept of one overarching power, leading to monotheism. Tylor had simultaneously been promoting the theory of the cultural evolution of societies from savage (i.e. hunter-gatherer) to barbarous (i.e. domestication of plants and animals) to civilized (i.e. possessing writing). Thus monotheism was merely the animism of civilized societies. Tylor suggested that contemporary "primitive" (i.e. small-scale, non-urban, technologically simple) cultures were akin to ancient "savage" societies and would undergo inevitable stages of development culturally and religiously. It became commonplace among anthropologists to think that the study of such "primitive people," who were regarded as somehow retarded on the path of cultural progress (and even mental development), would provide clues to the past, revealing how the earliest of our ancestors actually thought and acted. The quest for the origins of religion among human beings was a vibrant theme in the early anthropology of religion.

Certain of Tylor's ideas were effectively criticized by the folklorist Andrew Lang (1844–1912). Lang, who had initially followed Tylor's ideas, later pointed to evidence that various primitive societies practiced monotheism at the outset and did not begin with polytheism or more rudimentary forms of animism. The Catholic priest and anthropologist, Father Wilhelm Schmidt (1868–1954), in support of this observation, actually tried to argue that all primitive societies were originally monotheists, and that monotheism was the original form of all religions. To some extent, theorizing on the evolutionary development of religion, conducted by those aligned with

Tylor's ideas, was a type of response opposing other Christian-influenced assertions that the religions of primitive societies were degenerate forms of an original mono-theism. Theories on the origins of religion also emerged from other disciplines, such as from Max Müller (1823–1900), a philologist (*philos*—love + *logos*—word) who specialized in the study of Sanskrit and Indo-European languages. Müller speculated that our early ancestors were awe-struck by and worshipped forces of nature, such as the brilliance of the sun or of lightning. However, eventually, through a common error produced by all language, in which the word is mistaken for the thing itself, and where the thing's qualities tend to be personified, these natural forces began to be regarded as governed by supernatural agents or deities. Mythology was thus a "disease of language." It was soon apparent that such theories on the origins of religion were either proved to be incorrect, only partially true, or simply unpro-ductive notions because they could not be tested, testing being the hallmark of science, with which anthropology strives to be in alignment. However, new thematic concerns developed in the anthropological study of religion.

James George Frazer (1854–1941) was a prolific writer and a classic example of the "armchair anthropologist." It is said that he spent about twelve hours every day for sixty years, without a single day of rest, in academic study, and had a personal library of over 30,000 books. Widely read and extremely erudite, Frazer made marked contributions to our understanding of religion, particularly myth and ritual, through his monumental work, *The Golden Bough*. It is a highly readable encyclopedic study, full of comparative ethnographic data, for Frazer strove to find patterns in beliefs, practices, and institutions across cultures. For instance, Frazer offered useful categories for magical practices, among which he discerned two main types. Homeopathic or imitative magic is based on the law of similarity, as in the example of drums being beaten to resemble thunder to induce rain. Contagious magic, however, is based on the law of contact or contagion, as when a sorcerer uses fingernail clippings or burns an item of clothing that has been in contact with victims to make them suffer. Frazer noted that these categories are often combined, and he thus used the term "sympathetic magic" for both, since they are based on a belief that things are connected to each other through some hidden relationship.

Frazer also accepted Tylor's scheme of distinguishing between magic, science, and religion, but placed these three in an evolutionary sequence. Magic, he argued, was the most primitive, since it recognized a simple congruence or similarity between certain ideas, such as using a voodoo doll to represent a person. Magic, he thought, was a kind of pseudo-science, based on an incorrect understanding of the natural laws in the world. Religion reflected a higher order of thinking, indicating an intellectual evolution in a society, but was also more primitive than science, which he argued would progressively surpass religion in the most culturally developed societies. Such ideas are still prevalent today, even though the studies of field-working anthropologists and sociologists suggest that they are incorrect. Frazer's comparative work has been criticized by anthropologists who recognize that in his quest for finding universal patterns Frazer had not given enough attention to the specifics and contexts (and therefore rather significant differences) of particular cultural behaviors. The sharp distinction that Frazer, Tylor, and others had drawn between magic and religion was also brought into question. Studies demonstrated that the kinds of practices and underlying attitudes that were classified as magic—or more negatively labeled as "superstition"—were abundant in most of the major religions. The more one examined the evidence, the more unreasonable it appeared to place magic and religion into firmly separate categories.

Some scholars have also pointed to characteristics within science, such as patterns of authority, attitudes towards specialists, faith-like tendencies to accept unquestioningly, and so on, that resemble religious attitudes and behaviors. While these are not intrinsic to the method of modern science, which discourages blind faith and encourages experimental verification, the culture of the scientific establishment, and particularly the way it is regarded by some sectors of non-scientists, lead some to suggest that science is not far removed from the category of "religion." For instance, some members of certain religious groups see science as promoting a worldview that challenges their own, and thus relate to science as if it were another rival religious system. Others, rejecting religion but not adequately understanding the attitude of healthy skepticism in the scientific approach to understanding, treat the opinions of renowned scientists and the content of articles published in renowned scientific journals as unquestionably sacrosanct.

From the perspective of the discipline of religious studies, it is instructive to recognize that, unlike modern science, religion is not one, fairly clearly defined and agreed upon, uniform set of attitudes or practices. When people (including scientists) attempt to compare or contrast religion and science, they are often erroneously only comparing faith-based religious traditions against the imperative in science not to accept anything on blind faith. Religion is assumed to mean "Christianity," or "Islam," which, of course, it is not. Comparing science and religion is like comparing skimmed milk from cows to, say, all varieties of cheese. The exploration of similarities and differences can be instructive, teaching us much about definitions, categories, relationships, and so on, but may ultimately be grounded in some agenda that seeks to establish the nutritional superiority or equality, or some such valorization, of one over the other.

More pertinently for the discipline of religious studies, research evidence seems to indicate that in the centuries since the introduction of the scientific method, despite its impressive explanatory power, and the widespread appeal of the technological advancements that it has provided, science has not replaced, but co-exists with, the human religious impulse. Thus the evolutionary scheme of the early theorists, in which science should replace religion in culturally advanced societies, does not appear to hold true. Instead there is a rise in religious fundamentalism in many parts of the world, where believers use satellite broadcasts, the internet, and advanced technologies developed through science. In other locales, although conventional religious practices, such as congregational church attendance and so on, may have eroded, these have been replaced with new approaches to spirituality, as in the rise of the so-called "new age" movement and religions.

Social-functionalist approaches

Returning to our survey of the history of major ideas in the anthropology of religion, we note that the early theorists proposed that the basis of religion was psychological or sensory. They also regarded religion as deriving from rational, although incorrect, inferences about personal (e.g. dreams) or natural (e.g. lightning) phenomena. A different approach to the understanding of religion was offered by Bronislaw Malinowski, known for his promotion of participant observation as a crucial method in the anthropological study of cultures. Malinowski also emphasized the need to study a society holistically, and to examine how its various institutions were interrelated. Attempting to study religious beliefs and practices in isolation from a group's political, educational, or economic structures, and such, leads to inadequate or even distorted understandings of how religion functions within that society. Malinowski wrote influential books based on his fieldwork among the Trobriand Islanders, a Melanesian culture. In his *Magic, Science, and Religion* (1925), he discussed the relationship among those three categories, arguing that all three were present in all societies no matter how primitive. He thus rejected the line of thinking put forward by Lucien Lévy-Bruhl (1857–1939) and others that pre-literate peoples had an archaic, irrational, and pre-logical mentality and were thus completely absorbed in a mystical state of mind.

Malinowski argued that magic, science, and religion always coexist because they serve different functions. For instance, when the Trobriand Islanders fished in relatively safe waters, such as lagoons, they simply relied on their technical skills. The same was true in the methods they used for planting and harvesting. However, they did perform magical rites when sailing in the open ocean. They also used magic after clearing the land before planting (to inhibit insects and disease), after planting (to ensure the seeds sprouted), and after the seeds sprouted (to ensure that they grew well). Thus science (i.e. rational, technical knowledge) was used in conjunction with magic. Malinowski proposed that magic developed as an emotional response to the frustration people felt with the limits of their technical know-how in practical situations. It gave them a feeling of control and confidence in processes over which they otherwise felt powerless. Thus science has a practical function, while magic serves a psychological function. Religion, too, he argued, has a psychological function, but deals with a different set of anxieties, such as the fear of death, which it seeks to alleviate. While science gives people a feeling of control over the natural world, religion provides them with a sense of control over their fate, and derives as an extension of their innate instinct for self-preservation beyond death. Thus religion also provides society with a certain stability, for it nurtures solidarity when the community gathers for religious rituals in situations, such as the death of an individual, which threaten to rupture the social fabric. Some of Malinowski's ideas were later criticized as being unwarranted extrapolations from a single example. Thus, although certain behaviors were true of the Trobriand Islanders, they were not necessarily true of all human beings, societies, and cultures. Also, although religion may at times help people cope with death, it is not the only mechanism for doing so, and while coping with anxieties may be one of its functions, it is not necessarily what constitutes the basis for religion itself. Malinowski's approach is often categorized as psychological functionalism, since it involved examining cultural phenomena, such as religion, to discern how these functioned in response to physiological and psychological needs.

Another style of functionalism, known as structural functionalism, is associated with the work of A. R. Radcliffe-Brown (1881–1955). Influenced by the social theorists Herbert Spencer and Émile Durkheim, Radcliffe-Brown emphasized the need to attend to the network of social relationships that provided societies with their structure. While psychological functionalists focus on individuals, social functionalism regards social roles and relationships as pre-eminently important. With regard to culture (and thus religion), Radcliffe-Brown stressed the need to explain or interpret social activities over theorizing about the origins of religion. The focus is on what is actually happening in a social group, as opposed to imagining how its ideas may have emerged. Just as the stomach's activity is to secrete gastric fluids, but its function is to break foods down so they can be assimilated by the body's tissues, the study of social activities can point us toward understanding their social functions. Like the stomach's digestive function, which plays a crucial role in the body's well-being, the function of any social activity plays its part in the well-being of a social system, which Radcliffe-Brown likened to organic systems. Although interpretation could focus on meaning (i.e. the beliefs that myths or symbols strive to express), rather than function (i.e. how these work to provide social order), he gave preference to the latter. This, he suggested, is because religious actions, such as rituals, are more worthy of attention than religious beliefs, since the latter are grounded in social attitudes or social values shaped and maintained by ritual acts. Actions such as these inform ideas.

Within a society's social values, that is, the shared interests of a particular group, one finds ritual values, and these in particular relate to the realms of magic and religion. Ritual values may be positive (if acts are prescribed) or negative (if they are prohibited). Furthermore, these ritual values should not be studied to establish whether they are magical or religious, or whether they alleviate personal anxieties or depend on a belief in supernatural agents. They are studied to understand how they reinforce the social networks that bind persons together into what constitutes a meaningfully ordered life. Religious rituals celebrate the features through which social integration occurs. Also, rituals are both expressive and symbolic, and it is necessary to uncover the meanings of these symbols, since shared meanings hold society together.

In an effective critique of Malinowski's rationale for religion, Radcliffe-Brown pointed out how magic and religion do not only serve to eliminate fear and anxieties, but can actually cause them, for people may fear the effects of malicious magical acts or the vengeful actions of divine spirits. To illustrate his ideas Radcliffe-Brown offered an alternate interpretation to Malinowski's psychological functionalism for certain food prohibitions associated with childbirth in the Andaman Islands, where he did his fieldwork. For a few weeks before and after the birth of a child, both parents are expected to avoid certain foods, such as pork or turtle meat, which are regarded as taboo. The term "taboo" derives from the Polynesian word *tabu* or *tapu*, and refers to a strong social prohibition, the breaking of which is considered offensive or even abhorrent. One might say that, in Radcliffe-Brown's terminology, fasting is a social value in Andaman society and that the pork or turtle meat have a certain ritual value. Their ritual value is negative since they are prohibited and serve as a taboo. If the soon-to-be parents eat taboo foods, the Andaman Islanders believe that the parents will get ill, or that such an act might be harmful to the baby. Malinowski's theory might suggest that the ritual prohibition or magical activity of maintaining the food taboo is a way of coping with the anxiety that parents feel in the period of unpredictable and potentially dangerous circumstances surrounding childbirth. However, Radcliffe-Brown suggests that without the taboo fasting rites, the parents (certainly the father) might not normally feel any anxiety. Society, however, expects that they should. The rites are there to generate a shared sense of anxiety and concern that brings the father into solidarity with the mother, and supports social connectedness. Another such example from a different context is ritualized weeping at funerals, where a society "expects" people to cry, and professional mourners may even be hired. Most scholars now recognize that it is an error to choose between individual and social rationales for activities, for both psychological and social functionalism may provide insights into the forces that shape religious culture.

E. E. Evans-Pritchard's (1902–1973) approach is also categorized as structural-functionalism, in that the activities of persons within a social group are studied to understand how these contribute to forming and sustaining the overall structure of their society. His approach is exemplified in his studies—one of which concerns their religion—of the Nuer, an East African tribal society. In his *Witchcraft, Oracles, and Magic among the Azande*, Evans-Pritchard demonstrates that the practices (i.e. witchcraft, oracles, and magic) of these sub-Saharan African people are not the result of pre-logical or mystical mentalities and other such ideas, but that they comply with the culture's own internal logic, which is not so very different from how civilized societies cope with the world. If a misfortune befalls a member of the Azande, such as a stone granary collapsing on people sheltered there, the Azande are quite aware of the kinds of reasons in natural law why that might happen. They know that the supporting timbers of the structure might have been weakened by termites and that those people were there because they sought shade to avoid the heat, and so on. However, these rational explanations do not adequately address the question of why that particular granary fell on those particular persons while they were in the structure. Why was there that particular conjunction of factors leading to the tragic event? This is where a phenomenon such as witchcraft plays a role in their conception of reality, for they believe that other members of their social group may have consciously or unconsciously bewitched those who were injured. Oracles may be used to determine who is responsible for the witchcraft, which exercises its effects, and whose damaging effects might also be cleansed, in what one could label as magical ways. Extrapolating from such observations, Evans-Pritchard argued that non-scientific (i.e. religious, magical, etc.) beliefs and practices play a role in offering explanations for those things that a society's scientific understanding is as yet incapable of providing. The Azande system of thought is thus intimately connected to social activities, social structure, and the lives of individuals.

Evans-Pritchard may be classified as a functionalist because, as in the preceding example, he demonstrated how witchcraft, oracles, and magic function within Azande social structure. However, he theoretically and methodologically takes functionalism further than his predecessors because he argues that the function of religion and religious activities is to provide meaning. Thus he theoretically bridges the styles of functionalism of Malinowski and Radcliffe-Brown and the interpretive approach later associated with Clifford Geertz. Evans-Pritchard also saw the anthropologist's role as akin to a translator of a foreign language, for anthropologists translate a foreign culture (language included) into a form that makes sense to persons in the anthropologist's own culture. Furthermore, he stressed that social structure must be studied in its historical context. Societies change over time, and psychological theories (e.g. Malinowski's), and social functionalism (e.g. Radcliffe-Brown's) often ignored these processes because they tended to focus on the immediate conditions of individuals or a social group. Evans-Pritchard also drew attention to the problems inherent in the insider-outsider perspective when studying religion. Outsiders, he argued, tend to see religion as a delusion and theorize that it arises from psychological, sociological, biological, or some such primary factors, while the theories of insiders tend to regard religion as a way of conceptualizing reality and living meaningfully within it.

Interpretive approaches

Among the most influential contributions to the anthropology of religion in recent decades are the theoretical works of Clifford Geertz (1926–2006), who is often regarded as the father of interpretive anthropology. His book *The Interpretation of Cultures* contains a number of seminal articles on a variety of topics that present his approach. Despite the difficulty inherent in defining religion, in his "Religion as a Cultural System," Geertz offered a particularly useful one. It illustrates the value of striving to think about categories and how to define them. Religion is:

> (1) a system of symbols which acts to (2) establish powerful, pervasive, and long-lasting moods and motivations in men [and women] by (3) formulating conceptions of a general order of existence and (4) clothing these conceptions with such an aura of factuality that (5) the moods and motivations seem uniquely realistic.

Although this definition has subsequently been criticized—perhaps unfairly—for not overtly or adequately addressing issues of social power, or not attending to historical processes, or not assisting the researcher in identifying just what is a religious symbol,

Geertz's explanation of his definition reveals much about the interpretive approach that he promotes.

Geertz stresses that one should try to understand the meaning of symbols that make up a cultural system (these systems include science, art, philosophy, ideologies, common-sense, and religion), not by imposing one's own ideas, but by trying to decipher what the symbols mean to the insiders of that culture. We are creatures suspended in webs of significance of our own creation. Just as a wink may be accurately, but superficially, described as a rapid closure of one eye (i.e. "thin description"), "thick description" of the act would seek to uncover its varieties of contextual meanings, such as warning someone, or greeting them, or humorously performing a caricature of someone winking, and so on. The more of these nuanced meanings of its symbols that can be unpacked, the better one is able to understand the cultural system being studied. Thus with regard to religion, the anthropologist might discover that what initially appears to signify one thing (when viewed through one's own cultural lens, or through an understanding of another cultural system although not the one under examination), could in fact, upon closer investigation (and this is best done by seeking the "native's point of view"), actually have quite a different meaning. To illustrate this point one scholar used the example of Jain *puja*, ritual worship, which in other contexts (e.g. Hinduism) might be interpreted as trying to please a deity or ask for favors through offerings of flowers, burning incense, and lighting a lamp. However, when Jains perform a *puja* to a Jain saint or Tirthankara, both with materials and in a form that resembles a Hindu *puja*, such an interpretation would be incorrect. Since the Tirthankaras are believed to have passed beyond the realms of worldly existence, they are beyond access and cannot grant favors to devotees. Thus Jain devotees actually perform the *puja* as a form of reverence for an ideal they themselves hope to attain and to obtain religious merit. Such interpretive analysis requires, among other things, sustained time within the culture, patience, good access to the language, and genuine efforts to decipher the meanings behind symbols and actions.

Geertz's definition of religion envisions it as a cultural system within a social group's broader culture. Geertz defines culture as "a historically transmitted pattern of meanings embodied in symbols, a system of inherited conceptions expressed in symbolic forms by means of which men [and women] communicate, perpetuate, and develop their knowledge about and attitudes toward life." Intrinsic to this definition is the observation that people are not just acted upon by their cultural symbols, but that they influence, add to, and transform them. Furthermore, the symbols of a religious cultural system act both as models which depict a vision of the world (a worldview) and serve as models for how one ought to behave within this envisioned reality. The symbols generate emotional states (i.e. moods) and are conducive to certain behaviors (i.e. motivations) which may or may not actually occur. When people reach the limits of their rational, analytic capabilities (e.g. uncanny events), their physical and emotional endurance (e.g. the existence of human suffering), or their moral insight (e.g. the persistence of evil), limitations that threaten to rupture their sense of reality, the religious symbol set steps in to make the world meaningful.

To achieve this construction of an encompassing worldview, in which the baffling, brutish, or hollow features of existence are rendered meaningful, religions may employ rituals, shared activities that help forge a vision of the "really real." Religions do not deny the problematic aspects of reality; they construct a world in which these are rendered tolerable. Even though common-sense constructs a more narrowly circumscribed, less outlandish reality, religious worldviews, which may include seemingly wildly imaginative notions about heavens, hells, divine beings, and other such ideas about the past, the future, moral values, rationales for evil, suffering, and so on, become understood by believers as the way the world truly is. The religious worldview comes to be regarded as more real than the common-sense or scientifically constructed perspectives, because the sentiments and actions that religious reality induces are more powerful and meaningful than those provided by the non-religious perspectives. For believers, the religious system reflects their most comprehensive sense of the actual order of the world. The ethos that the religious worldview generates, that is, the underlying attitude (e.g. mood, aesthetics, moral style) of believers towards themselves, others, and their picture of the world, reciprocally influences their worldview. So there is a circular series of reinforcing influences in which the symbol system (which is not static) induces feelings and actions by constructing an image of reality, and reinforces and sustains it to such a degree that the imagined reality appears more real than any other competing or subsidiary perspective, so that the feelings and activities thus generated contribute to the sustenance and creative development of the symbol system.

Geertz thus promotes a two-pronged approach to the anthropological study of religion. While much attention has been paid to social-structural and psychological processes, which he agrees are essential to the study of religion, religious activities such as ancestor worship are not just means of regulating political succession, and spirit worship is not merely a way of scheduling agricultural practices. He calls for attention to the analysis (i.e. interpretation) of the system of meanings embodied in the symbols that constitute a religion.

Among the contemporary critics of the symbol-centered approach to defining religion is Robin Horton, whose primary fieldwork has been in Africa. Horton sees religion as grounded in dependent social relationships, which are then extended beyond the human realm (animals aside) to supernatural entities. He is also aligned with the intellectualist tradition, first promoted by E. B. Tylor, which regards human behavior, including its religious dimensions, as derived from rational thought applied to complex issues. Furthermore, the religious realities of various peoples, although they may appear strange or irrational to Western scholars, should be taken at face value (i.e. this is what they actually believe to be true), rather than attempting to suggest that people are manipulating beliefs in order to secure political power, gain social status, profit economically, and so on. Of course, they may well be engaged in all of those pursuits, but these are done in both religious and secular contexts, and do not nullify their beliefs. It is also condescending and patronizing when Western intellectuals try to put a meaningful face on the odd belief systems of other cultures, because they still seem to convey that the Western system is true and best, while the other understanding of reality is functional (i.e. "it works for them") but untrue. Horton argues that the Western notions about reality are actually no different, and their oddity is particularly apparent when viewed through the lens of history (e.g. the earth-centered cosmos, creationism).

Structuralist approaches

The French anthropologist, Claude Lévi-Strauss (b. 1908), advanced another approach to the study of myths, rituals, religion, and other aspects of human culture. It is known as structuralism, because it seeks to uncover, through analysis, structures in people's ideas and activities that derive from deeper structures within the very way our consciousness appropriates and processes information. Anthropologists wondered why myths, if they are purely imaginative creations, and although they derive from different cultures, widely separated geographically or deriving from different historical periods, often seem to share similar themes or values. Thus Lévi-Strauss's style of structural analysis moves away from preoccupation with studying a particular myth or rite, and may examine hundreds of variant forms before attempting to decode the intrinsic patterns. In his *The Raw and the Cooked*, Lévi-Strauss notes that a pervasive pattern evident in the study of myths is the existence of bipolar structures in tension with each other. These may be such polarities as male–female, left–right, sky–earth, nature (raw)–culture (cooked), and so on, which through myth find a resolution to the tension of opposites. A well-known application of this approach was Wendy Doniger's study of myths of the Hindu god Shiva, who in his persona fuses the seemingly irreconcilable opposites of eroticism and sexual asceticism. Some have criticized Lévi-Strauss's approach as being too ambitious in trying to say something universal about the human mind, and have suggested that structural analysis is most effective when applied in a more culture-specific manner, as Doniger did in her study of Shiva. However, others feel that such attempts at broad generalizations are beneficial and serve as a useful remedy to the overly cautious micro-studies that characterize much anthropological research.

An extremely influential theoretical framework for understanding rites of passage was put forward by Victor Turner (1920–1983), an American anthropologist, in his *The Ritual Process*. Turner focused on the overlooked threshold or "liminal" period, a loosely structured and creative period, which, in ritual, demarcates the passage from one stable state to the next. Liminality is a "betwixt and between" state, characterized among its other features by "communitas." Communitas derives from the feelings of liberation to think and act creatively, and the freedom from constraints that are placed on those who occupy more static social positions. Thus the liminal period and its attendant communitas disrupt conventional structures allowing for the transformation of the individual into a newly constructed state. Turner went on to apply these concepts to a wide array of social phenomena, including adolescence (a life-passage example), the hippie movement (a historical, social, and cultural example), pilgrimage (religious ritual activity), and drama (performance studies). Using pilgrimage to illustrate his theory, one can imagine how pilgrims leave the constraints of their social group and set out for some distant pilgrimage site in a process that often involves ordeal and the breaking down of their traditional cultural supports. They may meet up and travel with fellow pilgrims, sharing in features of communitas, in which their individual statuses at home have yielded to an egalitarian status. No longer the rich merchant or the poor carpenter, now both are pilgrims. In the great Muslim pilgrimage, known as the Hajj, all pilgrims wear a white robe that further dissolves differences which would otherwise be evident through their appearance. Finally, when the journey is over, pilgrims return to their home societies, but their experiences and new statuses confer on them a capacity to transform and shape their social milieus. Thus, the liminal state is a breeding ground for personal and social change.

Another prominent contributor to the anthropology of religion is Mary Douglas (1921–2007), who strove to uncover broad structural patterns in symbols across cultures. Her approach is sometimes labeled symbolic anthropology, while Turner's approach has been somewhat clumsily called processual symbolic anthropology to highlight its focus on dynamic transition states. In *Natural Symbols* Douglas offered a remarkable structural schema through which to classify social and cultural organization, including elements of religion. She designated two categories: "group" and "grid," which at their poles may be either "strong" or "weak." "Strong group" is the high degree to which a social group exerts pressure to control its members (e.g. the military), and differentiates itself from others, while "weak group" is the reverse (e.g. hermits). "Strong grid" refers to a highly organized cultural system, which is broadly encompassing in its worldview, highly coherent, and consistent, and which circumscribes a person's life with rules and prescriptions. "Weak grid," of course, belongs to loosely articulated, less rule-bound cultural schemes. Religious systems may thus be plotted on the group and grid axes. Consider Catholic priests, who are constrained by both the religious community to which they belong and the highly systematized Christian worldview and its attendant regulations on the priesthood. They might be placed in the "strong group/strong grid" quadrant of Douglas's system. However, early Christianity, as it appears through the letters of the apostle Paul, might be characterized as "strong group" (i.e. closely knit), but "weak grid" (i.e. regulations still in flux, worldview not yet systematized).

In *Purity and Danger,* Douglas advanced her analysis of how symbols, such as those regarding ritual purity and pollution, reveal a universal propensity among human beings to install order into their surroundings, and how the ritual maintenance of these categorical distinctions provides social order. Purity and order are associated with sanctity, and disorder with unholiness. Taboos reflect potential violations of crucial features of the culture's classification scheme, and press those items or actions into the sacred/unholy or religious realm. Douglas illustrated her approach by examining the Jewish dietary laws found in the Biblical book of Leviticus, analyzing the nature of the animals that were permissible and prohibited (e.g. shellfish), and the underlying categories that seemed to inform these restrictions. For instance, a crab (prohibited) is akin to a fish (permitted), in that it lives in water, but unlike a fish it has legs like a land animal. Since it was problematic to classify the crab according to traditional, culture-specific categories, she argues, it was to be avoided. Similarly, through its prohibition, pork carries a certain unholy power for Jews and Muslims, since its consumption can defile one's religious purity.

Douglas also demonstrates how, when entities fall outside the clear categories, they are often regarded with ambivalence, being both feared and yet held to possess some uncanny, dangerous, and sacred power. Similarly, one finds in widely varying cultures, parallel attitudes to sexual ambiguity, social misfits, menstrual blood and other bodily outflows or by-products, and whatever else does not easily fall into a culture's norms of order. One might apply Douglas's theory to the Hijras of India, a group that considers themselves a third gender, being neither male nor female. Hijras are typically born male but dress as women and many eventually undergo a castration operation to remove their male genitalia. Falling neither into the simple categories of male or female, they are believed to have special powers relating to fertility, and are often asked to sing or dance at wedding celebrations. People fear offending them, for their curse might cause infertility or some other sexual dysfunction. Similarly, the Aghori ascetics of India seek to transcend the bonds that characterize the existence of ordinary people by embracing the very things that are shunned as polluted by Hindu society. They often reside close to cremation grounds (a ritually impure area in Hindu culture), use a skull cup as a begging bowl, and are even reputed to eat human flesh—an abhorrent food to Hindus—on occasion as part of their unusual spiritual practices. Whereas they are avoided by most Hindus and dreaded—but occasionally consulted—for the supernormal powers they are believed to have acquired, they may nonetheless be respected for their potential proximity to spiritual liberation.

Evidently, even as this brief survey of the approach reveals, anthropological perspectives can make valuable contributions to our understanding of religion. Because anthropologists often study small societies in remote locations, they enable us to learn about features of human religiosity less evident merely through studying the world's major religious traditions. Religious studies scholars have long had access to the religious writings of literate societies, but since anthropologists sometimes study non-literate groups, they are able to examine such religious phenomena as rituals and orally transmitted myths, which would otherwise be inaccessible. It is unfortunately still true that many religious studies scholars who are immersed in the study of scriptural texts are only vaguely aware of the value of field studies among religious practitioners who actually use or are influenced by those texts. Religious texts tend to articulate grand ideas, present doctrines, offer theological arguments, prescribe actions, and so on. Ethnographies, however, can reveal how those ideas find expression in the lived experiences of individuals, and to what extent the prescriptions are actually practiced, and demonstrate the context within which religious literature is itself generated. They may reveal religious beliefs and practices not mentioned in the texts at all.

Anthropological studies are thus crucial complements to the study of religious texts if one wishes to understand living religious traditions. As in most of the social sciences and humanities (and perhaps in all human intellectual endeavors), trends in anthropological methods have often resonated with the cadences of fashionable ideas in Western culture. But anthropologists have also made significant contributions to transforming misguided theories and trends. Anthropologists are still pioneering efforts to reveal the intrinsic limitations of the discipline's Euro-American-centered orientations, by wrestling with "insider-outsider," "self-other," "participant-observer," and other such categories, which in parallel form problematize all perspectives in the study of religion, so that our understanding of humanity's cultures may be more genuinely holistic.

Influential social-scientific theorists on religion

E. B. Tylor (1832–1917): English anthropologist; pioneer in the anthropological study of religion; theorized on animism as the basis of all religious beliefs.

Andrew Lang (1844–1912): Scottish folklorist who contributed to the development of the anthropology of religion through his emphasis on collecting and comparing the myths and legends of a wide assortment of the world's cultures.

J. G. Frazer (1854–1941): Scottish mythologist and classic "armchair anthropologist"; known for his contributions to the study of magic in various cultures; authored the influential *The Golden Bough* (1890).

Émile Durkheim (1858–1917): French founder of the modern discipline of sociology; theorized on totemism as the earliest form of religion.

Max Weber (1864–1920): German sociologist and political theorist on religion; noted for his studies of the religions of China and India, but particularly for his analysis of the relationship between capitalist economic systems and Protestantism.

Wilhelm Schmidt (1868–1954): Catholic priest and anthropologist; known for his theory of original monotheism.

A. R. Radcliffe-Brown (1881–1955): British social anthropologist, associated with structural functionalism as an approach to the study of societies and culture.

B. Malinowski (1884–1942): Polish-born anthropologist; known for his emphasis on fieldwork and participant observation in the study of societies and their cultures.

E. E. Evans-Pritchard (1902–1973): British social anthropologist; contributed to functionalism linked to the interpretive approach.

Claude Lévi-Strauss (b. 1908): French anthropologist; pioneer of structuralism as an approach to the study of human social and cultural creations, such as myth and ritual.

Victor Turner (1920–1983): Scottish-born American anthropologist; known for his theoretical contributions on rites of passage, which he effectively extrapolated to analyze a variety of phenomena, including social movements and performance.

Mary Douglas (1921–2007): British social anthropologist who made contributions on the interpretation of symbols and values through category analysis; renowned for her analysis of food taboos in the biblical book of Leviticus, and her discussions of purity and pollution.

Clifford Geertz (1926–2006): American anthropologist; regarded as the father of interpretive anthropology; provided an influential definition of religion as a cultural system.

Peter Berger (b. 1929): American sociologist associated with the notions of social reality as a creation within the consciousness of individuals, and his analyses of secularization processes.

Rodney Stark (b. 1935): American sociologist of religion, known for his work on religious cults, and the development of early Christianity.

Sociological, political, and economic approaches

Émile Durkheim (1858–1917), a French scholar, is often regarded as a father of modern sociology, the study of human societies. Near the end of his life Durkheim wrote *The Elementary Forms of the Religious Life*, in which he offered an interpretation for the nature of religion. Durkheim noted the tendency of human beings to set apart certain aspects of reality and grant these a special status, which he designated as the category of the "sacred." There was nothing intrinsically sacred about these features, beliefs and practices, because what was held to be sacred by one society was not necessarily sacred (i.e. thus "profane") to other social groups. However, he understood religion to have a cohesive effect on societies, and thus defined religion as a coherent system of practices and beliefs pertaining to sacred entities, which unites the adherents of that system into a collective known as a "Church." He also strove to discern the most basic form of religion among human societies, and with the data available to him at the time (primarily studies of one Australian aboriginal tribe), determined this to be totemism.

Durkheim noted that the totem (often an animal, vegetable, or plant) stood as a symbol of a kinship group or clan's god (i.e. "the totemic principle"), and also represented the clan itself. He eventually surmised that the god of the clan was therefore nothing other than the clan itself. Extrapolating to other societies, he suggested that in most religious traditions, the society's god is, in truth, simply the social group, personified and offered to the imaginations of the group's members as their totem, the symbol of their collective selves. The members regard the totem with reverential awe, and all items related to the totem share in the totemic principle— in its sacred power. A social group, he suggested, is beyond the full comprehension of any individual member, and during large gatherings, individuals experience a host of feelings, or a "collective effervescence," which they might imagine to derive from a deity. In essence, the concept of a soul, or the feeling of relatedness to something greater and divine, merely derives from the totemic principle (i.e. the god which is the social group) as conceived or perceived within each individual. By implication, people, often unknowingly, worship their religiously structured social group as their god, because they derive feelings of power, security, and so on from it. Were one to apply Durkheim's theory to Christianity, for example, one might suggest that Christ (i.e. the totemic principle or god for Christians) is not much more than a symbol of the collective community of the Christian faithful (i.e. the Church), who experience deep feelings of awe, reverence, and such, particularly when gathered for communal worship.

Of course, there are many shortcomings in Durkheim's understanding of religion. It was methodologically flawed because he derived his theory from a very narrow and atypical religious system, namely, totemism among an Australian aboriginal group, and then extended his findings to all human societies and religions. His category of "profane" seems to be poorly explored and is simply a default of what is not regarded as "sacred." In many instances in particular societies, it is not easy or even reasonable to separate one category from the other. For example, certain illnesses may be held to have both religious and non-religious causes and cures. Are they thus sacred or profane? Durkheim's theory is so broad that it could be applied to virtually any social group, such as sports teams and their fans, and while these have many of the characteristics of creating unity and generating strong emotions under the banner of the team's emblem (e.g. the St. Louis Cardinals), the nature of sporting events strikes most people as somehow different from the nature of religion. His understanding is so centered on social unity that it does not adequately shed light on individualist approaches to religion as embodied by renouncers, mystics, and the like. Quite importantly, Durkheim equates religion with one of its functions (i.e. social cohesion), and here too he ignores religion's capacity to divide rather than unite members. Nevertheless, Durkheim's thought has valuably directed scholarly attention to the many, and often crucial, social features of religious phenomena.

Religion, economics and politics

Another influential social analyst was the German theorist Max Weber (1864–1920), whose contributions lead many to consider him equally as a political economist and as a historian. He is often associated with the notion of *Verstehen*, the German word for understanding. This is because Weber spearheaded the need to understand by interpreting the meanings that individuals provide for their social actions. In contrast to history, which emphasizes causal connections between events, sociology should seek to uncover patterns in the systems of meanings that govern the activities of people in social groupings. In his focus on the interpretation of meaning, Weber prefigured the theoretical approach of the interpretive anthropologist Clifford Geertz. To aid in the process of interpretation, Weber proposed the notion of ideal types. Ideal types are models that can serve as yardsticks against which actual individuals or social phenomena may be compared. Just as certain persons may have such strong musical talents as to be considered virtuosos, while others are less musically gifted, Weber suggested that individuals have a range of religious affinities and capacities. Through his studies of the religions of India, China, and the West, Weber attempted to extract usable typologies of religious functionaries and processes. For instance, among prophets he distinguishes between two main types, the exemplary and the emissary. Exemplary prophets teach by example about the attainment of experiences, often centered on a contemplative lifestyle that they themselves have had. One might consider the Buddha as having such characteristics. Emissary prophets, by contrast, carry a message that they believe they have received from an active divine source, and feel compelled to transmit the teachings to others.

One of Weber's most influential contributions to the study of religions was his *The Protestant Ethic and the Spirit of Capitalism*. There Weber convincingly argued that the values of certain branches of Protestant Christianity (particularly Calvinism), which promoted hard work and frugality, and which indirectly, if not explicitly, saw economic success as a sign of a favorable status in the eyes of God, had meshed with capitalistic economic structures, and actually contributed to shaping the character of capitalism in the West. His study was significant because scholars discerned parallels in other non-Christian cultures, such as in Judaism and in Chinese societies, and demonstrated that religious values may be so intimately intertwined with economic realities in a society that these features ought not to be ignored.

The relationship of religion to economic and political structures in society was also discussed by the German philosopher and social activist Karl Marx (1818–1883). Marx's most influential book is *Das Kapital* (*On Capital*), which presents his theories on economics. Essentially, Marx argued that the capitalist economic system, in which capitalists profit from the labor of workers, although mutually beneficial to both, ultimately tends to favor the capitalist at the expense of the laborer. Were the workers to control the means of production of goods, which could only be accomplished by a revolution—since those who had their hands on the reins of power would not relinquish them without a fight—the wealth of a society would be more equitably distributed. Enormously influential, his writings inspired the social revolutions in the former Soviet Union and China.

Marx is renowned for his saying that religion is the "opium of the people." He saw religion as a response by people to escape from the injustices of the social and political realities they experienced. The existence of religion in a society was a clear sign of social injustice and genuine suffering. However, what was particularly malicious, according to Marx, was the capacity for those in power to use religion to continue to keep the masses oppressed. The critique of any social, legal, or political system should have at its foundation a criticism of religion, because religion offers the core illusion which turns people's concerns away from actual human realities and needs. Like an opiate, fabricated and administered by people to themselves, and manipulated by some for its effects on others, religion is an effort to assuage humanity's suffering through flight into a dreamlike state, where people are kept asleep to the actual conditions of their exploitation and social abuse. Interestingly, some later theorists have seen Marx himself as akin to a latter-day prophet of a secular religion, rousing his fellow human beings to free themselves from delusion, and follow a path that held the promise of a utopian future centered not on a god in some heaven, but on humanity here on earth. Marx's appraisal of religion has been criticized for reducing the full compass of human spirituality to its negative consequences and to its foundations as merely embedded in social and economic causes. It also ignores the socially integrative and stabilizing functions of religion, and the many roles religions have sometimes played in uplifting the poor in societies and in inspiring the growth of facets of culture such as music, art, architecture, and literature.

It is instructive to note how, enamored by the successes of the scientific method, many early theorists sought to apply it not merely to the study of nature, but to a wide range of human phenomena. This led to the development of a variety of disciplines, such as the study of social organization (sociology), culture (anthropology), politics (political science), economics, consciousness (psychology), religion (*Religionswissenschaft*) and so on, in which the scientific method is applied with varying degrees of rigor. More significantly, many of the early studies display a negative disposition towards religion, which is seen as an aberrant human activity, deriving from perceived weaknesses in the human constitution, such as ignorance, fear, or fantasy. Such pejorative attitudes still persist among a cohort of scientists and social scientists. Religion exists and persists because people misunderstand the laws of nature and how human societies operate (which scientific study will reveal), because they fear the unknown (and there is nothing to fear but fear itself), or because they escape into illusions of their own designs in order to cope with harsh reality. While these explanations and many others certainly hold true in many instances and do contribute to our understanding of religion, most religious studies scholars understand that they do not adequately account for the human religious response. They are therefore regarded as reductionist explanations, since they reduce the complexity of the phenomenon of religion in human societies to overly simplified causes, functions, or effects. It would seem strange, if not absurd, if one were to propose simplistic dismissive rationales for why human beings make music or produce art, why we philosophize, or work. However, religious authorities or attitudes have often stood in the way of scientific endeavors (Galileo's trial by the Catholic Church, and the ongoing evolution versus creationism debates, are telling examples), occasionally triggering a response in kind by the scientific community.

Contemporary sociological approaches

The contemporary period entertains, for the most part, a much more nuanced and embracing approach to the study of religion among social scientists. Attempts at grand theory and universal explanations of causes and functions have yielded to efforts to offer more limited perspectives and insights into religion. To some extent this seeming humility derives from a shifting scientific paradigm and the contributions of postmodern theories in the social sciences. Each scientific observer is "situated," observing phenomena from a particular vantage point. Their perspectives are not the only, correct, and true ones. Just as relativity theory demonstrates that even a measurement of time by a stationary observer will differ from a measurement by one who is moving, postmodernism suggests that our appraisals about life, the human predicament, and so on are always colored by the particulars of our own conditions. Does this mean that men cannot adequately, and thus should not, study women? Or that Muslims should not study Buddhists? Or that atheists should avoid the study of religion? Of course not! However, it does mean that each study provides only a partial perspective, offering its own valuable, but limited, viewpoints on the items examined. The structure of this text is designed to highlight such an orientation toward the study of religion, introducing students to a variety of perspectives, and implicitly suggesting that exposure to the widest array of disciplinary approaches will enable us to better understand the phenomenon of religion.

A compelling sociological perspective on religion is offered by Peter Berger (b. 1929) in *The Sacred Canopy*. According to Berger, religious symbols and their meanings construct a reality that envelops ordinary reality, forming a sort of protective canopy of sacredness and order, under and through which the drama of human life unfolds and is made sense of. Religious authorities maintain the structures of this sacred reality, which is infused with such power that it inculcates the meaning systems of individuals and groups, who contribute to its preservation. Ordinary actions are understood and explained in relation to the sacred reality, and rituals are means of forging the two realities into one. Extraordinary events are also explained within this sacred framework. Berger tends to separate mystical experience, which seems to share commonalities across vast social, cultural, and historical divides, from so-called organized or social religions. Secularization, he suggests, has begun to erode the fabric of the sacred canopy, leaving individuals without the sheltering home that religious worldviews once provided. Berger later acknowledged that this breakdown has not led to the demise of religion in favor of secular structures such as bureaucracies, as he once thought it might, because new religious forms appear to be emerging to take the place of the older mainstream religions. Nevertheless, the fragmentation of major overarching religious worldviews has led to a privatization of religious realities, and the mind which once felt at home in the religiously constructed world is left feeling homeless. Berger's approach to the study of society is regarded as humanistic (rather than being a social science) and he proposes that societies themselves are modes of consciousness, constructed by individuals primarily through the use of language, the most powerful of symbol or sign-making systems. Interestingly, he proposes that the discipline of sociology is itself a mode of consciousness, and that one of its operative motifs should be to debunk the social structures that it studies. By this he means that the study of any social structure requires one to look through what is often taken for granted as real, true, ordinary, or accepted, to uncover the reality constructs therein that have been shaped by human consciousness and embedded into individuals' understandings of their social worlds. The examination of unquestioned notions of respectability, of marginal or devalued viewpoints, and of suppressed modes of speech can aid in uncovering the bricks and mortar of these social constructions.

Also in the contemporary period, scholars such as Rodney Stark have studied the rise of religious movements and the forces that drive religious conversion in individuals and in social groups. Certain sociological theories propose that religious conversion is grounded in ignorance, in some flaw in one's capacity to reason, in escapes from reality, and so on. However, Stark's is among the voices that propose that rational choice contributes intrinsically to such religious realities. This approach has been hailed by some as a dramatic shift in the direction of sociological theories about religion. The theory suggests that people act rationally when choosing religious paths, and the social realities and historical processes of religious movements may also be better understood if one looks for the rational motivations behind the behaviors of religious groups. Even acting in accord with strict moral laws that govern one's own life (e.g. asceticism, celibacy), or acting altruistically for the benefit of others (e.g. charity, martyrdom), which at first glance seem contrary to the rational norms of survival or self-interest, may actually be options selected by adherents because they reasonably think that these are appropriate choices (based on the information available to them, and their understanding of it). Rational self-interest is often at the root of individual and social motivations, and religion is no exception. This theory is most certainly not proposing that rational choice is the only factor in shaping religious conversion, adherence, and behaviors, but that it is a crucial and often overlooked component.

In collaboration with Stark, W. Bainbridge also put forward a theory that all religious movements that have connections with the non-religious or secular social elite (e.g. wealthy merchants, members of the ruling class), themselves undergo processes of secularization. These movements progressively lose their links with supernatural realities as they accommodate themselves to secular culture in order to gravitate to the centers of power. New religious movements better servicing the needs of the (typically, non-elite) populace by providing meaningful links to supernatural realities soon arise to take the place of the large, secularized religious organizations. Having lost their credibility with the masses, entire secularized religious movements may collapse as they confront certain newer religions that have successfully gained in popularity. Eventually, even these new sects, characterized by emotional intensity and often offering a critique of the elite mainstream, might themselves fall victim to the same processes of secularization, as they grow in size and power, join the elite, and lose their vitality.

One more noteworthy contemporary theorist, who could arguably be placed within several other divisions of this book, is Jonathan Z. Smith, who is often described as a neo-Durkheimian, because of his interests in the social, human-centered traits of religion. Smith's theorizing is wide-ranging. Quite significantly, with regard to the concerns of this text, he suggests that religion and its scholarly study are relatively recent phenomena, and a creation of academia. While the archeological and historical record, and even contemporary observations, do show people engaged in relating in various ways to deities, including reciting words, performing activities, adhering to ideas, and so on, it is the scholar of religion who designates any such datum as "religious," and therefore worthy of study as such. Therefore, the study of religion requires the student not only to select something to focus upon, but to demonstrate convincingly how this object of study serves as an effective example in his/her imaginative generalizations and comparisons about "religion." These choices do not have to comply with what particular groups consider to be their "community" proper, or their approved "canon" of literature. There is nothing expressly regarded as "outside" the scholar's range of choices. The scholar should not be constrained by the definitional criteria of religious "insiders." An extension of this is Smith's argument that all of academia, and the disciplines of religious studies, anthropology, and so on, within them, reveal a Protestant or anti-Catholic bias. By this, he is not referring to the Protestant or Catholic traditions per se, but attitudes they exemplify. He means that there has been a long-standing tradition of giving preferential attention to philosophical thinking over ritual activity and material reality (e.g. Protestant vs. Catholic). The history of scholarship demonstrates a preoccupation with the origins of a religion, as if authentic religion is to be found there, just as Protestant Christianity is focused on the Bible, rather than in the full historical sweep of a religious tradition throughout its existence. Theological arguments, metaphysical notions, and so on are seen as carrying the stamp of what the religion is really about, while the things that people do, individually and collectively, the objects that they manipulate and their bodily engagement with these (e.g. in Catholic sacramental practice), are seen as secondary and less important religious phenomena. As a result, social, historical, and political features of religions also get marginalized.

Smith is also noted for his critique of comparative studies in religion, such as those by Joseph Campbell and Mircea Eliade, which seek to demonstrate shared propensities among human beings across disparate cultures. Smith emphasizes that there is much to be gained by looking at the differences rather than the commonalities. For instance, there are often fiercely defended (even to the point of violence) distinctions on fine points of theology or morality between certain sub-sects of religious groups who to most casual outsiders would appear to be virtually indistinguishable from one another. Yet these procedures of drawing distinctions between "them" and "us," or of "othering," and of boundary creation, are a hallmark of human behavior and often particularly linked to religion. Another feature that is central to Smith's varied contributions is his insistence that the scholar of religion should not be content merely with accumulating data, or even discerning patterns, structures, and so on. Rather scholars should persistently pursue the question "so what?" with regard to their observations, in order to elicit even more textured understandings of human religiosity.

4

How people experience religion

Perspectives in the study of religious consciousness and perception

Phenomenological approaches
Blurred boundaries: irreducible religious essence
Pioneers in the history and comparison of religions
Recent influences
Psychological approaches
Early seminal theorists
Sigmund Freud: religion as illusory wish fulfillment
Freud: science displaces religion as civilizations mature
Criticism of Freud
Carl Jung: religion as imperfect therapy
William James: importance of religious experience
Comparing approaches
Later twentieth-century contributions
Buddhism and psychology
Cognitive and related "hard science" approaches
"Neurotheological" approaches

Phenomenology is an obscure term, related to a modern philosophical movement led by Edmund Husserl (1859–1938) in which human consciousness is studied through the subjective experience of its interaction with phenomena. Phenomena, in turn, are the objects of a person's perceptions or items of reality as they are perceived by a person's senses or mind. Before exploring the significance of phenomenological approaches to the study of religion in greater detail, this introductory section examines why these approaches have been grouped with psychological approaches and how both relate to the sociological and anthropological approaches surveyed in the previous section.

First, it is worth noting that the phenomenological and psychological approaches examined in this chapter were developed in conjunction with the sociological and anthropological approaches. That is to say that the timelines of major thinkers and influential works in each of these four approaches significantly overlap with one another, each approach describes its methods as scientific rather than theological, and all four approaches continue today. Moreover, these approaches have interacted with each other and have continually refined their assumptions and methods over time. For example, phenomenologists of religion might use for their own theories data collected by anthropologists; however, in their use and interpretation of this data they may strive to correct what they perceive to be overly reductionistic anthropological, psychological, or sociological interpretations. Reductionism is a term that connotes the intellectual tendency to explain the complexities of a phenomenon being examined through an account that simplifies its causes or nature. That is, the reductionist anthropological, psychological, or sociological account of religion would assert that religion originates and functions for cultural, psychological, or social reasons respectively. The phenomenologist might object that her social scientist colleagues' explanations addressed only parts of the complex whole and missed or misrepresented the essential *religious* quality of a religion, ritual, or myth.

With such tensions and different interpretations in mind, as well as the basic distinction between the emphasis on description in phenomenology and explanation in psychology, the pairing of phenomenology with psychology might seem surprising. However, they share a number of things in common, including a focus on religious consciousness in general and religious experiences and perceptions in particular. Both also differ from sociological explanations, although in different ways. Psychologists are likely to critique sociological theories as inadequate to the individual's experience, needs, and thought processes, whereas phenomenologists argue for greater attention to the religious dimension itself—of both groups and individuals—rather than understanding religion primarily according to its social function. One criticism invokes the practitioner's interior life and the other acknowledges, as essential and irreducible, the religious phenomena—the rituals, myths, concepts of sacred space, and expressions of the divine. However, even here there is important overlap between categories because, like psychologists, phenomenologists often emphasize the experience and perception of these religious phenomena.

The pairing of phenomenology with psychology of religion can also highlight juxtapositions in terms of irreducibility, bracketing of truth claims, and sympathetic descriptions. While "sympathetic descriptions" could mean merely reproducing insiders' descriptions of their religious traditions, without any critical analysis, such descriptions would add nothing to scholarship beyond the reporting of data. More typically, sympathetic description refers to a sensitivity that tries to understand and take seriously the insiders' perspective without limiting interpretation to insiders' views or categories. "Bracketing" suggests a suspension of judgment (taking certain questions and evaluations out of play). "Irreducibility" refers to a reluctance or inability to simplify something out of concern for losing an essential quality, or distorting it beyond meaningful recognition in order to fit a model. Thus, phenomenologists would resist "explaining away" religion only in terms of psychological conditions as strongly as they would reject reductionistic sociological explanations. However, phenomenologists are quite willing to acknowledge psychological dimensions to religious practice and belief—as well as sociological, political, and other influences—as long as there remains something distinctly religious that is not subsumed by or reduced to these non-religious explanations. Although the pheno-menologist seeks to preserve and emphasize this distinctly religious dimension, the "sacred" in Eliade's writings and the "numinous" or "holy" for Otto (to name two major theorists and their concepts, which we will explore below), this approach is best known for "bracketing" claims of truth rather than affirming or rejecting the theological claims made by religious insiders. Phenomenologists are often sym-pathetic to the religions they study in terms of trying to understand the ideas, language, myth, rituals, beliefs, and practices of insiders, but they are not compelled to affirm, reject, or limit themselves to the insiders' interpretations. Psychological approaches are not bound to this bracketing or sympathy. Although some psycho-logists of religion do bracket the reality of an external sacred power, others confidently assert that religion is simply an illusion, a mental affliction, or a projected human construct derived from psychological needs, wish fulfillments, and stunted development.

Psychological approaches can also focus on individuals' perceptions, experiences, or even brain activity while engaged in religious practice, without denying or dismissing the possibility of an external religious reality or the positive potential that religion can play for practitioners' mental health. However, even such positive evaluations of religion seek a psychological explanation beyond practitioners' interpretations or explanations of religious experience. The scholar of either phenomenological or psychological approaches analyzes various dimensions of religion to better understand individual people, their experiences, beliefs, and traditions as well as religious patterns, origins, and functions. Moreover, these approaches share origins and ambitions that justify grouping them together. At the beginning of the nineteenth century, Hegel defined phenomenology in terms of knowledge as perceived by consciousness. His *Phenomenology of Spirit* asserted that close study of diverse phenomena reveals an essential spirit that unifies and directs the various manifestations. Many of the seminal figures in the development of religious studies described their studies in terms of the "science of religion" (*Religionswissenschaft*) and used phenomenological approaches. By the end of the nineteenth century, the phenomenologist Pierre Daniel Chantepie de la Saussaye had even linked the approaches together by asserting that psychological and phenomenological approaches complement each other in the pursuit of a science of religion.

Psychology of religion, like the discipline of psychology as a whole, is rooted in nineteenth-century expansions of scientific modes of study which aimed at a better understanding of human beings and their culture and society as well as the natural world. In *Psychology and Religion: West and East*, Carl Jung asserts that in his study of religion, he restricts himself to "the observation of phenomena" without engaging in "metaphysical or philosophical considerations." He further invokes phenomeno-logical approaches in this work by insisting that he is an empiricist and that his scientific approach to psychology represents a "phenomenological" standpoint "concerned with occurrences, events, experiences—in a word, with facts" rather than judgments. Some of the notions of science and technologies used to test hypotheses and establish "facts" have changed between the time of Jung and his predecessors and today. Contemporary studies of religion through cognitive science and even "neurotheological" analysis are more recent movements that examine religious consciousness in terms of cognitive processes and brain activity. These approaches employ cutting-edge scientific techniques, language, sensibilities, and machinery; however, the resulting explanations and interpretations about religion and religious consciousness have not rendered all earlier approaches and methods obsolete. We will explore several of these recent movements alongside phenomenological and psychological approaches in this survey of perspectives in the scientific study of religion that focus on religious consciousness, perception, and experience.

Phenomenological approaches

The introductory paragraphs above described phenomenological approaches and some of their telling characteristics. These included bracketing truth claims and acknowledging that other approaches might offer partial explanations or descriptions while asserting that there is something irreducibly *religious* about religious phenomena. That is to say that religion is *sui generis*: it is of its own kind. Because phenomenologists typically maintain that religion is its own unique category, they argue that something would be lost if religion were only studied as one focus among many in departments such as anthropology, sociology, psychology, and history. Each of those departments, and each approach to the study of religion, adds important insight about religion, but for the phenomenologist, religion cannot completely be explained by or reduced to its socio-economic, psychological, or cultural dimensions. Phenomenologists of religion argue that to attempt such reduction misses the most essential *religious* aspect. Scholars who employ this approach are also among the most passionate advocates for departments of religious studies rather than leaving the study of religion to the theoretical perspectives, methods, and perhaps the margins of departments of psychology, anthropology, sociology, and history. For example, these departments might ignore religion or study it restrictively: psychological perspectives would likely be restricted to explanations of religion in terms of psychological causes and functions; religious accounts in anthropology might be restricted to participant-observer ethnographic methods; and religion could become marginal in sociology if the department did not include a sociologist of religion, or could become marginal in other ways in history if an historian only incidentally made reference to religion as a relatively minor factor among many others that shape historical context, dynamics, and events. A religious studies department, it is argued, will be more fully and comprehensively focused on the study of religion, with the resources and institutional standing to avoid haphazard study or a slide to the margins. Phenomenologists go one step further in arguing that uniquely *religious* dimensions should not be neglected within religious studies itself, much less within the university as a whole.

Although phenomenological approaches have been quite influential for religious studies scholarship and teaching, the term phenomenology baffles students, and its meaning is far from clear to many religious studies scholars. This lack of clarity stems both from the obscurity of the term, and the imprecise and shifting meaning that it has when applied to the study of religion. Phenomenon, of which phenomena is the plural, refers to a thing as it is experienced or perceived by our senses. Such a thing can be observed or apprehended by the senses, though this perception of the object is not the same as the object itself. That is, our perception is shaped by our senses, experiences, tastes, preferences, history, culture, mind, cognitive functions, etc. The intrinsic essence of the thing in itself is mediated through these lenses. Therefore, phenomenology is a study of phenomena, not of things as they actually are without regard to how we perceive them. By acknowledging that descriptions of consciousness and experience are mediated by perception, phenomenological investigations in philosophy and religion typically bracket the question of whether or not the phenomena that are experienced are ultimately real in some objective sense.

Blurred boundaries: irreducible religious essence

That said, some phenomenologists of religion seek to grasp and describe a religious essence, which they perceive in the traditions they study and from patterns that they detect in wide-ranging religious data from myths, rituals, texts, temples, dances, practices, beliefs, and ideas of gods and sacred space. A good number of seminal thinkers in the history of religious studies fit this category. Many are sympathetic to religion and to the priorities, language, categories, and explanations of religious adherents. They do not restrict themselves to the interpretations of insiders, but they are more likely to consider and value insiders' perspectives and perceptions relative to other approaches in the academic study of religion. Scholars inside or outside a religious tradition can conduct phenomenological observation, analysis, and interpretation of patterns in religious practice and belief. Those outside the tradition may need to pay closer attention to insiders' sensibilities, but those inside the tradition may need to guard against confessional perspectives where normative statements about their religion transgress the boundaries of academic analysis in a secular setting. In light of the statements above concerning sympathetic disposition toward religion and religious insiders as well as assertions regarding an irreducible religious essence, it is not surprising that this boundary between secular and theological approaches has been blurred by a number of influential phenomenologists.

Rudolf Otto (1869–1937) is a classic example of a scholar who blurs this distinction. Whereas some phenomenologists approach the study of religion from a background in philosophy or with a careful adherence to the objective ideals of the scientific study of religion, Otto is one of the early religious studies scholars who first trained as a theologian. This theological disposition, in combination with his focus on experience, asserts itself in his famous work, *The Idea of the Holy* (1923), in which he invited the reader "to direct his mind to a moment of deeply-felt religious experience, as little as possible qualified by other forms of consciousness. Whoever cannot do this, whoever knows no such moments in his experience, is requested to read no farther. . . ." Otto privileges the insider's access to experiences of this religious essence and elsewhere argues against the capacity of scientific study objectively and comprehensively to grasp, understand, and explain religious experience from the outside. His contention may strike many as reasonable or intuitive. His dismissal of those who have not had such a religious experience can further be understood as a rejection of secular theories and theorists, such as Sigmund Freud. Freud acknowledged that he had never had an "oceanic" experience, and his psychological theories marginalized powerful and mystical religious experiences. Nevertheless, Otto's restriction is exclusivist and normative in ways that conflict with the standards of the secular scholarship of religion and with social scientific ideals of open, impartial, repeatable, and verifiable analysis.

Reason and rational elements factor into Otto's analysis, but as a complement to, rather than a dispeller of, supernatural and non-rational elements of religious meaning and experience. Whereas aspects of religion, of the holy, are accessible to reason, he used the term "numinous" to designate the religious dimensions, or "overplus of meaning" beyond reason's reach and rational articulation. In some ways, he may seem more at home in the section on theological approaches; however, his methods and description of an irreducible essence of religion, the "numinous," were quite influential to the development of the phenomenological approach. Moreover, he focused on how individuals perceived and experienced religion. For example, he analyzed how people experienced this numinous reality not through rational comprehension but instead in terms of "mysterium" and "tremendum," characterized by overpowering feelings of awe, terror, fascination, and urgency when confronting the "wholly other" mystery. Otto's descriptions of awe, fear, and trembling in the face of divine power rely on Christianity but are intended to address experiences and perceptions of the divine from various traditions. That is, his language and insights, such as linking feelings of awe with the awe-full majesty of the unapproachable creator god, are refracted through Christianity, but attempt to speak to a unified religious dimension beyond his own tradition. He did travel widely and promoted the comparative study of religion with a sympathetic and relatively open disposition, which is characteristic of phenomenologists. He noted differences but also stressed larger patterns and similarities across traditions. Nonetheless, he compromises any sense of even-handed comparison by explicitly claiming Christianity as a uniquely superior religion. His terms and descriptions of religious experience and his insistence upon a separate essence of religion remain influential, while his discussions of the origins, development and fulfillment of religion have exerted much less influence in religious studies.

Other major early phenomenologists, such as the Dutch scholars P. D. Chantepie de la Saussaye (1818–1874) and Cornelius Petrus Tiele (1830–1902), studied theology and served as ministers before advocating phenomenological approaches that extended beyond Christianity to categorize and compare religious phenomena.

They directed their studies toward understanding religion as a whole rather than toward promoting one tradition at the expense of another. They promoted the scientific study of religion though they did not claim that such study could fully explain religion or grasp its essence. Gerardus van der Leeuw (1890–1950) also spent time as a minister. His dissertation and later books, including *Religion in Essence and Manifestation: A Study in Phenomenology*, contributed to this phenomenological approach in the academic study of religion. He carefully examined religion as an object of study, as well as the subject who experiences religion, with an emphasis on the power of the sacred. He studied religious practitioners' traditions along with their feelings of fear and attraction while setting aside, or bracketing, specific truth claims made by a particular religion or about the sacred in general. Such bracketing is especially characteristic of phenomenology, and arises from the effort to understand religion without necessarily trying to explain it, much less refute or promote it. That said, van der Leeuw's writings reveal Christian theological assumptions that help to organize and interpret the vast data he collected from various religious traditions.

Pioneers in the history and comparison of religions

Whereas van der Leeuw was the pre-eminent phenomenologist in the first half of the twentieth century, F. Max Müller (1823–1900) and Mircea Eliade (1907–1986) were dominant figures in the history and comparison of religions in the latter halves of the nineteenth and twentieth centuries respectively. Their influence exceeds the boundaries of phenomenology, but exhibits crucial phenomenological characteristics of description and the gathering of vast amounts of diverse data from which to ascertain patterns, connections and essences of religion as a whole. Müller was the founding father of the scientific study of religion (*Religionswissenschaft*) separate from traditional perspectives of theological and philosophical approaches. He spent most of his life and career at Oxford, but also demonstrated his German academic training with close analysis of religious texts from around the world. This comparative dimension was central to his study. He adapted Goethe's famous phrase about language, "he who knows one knows none," to the study of religion. Study within one tradition is not truly to study or know religion. It is only through comparison that one comes to understand one religious tradition, other traditions, or the category of religion as a whole. His tireless efforts on behalf of the scientific study of religion yielded many influential books and essays, including the massive *Sacred Books of the East* series of primary texts in translation. This series, which began in 1879 and eventually reached fifty volumes, provided Westerners with access to Asian traditions, such as Hinduism, Buddhism, Daoism, Confucianism, and Zoroastrianism, which were little known in the late nineteenth century.

Mircea Eliade interpreted, connected, and categorized myriad myths and symbols from religious traditions throughout the world. He sought out phenomena that manifested a sense of the sacred as distinct from the profane. For Eliade, religion concerns experience of the transcendent, sacred mode beyond the everyday, profane mode of existence, which is ordinary, relative, and bound by history. Rituals, practices and myths provide access to sacred experience, sacred place, and sacred time. Eliade was at least as prolific as Müller. He edited the highly acclaimed sixteen-volume *Encyclopedia of Religion* and numerous influential books, from classics such as *The Sacred and the Profane: The Nature of Religion, The Myth of the Eternal Return,* and *Patterns in Comparative Religion,* to massive works that demonstrated the scope of his scholarship, such as *From Primitives to Zen* (now known as *Essential Sacred Writings from Around the World*). His work on shamanism, yoga, myths, and other sacred writings brought attention to sources and traditions that were often new to religious studies. However, his contributions went beyond the vast data that he gathered and described, to the theories and methods he employed in connecting this diverse data into a framework for understanding the meanings and logic of symbols that represent how the sacred manifests itself throughout the history of the various religious traditions. Unlike historical explorations that emphasize a particular historical context, Eliade asserted that many concepts, types, patterns, and manifestations of the sacred are the same across time and space.

Although very much a comparativist, Eliade preferred "history of religion" for a title to describe the discipline of religious studies. Eliade combined analysis of the history of various traditions with the language, experience, and insights taken from religious participants and their symbols and myths. He insisted on the autonomy of religion as irreducible and on the need to understand religion through its symbols, categories, and interpretations. In other words, he did not believe that religion could be reduced to a psychological or sociological theory, or that it could be most fully understood through the tools of those other disciplines. According to Eliade, the other disciplines can capture economic, linguistic, artistic, and other aspects of religion, but they miss the essential element of the sacred. This remains a point of contention in religious studies between phenomenologists in the mode of an Eliade, Otto, or van der Leeuw, and social scientific scholars who cringe at the idea of a privileged, sacred essence beyond the grasp of an outsider's secular analysis.

Eliade's influence extends even further beyond his writings to the students of religion whom he trained at the University of Chicago. Eliade helped to build an especially strong program in Chicago, which produced many of the scholars who filled the rapidly growing number of positions in this relatively new discipline. However, Eliade's extensive influence has waned in recent decades with greater specialization, area studies, postmodernism, and critiques that his methods were anti-historical and uncritically selective. These critiques have reduced the influence of research in comparative studies and phenomenology of religion more generally. In fact, criticism of this approach has come from distinctly opposing directions. On the one hand, there are those who think that attempts like Eliade's to reveal universal structures have been inadequate to the diversity and specific context of each tradition. On the other hand, critics from social scientific approaches assert that there is inadequate reduction and rigor in what appears to them to be a subjective selection of data and interpretation without sound scientific method.

Influential phenomenologists of religion
───

P. D. Chantepie de la Saussaye (1818–1874) and **Cornelius Petrus Tiele** (1830–1902): Dutch scholars who shifted from theological ministries to early advocacy of phenomenological approaches that categorized and compared religious phenomena beyond Christianity.

F. Max Müller (1823–1900): German scholar at Oxford and founding father of the scientific study of religion (*Religionswissenschaft*); compared and analyzed religious texts from around the world; the multi-volume *Sacred Books of the East* exemplifies his vast contributions.

Rudolf Otto (1869–1937): German scholar; theological training and phenomenological perspectives; used "numinous" to designate religious dimensions— including feelings of awe and terror—beyond the grasp of reason and scientific explanation; wrote *The Idea of the Holy* (1923).

Gerardus van der Leeuw (1890–1950): Dutch scholar, theologian, and author of *Religion in Essence and Manifestation: A Study in Phenomenology*; studied many religious traditions while setting aside, or bracketing, specific truth claims of a particular religion or about the sacred.

Mircea Eliade (1907–1986): Romanian scholar of the "history of religion" at the University of Chicago; interpreted, connected, and categorized myriad myths and symbols from religious traditions throughout the world; focused on phenomena that manifested a sense of the sacred as distinct from the profane, including rituals, experiences, and ideas of sacred space or time.

Ninian Smart (1927–2001): Scottish scholar of religion; encouraged an imaginative empathy with adherents to better understand them and their religious experiences; rather than seeking a single essence, he explored multiple dimensions of religious perspectives, rituals, beliefs, myths, ethics, institutions and experiences.

Recent influences

Nonetheless, these comparative and phenomenological modes continue to exert great influence, both at the popular level through documentaries and books, such as *The Power of Myth*, a book and PBS television series based on Bill Moyer's interview with Joseph Campbell, and in the way religious studies is taught in the university. Ninian Smart (1927–2001) is a pre-eminent example of this enduring influence at university level, as well as an exponent of a nuanced phenomenological approach that avoids the attempt to isolate a religious essence, for which many earlier scholars in this approach have been criticized. He avoids the critique of pursuing an overtly religious agenda in the study of religion, but by bracketing the possibility of super-natural elements in religion, he does not avoid all criticism from religious studies scholars who seek to bolster the scientific rigor of their discipline by treating religion exclusively as a natural, human phenomenon.

Smart exerted considerable influence through his books, including textbooks such as *The Religious Experience of Mankind* and *The World's Religions*, as well as through the many students and graduate students whom he trained and who have since become major scholars and teachers in the field. Smart encouraged students and scholars to "walk in the moccasins" of the religious insider, to better understand his or her perspectives, rituals, beliefs, myths, ethics, institutions and experiences. He argued for an imaginative empathy with adherents of all traditions to better understand them, including their religious experiences and intentions. This required the phenomenological bracketing, known as *epoché*, where suspension of one's own beliefs and an openness that neither confirms nor denies truth claims assists one in empathetically engaging with another's worldview. In this way he was able to avoid some of the biases of his predecessors, including the bias of interpreting other religions through a Christian lens and the undue emphasis on religious belief in particular at the expense of other dimensions of religion. He is admired for promoting a popular mode of religious studies that values diversity in keeping with liberal ideals of religious pluralism. However, Smart was also a critical scholar and teacher who did not advocate simply repeating the insiders' explanations. Instead, he discussed religious traditions as complex organic entities with interrelated dimensions of doctrine, experience, mythology, art, ritual, ethics, and social institu-tions. Rather than one central essence of religion, each religious tradition exhibits these dimensions with some aspects emphasized more than others from one tradition to the next. Religion is not a static unified whole, nor are the various religions identical to one another. Instead, religions are related to each other according to Wittgenstein's idea of "family resemblance." For this relationship there does not need to be a single defining trait shared by all members, but instead various members can be recognized as part of the same family, because they resemble each other by sharing some characteristics with one family member and others with another. Smart's cross-cultural comparisons aim to indicate these resemblances while also acknowledging the specific context and worldview of each tradition.

Psychological approaches

Psychological approaches to the study of religion are fairly diverse in their claims, but largely unified in attempting better to explain or understand religion by focusing on the mind, perception, experience, and consciousness of the religious individual. Some approaches can be described as reducing religion to its psychological dimension, such as "explaining away" religion as illusory wish fulfillment projected onto reality and mistakenly believed to be real. Others, such as studies that illustrate how existing beliefs influence the way in which religion is experienced, demonstrate how psychology shapes religion without necessarily claiming that all of religion can be reduced to a psychological origin or explanation. This chapter will first explore some of the classical theories and theorists in the psychology of religion and then explore topics and recent methods that are related to this approach. Sigmund Freud (1856–1939) and Carl Jung (1875–1961) are seminal to the formation of psychology as a discipline as well as psychological approaches to the study of religion. In addition to these two, we will survey the thought of their older contemporary, William James (1842–1910), and briefly mention subsequent scholars whose approach was influenced by these pioneers.

Early seminal theorists

Sigmund Freud: religion as illusory wish fulfillment

Freud developed the theory, therapy, and emerging field of psychoanalysis, led an influential group of psychologists centered in Vienna, and remains the most widely recognized name in psychology even today. His fame encompasses a fair bit of notoriety from knowledgeable critics and from lay people with limited and at times distorted understanding of some of his seminal theories—especially those, such as the Oedipus complex, involving sexual urges, infantile dependencies, and frustrated instincts. His views on religion are less well known, but were closely related and important both for his own life work and for religious studies.

Freud was very bright and ambitious. Even before developing psychoanalysis and writing numerous influential books, he was a doctor and a clinical neurologist who specialized in psychopathology. Freud continued with his clinical practice and interest in various neuroses, but he simultaneously directed his formidable intelligence, education, insights, and theories toward addressing larger questions of human civilization and religion. These topics were interrelated for Freud and he believed that his psychoanalytic insights were as usefully applicable to understanding religion as they were to resolving patients' neuroses. In *The Future of an Illusion* (1927), he speaks of religion as illusory wish fulfillment that transforms forces of nature into anthropomorphic gods who are powerful and potentially destructive, but can also be approached and appeased. Freud indicates that monotheism, with god as a father figure, is especially conducive for developing a sense of a special relationship between god as parent and chosen people as children. The creation of gods and religion, according to Freud, also provides convenient solace and incentives that soften life's hardships, and protection and recompense for present and past suffering as well as future rewards for good behavior. In a sense, religion assists society's civilizing project by promoting moral precepts that guard against some of the baser instinctual desires of the individual and by attempting to domesticate some of the wilder forces of nature. Religion imbues civilization and individuals' lives with a sense of higher purpose, a divine hand guiding the helm, and an authoritative source of moral precepts beyond human society itself.

Despite Freud's praise for civilization and the link he establishes between its formation and that of religion, he remains critical of religion precisely because he thinks that it is illusory. That is, he asserts that it cannot be authenticated. Religious claims and beliefs are not necessarily false, but according to Freud they are quite improbable, and the inability to authenticate or refute religious claims leaves them in the category of illusion and well short of his preferred rationalist and scientific standards. In *The Future of an Illusion*, Freud appears to make the same bracketing move as phenomenologists who refrain from judging the truth claims of religion; however, his initial distinction between illusion and delusion falls away, as they are seen as ultimately the same in failing to measure up to objective, scientific knowledge. In this same work, Freud asserts that "scientific work is the only road which can lead us to a knowledge of reality outside ourselves." This rationalist ideal and the pre-eminence of science was increasingly common in Freud's age, but he speculates that there have always been doubts about the authenticity of religion and the gods, and that these doubts have been suppressed by individuals and societies. Freud explains that religious beliefs have been insulated from doubts and critiques because the related issues of meaning and purpose are so important even while the evidence is so tenuous and the logic in support of religious claims is often circular.

Freud: science displaces religion as civilizations mature

For Freud, the power of these urgent and ultimate wishes and the collective hold of the related illusion have propped up religion and led to suppression of these doubts. They have also led to the elevation of particular experiences and claims of faith over reason. Unlike the theological perspectives that privilege faith above reason or maintain that reason is ultimately supportive of faith claims, Freud distinguishes reason as separate from and superior to faith. Moreover, he finds individuals' inner experiences inadequate evidence for religious claims. For Freud, another's personal religious experience has no particular significance for those people, including Freud, who have not had such an experience. This disposition toward the insider and his or her experience is a departure from Otto and some other phenomenologists and theologians, who privilege insiders' experiential access to the most important religious essence, which is inaccessible to external observation and scientific analysis. Freud retorts at the end of *The Future of an Illusion* "an illusion it would be to suppose that what science cannot give us we can get elsewhere."

As Freud studies the past, present, and future of civilization, he theorizes about the past and future role of religion. Its future, for Freud, is quite limited. People, and civilization as a whole, will no longer find religion's illusion adequate and will benefit from a more penetrating and objective understanding of what is "really" happening. For Freud, both civilizations and human beings mature. In fact, he theorizes certain parallel developments where the illusions and neuroses of a child, including the ambivalent fear and reverence with which a boy might relate to his father, are recapitulated in early civilization's primitive religion and subsequent developments of a father-figure god who inspires similar ambivalence. Just as Freud, as a full grown and self-aware adult, can dispel the illusions of childhood and penetrate the artifice of religion, so he thinks that civilization as a whole can reach a similar maturation at the expense of religious belief. For Freud, we as a society have outgrown religion. In the terms Freud developed in his practice, to remain "fixated" on religion or to "regress" back to earlier stages, where religious belief may have been an inevitable, child-like developmental stage, would indicate a neurosis best overcome through therapy.

His theories of religion, articulated in books such as *Totem and Taboo* (1912–13) and *Moses and Monotheism* (1939) as well as *The Future of an Illusion*, contain this type of argument, where insights produced or reinforced by his wide reading and psychiatric practice are applied to diagnosing not just individuals, but psychological dimensions used to explain the origins and progressive development of religion and of civilization as a whole. In *Totem and Taboo*, the instinctual urge to displace the father described by Freud in the Oedipus complex is used to explain totemic religion with its related concept of powerful taboos. In parallel with killing the father and marrying the mother, Freud speculates that in prehistoric times frustrated younger males killed the dominant male of their "primal horde" in order to satisfy their sexual desires with the females under his control. This early clan or tribal model of extended families ruled by one dominant male stemmed as much from observations of apes and other animals as from ethnographic evidence of human groups. Consistent with other influential anthropologists and scientists of his age, Freud not only accepted Darwin's explanation of the evolution of species, but assumed social evolutionary principles where less developed social arrangements progressively gave way to more advanced societies. The Oedipal uprising in *Totem and Taboo* provides the catalyst for abandoning a relatively primitive and animal-like interaction for a more civilized social arrangement. That is, Freud claims that the guilt of the young males (following killing and consuming their own father) eventually led them to reinstate the father as a totem animal to be worshipped, and to create taboos against incest and killing or eating the totem animal. This more advanced social arrangement arises from the recognition that the brief ecstasy the young males may have enjoyed by impulsively indulging their frustrated desires was unsustainable. The protection and security of the "primal horde" is sacrificed if members kill each other to fulfill sexual or other urges. The illusory wish fulfillments of religion allowed a restoration of security by restoring the dominant male and his authority (as a totem or a god) where allegiance to this authority in turn required precepts against killing, cannibalism, and incest. Through this Oedipal analogy, Freud explains the origins of religious totems, taboos, and even of "more advanced" societies characterized by better regulated violence and marriage outside the clan or tribe.

Similarly, in *Moses and Monotheism* Freud recounts developments in Judaism and Christianity as seen through his psychoanalytic lens. He departs from historians, theologians, and other biblical scholars by speculating that Moses may not have been a Hebrew devoted to Yahweh. Instead Freud postulates Moses as an Egyptian prince and monotheist devoted to the god Aten, who leads the Hebrews out of oppression only to be betrayed. Here we move from Freud as maverick historian to his still controversial but more recognizably psychoanalytic claim that frustrated followers murdered Moses and displaced his god with Yahweh, whom they served with more primitive rituals. Freud credits later prophets with recovering the earlier monotheism, which he explains according to psychological notions of neuroses, guilt, repression, latency, and the inevitability of repressions resurfacing.

Criticism of Freud

Freud's explanations of Jewish and Christian developments in this book reveal some of the key limitations to his approach. Despite his early work on totemic religion, his insights are directed to the monotheism of Judaism and Christianity in particular rather than to diverse expressions of religion as a whole. Not only does he rely on a monotheistic father-figure god, but he also presumes that observations of individuals in psychoanalysis provide an unproblematic analogy to entire groups of people across vast spans of space and time. His analogies connect his insights about individuals' neuroses with his speculation about the religious and societal development of humankind. However, critics question both side of the analogy—his psychoanalytic conclusions about individual development and his grand theories about religion or civilization—as well as what they perceive to be a woefully inadequate logical or scientific basis for these interpretations, much less for the leap from individual case studies to society as a whole.

Despite this ongoing criticism of his work, Freud's influence can be best understood not so much by the specific content of his theories on the origins of religion, which have been widely rejected, as by his psychoanalytic method, rhetorical style, and confidence in "explaining away" religion. For Freud, not only was religion produced by humans rather than a divine, external authority, it was a defective product of an early stage of development. Moreover, Freud's approach is reductive in the sense that his questions and psychoanalytic methods reveal the psychological basis and motive for religion as well as the therapy to overcome it. Despite occasional references to the benefits of religion or distinctions between illusion and delusion, Freud ultimately seeks to dispel religion as an intellectually dishonest illusion, comparable even to an obsessive neurosis.

Religion as a sort of collective neurosis, according to Freud, should be overcome in the interest of knowledge vanquishing ignorance, even if religion has provided some services, such as consolation, motive for morality, "taming of the asocial instincts," and other relatively positive side effects. Freud acknowledges these benefits, but argues that religion has not done enough and that the usefulness of its function has been outgrown. He asserts that it has failed ultimately to provide happiness, morality, or other benchmarks of satisfaction and that there is greater risk than reward in maintaining the illusions of religion. Freud understands human and social development to occur in stages. Whereas such a "neurosis" may be inevitable in the ignorant infancy of a person or a society, Freud deems it unfit for adults or mature civilizations. Problems arise if healthy progress is stalled by fixation or even reversed by regression, sliding back to an earlier stage of development. In either case, Freud asserts that his psychoanalytic insights and therapy can help both the individual and the larger society. Thus, he sees his role in dispelling the illusion of religion as ultimately healing and constructive. He further reinforces a modern, rational assault on religion by adding a "psychological foundation to the criticism of my great predecessors" in order to advance the scientific spirit and move civilization forward.

Freud's theories were always controversial, but their influence has diminished over time and critics have also taken to task the claims of Freud and his followers concerning the scientific credentials of their method. Subsequent psychoanalytic approaches to religion have pursued similar questions about the nature of religion and the motives and mental health of religious belief, but they have generally been more nuanced while emending or ignoring many of Freud's most controversial claims. Moreover, Freud's theories represent just one of an expanding multitude of psychological approaches. Many of the more recent developments in psychology as a discipline, including psychological approaches to the study of religion, can be characterized as considerably more quantitative with "hard science" credentials, such as hypotheses that can be tested empirically. Psychologists of this stripe differ most radically from Freud's methods and conclusions. However, even among more qualitative approaches during the peak of Freud's influence, there were high-profile departures from Freud's views. The Swiss psychologist, Carl Gustav Jung, exemplifies such a famous departure with implications for the interpretation of religion.

Carl Jung: religion as imperfect therapy

Jung and Freud shared a general commitment to advancing self-understanding and its broader applications as well as more specific interests and views, such as the importance of dream analysis. Moreover, each inspired schools of psychologists to form around his insights and methods. Thus, the schools of psychoanalysis pioneered by Freud and Jung's analytic psychology continue to outlive their founders and are added to and revised by subsequent generations of psychologists. Each forms a psychodynamic system that purports to help the individual achieve healthy development, integrity, and self-understanding. It can be argued that religion includes similar objectives, and part of these psychologists' interest in religion stems from this sense that they had devised a therapy to exceed or supplement the limitations of religion. Despite these similarities, there were important differences as well, such as the broad, deep, rich, complementary, and positive sense of the "unconscious" for Jung relative to Freud's emphasis on the "subconscious" as a repository of suppressed desires and base instincts at war with mature, civilized, social behavior. Jung broke from Freud, but like his elder colleague, he applied his insights to religion and society as well as to himself and to his patients. The two great psychologists held quite different interpretations and theories of religion. Both located the origins of religion in the unconscious, but Jung took the reality of religion more seriously and positively than did Freud.

Not only did Jung have a greater respect for religious ideas, symbols, and experiences, but he also found commonalities in individuals' experiences and the symbols of disparate traditions in various times, which reinforced his theory of universal archetypes that emerge from a collective unconscious, which was more broad and deep than the individual's personal unconscious. These unconscious depths combined with the conscious ego to form the self. Many might mistake the conscious ego for the self, as the former includes personality and identity including sensations, feelings, and memory, whereas the more complete "self" operates under the radar of consciousness. Even the conscious ego remains hidden to others as they experience the persona presented to them, which is shaped by various factors, such as social convention, politics, religion, class, nationality, gender, and occupation. The persona too had a complementary hidden dark side.

This sense of complementariness and totality is evident throughout Jung's writings. For Jung, the objective of "individuation" resonates with religion and religious ideas. Individuation refers to a coming together of the complementary conscious and unconscious aspects of the self. Becoming more conscious of the self, including the deep riches of the unconscious dimension, can be described as a process of self-realization. The relationships and connections are always there, and the goal—to borrow a key term in Buddhism—is to "awaken" to this more full and accurate understanding of the self and reality. The unconscious communicates through symbols, according to Jung. Dreaming is an especially useful intermediate state for this communication. Symbolic mental images from dreams can be interpreted according to the individual's context and perspective in order to illuminate the collective and personal unconscious while advancing the process of individuation. Religion, too, is an instructive repository of symbols that can be read as expressions of archetypes—including the idea of the completeness of God as a model of the whole self. Jung indicates that this idea of wholeness and perfection can also be symbolically represented by heroes, magical animals, and objects, or even a *mandala*—the geometrical cosmic maps of Tantric Buddhism and Hinduism. Religion also provides a realm for experiences, ideas and states of consciousness beyond the conventional limits of the ego consciousness. Jung recalls the pheno-menologist Rudolf Otto by identifying religion as the attitude of a consciousness that has experienced a sense of an external, sacred, *numinosum*.

From the 1930s through the 1950s, Jung wrote half a dozen books directly relevant to his psychological approach to understanding religion. In addition to works such as *Psychology of Religion* (1938), *Answer to Job* (1956), and *Psychology and Religion: West and East* (1958), Jung also contributed the opening chapter of *Man and His Symbols*, a book written by Jungians and directed to a more general audience. Where an ardent atheist might find satisfying Freud's dismissal of religion as an illusion to be outgrown in healthy development, religious believers and practitioners are more likely to take comfort in Jung's insights and interpretations, which suggest that religion can be therapeutic. Where Freud's gaze was directed to Jewish and Christian monotheism in particular, Jung's focus on a universal unconscious has won admirers from Eastern and Western traditions including those with mystical inclinations. Freud recommends therapy to overcome the neurosis of religion. Jung, on the other hand, asserts that religion functions as a therapy to overcome imbalance and realize a healthier and complete sense of self. In the modern age, its therapeutic potential has been eclipsed by therapies such as Jung's own analytic psychology, but religion is not the neurosis for Jung that it is for Freud.

In fact, for Jung, any manifestation of archetypes serves the compensatory purpose of the unconscious correcting an imbalance in consciousness. For example, manifestations, often particular to the individual, of the *anima* (the feminine part of a man's personality) or *animus* (the masculine part of a woman's personality) archetypes may appear in dreams to restore balance. The three primary archetypes are these two, along with the shadow, which represents negative qualities that are hidden, rejected, or projected onto others. These archetypes shape perception, but they cannot be perceived directly. Dreams, imagination, myths, and religious experience provide access to archetypal images, such as the sun, mother, father, sage, trickster, child, an animal, birth, and other important rites of passage. Archetypal images appear directly in dreams. Dreams, however, are irrational and require the therapeutic process of individuation to understand the unique significance of these images for one's self. This process involves self-realization—including awareness of the links and communication between one's consciousness and unconscious—and establishing a critical distance from the images to allow interpretation. According to Jung, religious experience also offers immediate access to these archetypal images. This direct access can be intense, confused, and can appear as a form of psychosis. However, when organized religion is mediated through ritual and doctrine, the archetypal images are no longer directly communicated. This form is less revealing but also less dangerous than immediate religious experience. It is, in a sense, an incomplete move in the direction of distance and understanding of the manifestations of archetypes that can be pursued more fully and successfully through Jung's therapy of individuation. Jung's psychotherapy is not only sympathetic to religion—the two overlap. The overlap, however, is not complete. Jung is ultimately urging his modern audience, many of whom have abandoned religion in their embrace of science, to pursue therapy rather than to return to religion in order to reconnect with their unconscious.

William James: importance of religious experience

Jung was by no means the first major psychologist to view religion and religious experience positively. William James, an American psychologist and philosopher at Harvard, was a pioneer of scientific psychology in the late nineteenth century. His nationality is notable in the sense that most seminal figures in the early developments of religious studies were European; however, Americans have been at the forefront of some of the experimental and "hard science" approaches to understanding religion. After he published *The Principles of Psychology* in 1891, James examined religious experience from a psychological perspective. This focus on experience arose, in part, out of interest in conversion and differentiating religion from irreligion. His conclusions emphasized the potential value, importance, and benefits of religious experience. He disseminated his findings in the prestigious Gifford Lectures, which he delivered at the University of Edinburgh in 1901–2. His most famous work for the academic study of religion, *The Varieties of Religious Experience* (1902), emerged from these lectures.

Some of his observations and insights relied on personal introspection and clinical case studies, though much of this work responded to a wide array of readings from psychological materials, biographical accounts of religious leaders, translations of sacred texts, and other sources that informed his assessment of the psychological dimensions of religion. James focused on "immediate personal experience" of religion rather than doctrine, origins, texts, or ritual. He declared these other aspects to be secondary developments, and he asserted that the religious experiences, feelings, urges, and propensities form a compelling subject for psychological study. Moreover, he chose to focus on religious "geniuses" and their original, "pattern-setting" experiences, which display these religious propensities in their most extreme and fully developed forms. He acknowledges that such figures may be eccentric and unstable in some senses, but for his purposes, it is important only that they are sufficiently articulate to communicate their religious experiences.

While the "healthy-minded" religious adherent encountered neither spiritual crisis nor conversion, the conversion, awakening, or rebirth of the relatively tormented "sick soul" could lead to a dramatic and positive spiritual strength. James indicates Buddhism and Christianity as the religions that have most fully developed the relatively pessimistic aspects associated with the "sick soul" or "twice-born." This latter term speaks to the possibility of transformative "deliverance: the man must die to an unreal life before he can be born into the real life." For James, the direct, and especially intense, experiences and ideas of extraordinary mystics and religious founders carry particular authority and power. James acknowledged that mystical experience includes a "noetic quality"—perhaps better described at "metanoetic" (beyond the intellect)—of deep insight into truth and reality beyond the reach of rational, discursive thought. Such experiences are also characterized by ineffability— being beyond words or description. This term refers to the inexpressibility of such an experience. Merely describing it in words cannot communicate the feeling, the experience, to someone who has not shared it. James acknowledges that some have had this experience and others have not. As with his discussion of "healthy minded" and "sick souls," he resists setting one group above the other in any absolute sense. However, he validates the claims of religious experience, taking a stance quite different from Freud's, by asserting that there is no philosophical justification for determining that a "mystical world" is unreal just because not all have experienced it or because it cannot be easily communicated or revealed to the discursive mind. Moreover, James indicated that the power and authority from the unmediated insights and experiences of mystics and religious founders is primary, and that it then deteriorates through the mediation of later religious organizations and interpretations. In the concluding lecture, which formed the final chapter of *The Varieties of Religious Experience*, James characterized the religious life as maintaining "that the visible world is part of a more spiritual universe from which it draws its chief significance" and that "union or harmonious relation with that higher universe is our true end." He added that religion facilitates this goal and contributes "a new zest" to life, enchantment, earnestness, heroism, peacefulness, and love.

Like Jung, James understood his psychological approach to religion to be an empirical form of study. Both men also shared a positive view of religion as potentially transformative in helping to create a more complete self larger than, but unified with, the more limited conscious self. Both were also more open than Freud to applying their insights to religious traditions beyond Judaism and Christianity. Admittedly, James's case studies and personal introspection often emphasize a Protestant perspective, as suggested by his definition of religion as "the feelings, acts, and experiences of individual men in their solitude, so far as they apprehend themselves to stand in relation to whatever they may consider the divine." He prefaces this definition with a discussion of the impossibility of fully or adequately defining the term and acknowledges that his own is rather arbitrary and responsive to his present study. Not only are women subsumed in the use of "men" to stand for all humans, which was common at the time, but the emphasis on solitude in James' definition privileges Protestant ideas of direct access to God and the Bible free from mediating priests, rituals, or communal ceremonies and institutions. The latter part of the definition, however, suggests his openness to "whatever they may consider divine." His text bears this out as he acknowledges that religion and religious experience do not require the actual existence or even the idea of a god or gods. He notes that Buddhism is officially atheistic even if the Buddha performs a similar role in popular devotion. James uses the transcendental idealism of Emerson as another example of religion where god is an abstract divine quality of the natural universe.

These references are typical of his work as James invokes a wide range of religious and philosophical systems with impressive command of diverse traditions for his era. For example, his analysis of mystical union explicitly states that this especially exalted religious experience is not restricted to any particular theology or philosophy. He illustrated how Hindus and Buddhists as well as Christians and Muslims have cultivated mystic consciousness. Over the next several pages of his book, James elaborates and offers sources that range from Indian yoga and the nuanced difference between the Hindu use of *samadhi* and the Buddhist *dhyana* for higher states of meditative absorption to a long extract in translation from Al-Ghazali's writings on Sufism. In short, his studies of *The Varieties of Religious Experience* truly sought diverse source material for his conclusions. In self-deprecating introductory and closing remarks, he admits to being "ignorant of Buddhism" and does not claim to be a theologian, anthropologist, or a "scholar learned in the history of religions." Nonetheless, his contribution to religious studies from a psychological approach was impressive and discerning. Moreover, this work has stood the test of time better than most early classics in the academic study of religion in the sense that it remains more relevant and influential than most late nineteenth- and early twentieth-century works that have addressed the human religious response.

Comparing approaches

Scholars of psychological approaches to religion often differ in the types of religious experience, practice, or belief that they focus upon, as well as in their explanation of religion's origins, function, future, and positive or negative effects on individuals and society. Some think that religion can be reduced completely to its psychological aspect. For others, psychology explains much but does not exhaust the scope or understanding of religion. Some focus on the academic study of religion; for others, religion is but one of many fields that they attempt to map in their psychological explorations. Freud's conviction that God and religion are concepts created by humans due to their own needs, projected out and then naïvely accepted as originating from a higher authority, fits with other interpreters of religion from the nineteenth-century philosopher Ludwig Feuerbach to the twentieth-century sociologist Peter Berger. Similarly, he shares with earlier anthropologists, such as Tylor and Frazer, the dismissal of religion as illusory superstition lacking the reality, source, or authority with which believers imbue it. Although Freud devotes greater attention to questions of motive and psychological processes involved with religious beliefs, he labels them as illusory, ultimately unhealthy, and destined to be replaced by more rational explanations of reality.

In contrast, Jung and James are less dismissive of religion, even though they too explore and explain religious beliefs and experiences from a psychological perspective. While Jung agrees with Freud that gods arise from within the human psyche and are projected out, he does not agree that religion is a dangerous illusion to be dispelled by reason. In fact, in his chapter "Approaching the Unconscious" in *Man and His Symbols,* Jung directly contradicts Freud by declaring "Our present lives are dominated by the goddess Reason, who is our greatest and most tragic illusion." Jung turns Freud's conclusion on its head and suggests that not only is reason the dangerous illusion, but its devotees venerate it like a projected goddess.

Academic and popular studies of religion, such as those by the famous comparativist Joseph Campbell (1904–1987), are indebted to Jung's concepts of archetypes and his positive evaluation of religion and myths as important experiential and cultural modes that communicate universal, symbolically rich meaning necessary for self-realization. Campbell has reached a wide audience, well beyond the boundaries of the academy, through books such as *The Hero with a Thousand Faces* (1949), *The Masks of God* (4 volumes, 1959–68), and *Myths to Live By* (1972) as well as the book and PBS television series, *The Power of Myth* (1988). Campbell also edited *The Portable Jung* (1971), in which the publisher describes him as "the most famous of Jung's American followers" although the label "Jungian" is a poor fit for Campbell. William James's exploration of immediate religious experience and the deep insights but inexpressibility of unmediated mystical awareness has been extended to studies of Asian religious traditions, such as Zen Buddhism. D. T. Suzuki (1870–1966) is the most famous of the scholars, practitioners, and popularizers who emphasized the religious experience of unmediated perception of reality and a non-dualistic whole encompassing nature, one's self, and others. Through his numerous lectures and books, including *Zen and Japanese Culture*, Suzuki greatly influenced the introduction of both this Buddhist tradition and its Japanese artistic and cultural context into North America and Europe. Of course, *The Varieties of Religious Experience* influenced many Western scholars of religion as well, though James's subsequent publications focused on philosophy rather than religion or psychology in particular.

Later twentieth-century contributions

While Freud's assertions about Jewish and Christian developments in *Moses and Monotheism* were soundly rejected, his application of psychotherapy to religion continues to influence religious studies. Erik Erikson (1902–1994) was an influential psychoanalyst and developmental psychologist with an interest in understanding key religious figures according to a psychoanalytic model of stages of development. Erikson's *Young Man Luther: A Study in Psychoanalysis and History* (1958) and *Gandhi's Truth: On the Origins of Militant Nonviolence* (1969) offered his contribution to the academic study of religion during the rapid rise of religious studies in the 1960s and 1970s. In Erikson's model of eight stages of a human's life cycle, healthy development required adapting to each stage with its corresponding virtues while overcoming obstacles. Religion can help foster such healthy development of the ego into an increasingly meaningful and stable sense of self-identity. It can also influence an individual's development. His work on Luther demonstrated both directions of influence between religious and non-religious spheres in relation to crises in an individual's development. According to Erikson, Luther's troubled relationship with his father was linked to a nervous breakdown, which pushed him to a religious life and subsequent crises of self and purpose, before being resolved in a self-awareness that connected with God, free from the obstacles of his ego and thereby also resolving non-religious problems with his father.

Psychoanalytic interpretations of religion include other forays into psycho-biography. For example, Jeffrey Kripal (b. 1962) published a controversial work in this genre, *Kali's Child: The Mystical and the Erotic in the Life and Teachings of Ramakrishna* (1995). This work asserts that a psychoanalytic reading of the Bengali mystic and saint, Ramakrishna, reveals homoerotic aspects of his tantric approaches, visions, teachings, life, and interaction with disciples. The book has received strong praise and passionate criticism from the time it was published through to the present, where much of the back and forth plays out on the internet. In addition to offering an example of psychobiography, the scholarship and reception of this book also raise issues of insiders and outsiders in the academic study of religion. Kripal is a religious studies scholar and many of his detractors are followers of Ramakrishna. Some detractors claim their issue is with the adequacy of the scholarship itself—that Kripal is an outsider with insufficient access to or command of the language, context, and meaning of Ramakrishna's life and teachings to interpret it adequately. Other critics seem more personally involved in what they interpret as an outsider's attack on, and distortion of, the record of their saint. In either case, there is an insider vs. outsider dynamic not uncommon for religious studies. While not always as passionate, it is common for religious insiders to be uncomfortable with the questions asked and assertions made from the "outside" by scholars of religion.

Others could certainly be mentioned here, such as the influential work in psychoanalysis and anthropology of Gananath Obeyesekere. In *Medusa's Hair: An Essay on Personal Symbols and Religious Experience* (1981), Obeyesekere offers insight into the religious practices of Sri Lanka as well as theoretical breakthroughs for understanding symbolism. He employs methods of both anthropology and cultural applications of psychoanalysis, but he uses his ethnographic case study as evidence to revise the theories of symbolism offered by both approaches. René Girard (b. 1923) is another prominent theorist in the academic study of religion whose groundbreaking book, *Violence and the Sacred* (1977), has significantly revised earlier psychoanalytic ideas. Girard argued that violence and the sacred are inseparable and operate in the same way. Moreover, the origins of each can be located by his psychoanalytic understanding of mimetic desire—the motive force that concerns desiring that which others desire—and the power and function of sacrificing a scapegoat to unite the group and stave off uncontrolled violence, which could otherwise spread like an epidemic and tear society apart.

Girard describes violence as a dangerous contagion that is powerful, awe-inspiring, and inescapable. Controlling this violence enough to ward off crisis involves sacrificial substitution that redirects this violence in ways that are most effective if they are not fully understood. Religion allows for this through rituals that are not completely transparent or rational, but can be effective and necessary if they are able to restore social order. This solution uses ritualized violence to quell internal violence in a manner that brings society together without inviting further retaliatory violence. Although judicial systems have taken on this role of curing escalating violence, Girard maintains that a religious quality continues to pervade this system in order to achieve its same purpose. That is, there remains a carefully scheduled, sanctioned, ritualized violence deployed to end chaotic, contagious violence. Girard disagreed with Freud's explanation of religious origins by means of the Oedipus complex. However, he shared Freud's method of looking to myths and primal psychological motivations, including desire and the violence that can arise out of desire, to understand how religion arose and functions.

Abraham Maslow (1908–1970) was a key contributor to the humanistic psychology that became increasingly popular in the latter half of the twentieth century. Maslow is particularly well known for his theory of a motivation responding to a hierarchy of needs and values. His focus on human, rather than animal, subjects included a particular interest in especially well-adjusted, happy, and healthy individuals. Maslow posited that human beings' basic needs must first be met before motivation and opportunity for higher values can be realized. In this pyramid, the most basic needs are physiological—food, water, sleep, a hospitable environment, and even sex—followed by needs related to safety and security, love and belonging, and esteem. Although progressively higher than the basic needs, these latter ones are all "deficit needs" in Maslow's theory. Whereas a deficit in any of these areas, such as belonging or esteem, prompts the need, the yet higher level of "being needs" are motivated by growth rather than deficit.

These higher values include wholeness, truth, beauty, and self-sufficiency. Whereas lower needs are necessary for basic health, progressing through these higher needs is part of "self-actualization." In this regard, "peak experiences" are especially valuable, and mystical religious experiences represent the "peak experience" *par excellence.* Maslow's research concluded that not all "self-actualizers" have peak experiences and not all who experience these peaks are self-actualizers, but the ideal includes both having such experiences and continuously improving and self-actualizing. This emphasis on the value of peak experiences moved Maslow in the direction of transpersonal psychology, which looks to religious examples for transformation beyond normal states of consciousness. His book *Religions, Values, and Peak-Experiences* (1964) is most explicit in connecting his theories with religion. In the Preface to the 1970 edition, he indicates dangers of extremes in organized religions—"the 'mystical' and individual on the one hand, and the legalistic and organizational on the other." Maslow repeats warnings against the excesses of organized religion where convention, dogma, habit, bureaucracy, and the churches "may become the major enemies of the religious experience" and the peak experiencer. However, he also warns against the mystic becoming selfish or mean in pursuit of peak experience, or like a desperate junkie needing successively stronger stimuli to achieve this peak fix, or actually turning to drugs as a shortcut to such an experience, rejecting all guidance in a distorted way, or seeking the exotic in other places and traditions without recognizing that the "sacred is *in* the ordinary." These comments appealing for a holistic integration rather than faddish excess speak directly to the times in America. In addition to a rise in academic religious studies, the late 1960s were characterized by experimentation in Asian and other alternative religions, drugs, and sex without always differentiating among these practices and experiences.

Influential psychologists of religion

William James (1842–1910): American psychologist and philosopher at Harvard; studies emphasized the value, importance, and benefits of religious experience with particular focus on "immediate personal experience" of religion rather than doctrine, origins, texts, or ritual.

Sigmund Freud (1856–1939): Psychologist and influential intellectual based in Vienna; founding father of psychoanalysis; asserted that psychoanalytic insights fostered understanding of religion; indicated that religion provided several benefits to civilization but ultimately is illusory, akin to a childhood neurosis, and inadequate for scientific standards.

Carl Gustav Jung (1875–1961): Swiss founder of analytic (also called Jungian) psychology; evaluated religion more positively than Freud; propounded the notion of universal archetypes that emerge from a collective unconscious and the importance of individuation—a process where one comes to self-realization linking the individual conscious with the collective unconscious.

Erik Erikson (1902–1994): German psychoanalyst and developmental psychologist; in his model of eight stages of a human's life cycle, religion could assist in adapting to each stage; applied psychoanalytic model to key religious figures, such as Luther and Gandhi.

Abraham Maslow (1908–1970): American humanistic psychologist; considered that human beings' basic needs must first be met before motivation and opportunity for higher values can be realized; progressing through higher needs is part of "self-actualization"; mystical religious experiences represent the ultimate "peak experiences."

René Girard (b. 1923): French scholar; asserted that violence and the sacred are inseparable: their origins can be located in mimetic desire and the power and function of sacrificing a scapegoat to unite the group and stave off uncontrolled violence, which could otherwise tear society apart.

Buddhism and psychology

Before turning our attention to some of the latest intersections between science, religion, and psychological approaches in the West, it might be instructive briefly to survey close links between Buddhism and approaches focused on the mind, awareness, consciousness, and cognitive processes. Psychologists engaged in transpersonal psychotherapy and related practices with clear spiritual aims of self-realization beyond the confines of conscious awareness have found resonance between other forms of religion and their theories, practices, and goals. While some have highlighted supportive similarities in such mystical practices as Sufism or Kabbalah, links between Buddhism and psychology have been described as especially strong and have been pursued most extensively. In fact, Buddhism has appealed to a wide range of psychologists and psychological approaches, interests, experiments, and therapies. This has not simply been a recent preoccupation of Western psychologists read back onto the Asian tradition. Analysis of psychological and cognitive processes has been central to Buddhist thought from the time of the Buddha, approximately 2,500 years ago in India, through to the present, including this most recent appropriation in the West.

Many high-profile Buddhist teachers in the West also trained as psychologists. This is most evident with *vipassana* (insight meditation) teachers. Jack Kornfield, Joseph Goldstein, and Sharon Salzberg all trained under Asian Theravada Buddhist masters, but their Insight Meditation Society, with its retreat centers, forms of practice, and vast numbers of popular books, focuses on *vipassana* meditation. In the West, this practice's psychological emphasis on awareness and insight has been promoted often with little reference to its larger Theravada Buddhist context. Still further from its traditional religious setting, some other practicing psychologists who are not Buddhist teachers or authors nevertheless incorporate Buddhist meditation and insights into their clinical practices. In this context, meditation is often lauded for its therapeutic capacity to relieve stress and allow individuals to step back from the anxieties of their busy schedule, personal problems, or illness. With both groups in mind, one can argue for a sort of psychological approach to, or appropriation of, Buddhism. However, the relationship that is rooted more deeply in history could better be described as a Buddhist approach to key psychological concerns, such as states of mind, consciousness, awareness, and identity.

The story of the Buddha and his early teachings is often portrayed through an analogy where the Buddha is a physician diagnosing human beings' afflictions, and identifying the cause, cure, and prescriptive course of treatment. These core Buddhist teachings speak to a sense of dis-ease or suffering, which characterizes existence, and is caused by desire. Desire, including craving or attachment, results from ignorance of the impermanence and radical interdependence of all things. Buddhists speak of a mistaken idea, arising from this same ignorance about the nature of reality, of a separate, enduring self that desires, loves, hates, craves permanence, and suffers. Both cause and cure can be understood psychologically, and the constant encouragement to be aware of and awake to the often hidden workings of consciousness, feelings, perceptions, thoughts, attachments, and ideas about oneself and others fosters a sophisticated understanding of mental processes and their connections to beliefs, actions, and identity. The therapeutic treatment at the core of these Buddhist teachings prescribes an ongoing and interrelated eight-fold path where living ethically, practicing meditative contemplation, and working to better understand the teachings and corresponding insights into the nature of reality can reinforce each other and facilitate an awakening or enlightenment. This highest realization, which some psychologists might describe as self-realization or actualization, is actually a realization of "no-self" in the Buddhist context. In this early formulation of Buddhism, neither gods nor external powers are religiously—or therapeutically—important. Part of the appeal and link between Buddhism and many of the psychological theories already discussed includes an inward focus and emphasis on mental states, relationships, insights, and perspectives broader than the conventional concepts of the discursive mind and the limitations of ordinary consciousness.

Of course, to exaggerate the relationship or conflate Buddhism with Western psychology and related forms of psychotherapy would require distorting and over-simplifying both. Many psychologists would understand their discipline as capable of explaining Buddhism and many Buddhists would see psychology as just one aspect of their tradition. After all, Buddhism is a religion, or a group of related religions, that developed various strands and characteristics in multiple cultures over the course of more than two millennia. However, in the West, certain aspects of Buddhism have often been seized upon and emphasized while ignoring or distorting other cultural and religious aspects. Humanistic, rational, and psychological dimensions have been especially popular. The fascination with Zen in the West has included its psychological appeal as evident by the involvement of high-profile psychologists, such as Jung, who wrote the foreword to D. T. Suzuki's *Introduction to Zen* (1949), or Erick Fromm's book, *Zen Buddhism and Psychoanalysis* (1960), which he co-authored with D. T. Suzuki and Richard De Martino. The authors suggest that Zen and psychoanalysis are mutually supportive in important ways though not fully equivalent; after all, Suzuki suggests that Zen is considerably more expansive and can provide insights and benefits beyond the psychoanalytic healing suggested by Fromm. Franz Aubrey Metcalf's article, "The Encounter of Buddhism and Psychology," in *Westward Dharma: Buddhism Beyond Asia* (2002), notes that this dialogue between Buddhism and psychology has been continued by the Dalai Lama and his Tibetan tradition. Tibetan Buddhist monks have been involved with neurological experiments in American universities as a lab component of this dialogue, which has included the "harder-science field of neurology and the more philosophical field of cognitive psychology." These areas are addressed in the next section.

Cognitive and related "hard science" approaches

Whereas most of the attention devoted to religion by psychologists, including those surveyed above, could be categorized as qualitative social scientific studies, the quantitative "hard science" approach has also applied its theories and experiments to religion, influenced more by the natural sciences. There is, in fact, a surge of recent attention and experiments devoted to cognitive processes of the mind and measuring physiologically observable brain activity during religious prayer or meditation. Recent researchers in this "hard" scientific approach depart significantly from Freud and Jung, but they represent a vibrant current direction of research in the psychology of religion. They often strive for more repeatable and verifiable experiments guided by the scientific method.

Cognitive approaches have been increasingly influential for studies of religion rooted in psychology. Cognitive studies can be difficult to categorize as they often draw on expertise beyond one discipline. For example, Daniel Dennett's book, *Breaking the Spell: Religion as a Natural Phenomenon* (2006), explains the origins, functions and evolution of religion with reference to cognitive studies, including the roles of psychology and biology, as well as history and appeals to reasoned analysis from his own principal discipline, philosophy. Because this wide-ranging and lively work was written in a style intended to be inviting to a broader audience of non-specialists, we could address it in the later section of this book, which examines the popularity of recent publications that are largely critical of religion. However, it may be more fruitful to keep it here, as Dennett's work draws upon cognitive studies—including the evolutionary interplay among biological, social, and cultural components that shape and perpetuate the mind's processes—along with references to a wide range of psychological, anthropological, and other approaches in the academic study of religion. Moreover, the first two chapters of Dennett's book discuss what religion is and why science can and should study it. This position, that religion should not be set apart as taboo to rigorous investigation, is central to all approaches in the academic study of religion however much they might diverge in their methods and conclusions. In summarizing these first chapters, Dennett acknowledges "obstacles" and "misgivings" about the scientific study of religion, but he insists that we should pursue these studies precisely because religions "are among the most powerful natural phenomena on the planet," and that a better understanding of "how and why religions inspire such devotion" is necessary to determine how to "deal with them" more rationally. In *Breaking the Spell*, Dennett adds his voice to the chorus of calls for the scientific investigation of religion, which in turn is understood as a "natural phenomenon" rather than supernatural or of divine origin.

Pascal Boyer is one of the scientists and anthropologists referenced most frequently by Dennett in his cognitive studies approach to an overview of the origins, developments, and implications of religion. Relative to Dennett, Pascal Boyer's cognitive studies of religion are more firmly rooted in psychology and more neutral in asserting religion's harm or benefit, but he too straddles disciplinary boundaries with classes taught in both anthropology and psychology departments. For his research in cognitive psychology, he conducts experiments designed to better understand the mind's neuro-cognitive systems. Ongoing work in cognitive studies and evolutionary biology has informed his theories about the relationship between mind-brain and religion. He has published his findings and theories in books such as *Naturalness of Religious Ideas: A Cognitive Theory of Religion* (1994) and *Religion Explained* (2001). The term "mind-brain" refers to the multiple neuro-cognitive systems responsible for how we understand reality, and act in various settings and situations. It is understood to be considerably more complex than simple notions that view the brain as an organ, catalog of information, or blank slate gradually being filled by information and experiences in this lifetime. Instead, evolutionary biology is used to explain the development, over many generations, of properties that serve as constraints upon what is perceived and how it is processed and acted upon.

Boyer's cognitive theory of religion in *Naturalness of Religious Ideas* accounts for the development, spread, and perpetuation of similar religious representations across diverse cultures and traditions by examining the role and constraints of the mind-brain in acquiring and transmitting some representations rather than others. Thus even though a wide assortment of people may possess religious conceptions of unusual, supernatural entities such as spirits and ghosts, their shared "mind-brain" constraints still have these seemingly counter-intuitive creations possessing certain human characteristics, such as beliefs and desires, which are derived from intuitions about the natural world. *Religion Explained* extends this theory by analyzing how increasingly advanced understanding of the mind-brain allows for similarly greater insight into why religious representations arise and the function that they serve. In fact, Boyer points out that cognitive architecture constructed without particular reference to religion can account for religious concepts. Whereas questions about religion have been more central to some psychological studies, here explanations of religion can be seen as useful by-products of larger projects. Religion is not considered especially unique, or *sui generis* in the terms of many phenomenologists, but can be understood as a collection of natural instincts and cognitive processes. It is argued that the development of religion, or something similar, was essentially inevitable because it is so well suited to—or, more negatively, it so effectively exploits—these natural cognitive processes related to memory, moral-intuition, storytelling, etc. Moreover, Boyer argues that religion defies explanation without an understanding of these cognitive processes. Like earlier psychological approaches to religion, Boyer insists that the processes responsible for religious beliefs and experiences are primarily internal, but beyond the limitations of the conscious mind. The results of his experiments take issue with earlier theories that religion arises in response to a need, as well as with the contemporary physiological emphasis surveyed below, where religious activity is located in a specific part of the brain.

"Neurotheological" approaches

This latter physiological approach to understanding the interaction between religion and the mind-brain is dramatically apparent in Andrew Newberg's neuroimaging studies on Tibetan Buddhist monks and Catholic nuns to determine the correlation between brain activity and intense prayer, meditation, or visualization. These studies—he uses the term "neurotheology" to designate this seemingly unlikely pairing of brain science and theology—combine his expertise and interest in nuclear medicine, neurology, psychiatry, and the health benefits of spirituality. These wide-ranging but interrelated areas can be simultaneously and collaboratively pursued at the University of Pennsylvania, where he holds positions in each of the relevant departments and directs the Center for Spirituality and the Mind.

His research, with its provocative combination of "hard" science and typically less quantifiable spirituality, has attracted wide attention from the media. His co-authored books, *The Mystical Mind: Probing the Biology of Religious Experience* (1999), *Why God Won't Go Away: Brain Science and the Biology of Belief* (2001), and *Why We Believe What We Believe* (2006), introduced this neurological research along with accompanying "neurotheological" analysis and speculation. The last title responds to a question central to psychological approaches to religion. All of the theorists, at some level, are looking to the mind, conscious, unconscious, cognitive processes, experiences, and perceptions to understand what religion is, where it comes from, how it functions, and "why we believe what we believe." Newberg looks to both biological determinism and a variety of equally influential societal factors to answer these questions. This study goes beyond exploring the source of religious beliefs to assess how these beliefs shape us, and how they can lead to various benefits or harm.

Newberg's core questions restate the dominant themes found throughout psychological approaches to religion; however, the methods he uses to observe and map the physiology of the brain are novel in their capacity to link observations and explanations from the "hard" physical sciences with religious behaviors, activities, and experiences that have been studied more often by "softer" social scientific techniques. For instance, Newberg's studies demonstrate similar brain activity for Catholic nuns in prayer and Tibetan Buddhists in meditation. That is, the same areas of the participants' brains showed both significantly higher than baseline neurological activity in some parts and lower activity in others. These results have now been extended to include other nuns, atheists, and evangelicals while in the activity of speaking in tongues. The initial study graphically illustrates that elevated brain activity in the frontal lobes, as measured by blood flow and represented by SPECT imaging (single photon emission computed tomography), occurs during concentrated religious activity by trained adepts from these two different traditions, cultures, and genders. The images and accompanying interpretations explain that the increased activity in the frontal lobes is related to "focusing attention and concentration" whereas the parietal lobes, which show decreased activity during meditation and prayer, are involved in our sense of "orientation in space and time." In short, the functions associated with the areas of the brain that revealed significant increased or decreased activity during prayer or meditation fit with religious adherents' descriptions of the focused awareness and relative dropping away of time and space in intense or even mystical states of prayer or meditation.

Although the experiments, repeatability, predictability, and high-tech medicine and machinery demonstrate the scientific credentials of these studies, the interpretation of what they means enters murkier waters. It is the nature of science to keep pushing back the limits of knowledge, and cognitive science and neurological research promise to continue improving our understanding of the mind-brain. However, the analysis of what this means for understanding religion continues to leave ample room for speculation—theological or otherwise. To some, the studies suggest that human beings are "hard wired" for religion: that is, there is a capacity built right into the brain and a rather universal religious impulse is part of our genetic heritage, physiological architecture, and cognitive capacity. While it is exciting to be able to see and measure this activity more scientifically, the full extent of the conclusions that can be drawn from the experiments is less clear. Some might be persuaded that these studies objectively demonstrate that religion is "real" as an external force that is registered by the brain during prayer and meditation. However, such an interpretation jumps to conclusions that are possible but not necessary interpretations of the data. Jung and James also asserted that religious activity and experiences are important and that they can "really do something" transformative for the individual. However, Freud and Jung understood these experiences to arise from the human psyche, in connection with the vast collective unconscious for Jung. William James contended that a sacred power need only be larger than the conscious mind, whether located in one's own psyche or out in the universe. These more recent studies have not yet resolved this enduring question, as they locate processes and activity in the mind, which can respond to internal or external stimuli, "real" or "imagined"—distinctions that may or may not ultimately be resolved by these approaches.

5

Judging religion

Critical perspectives and evaluations

The study of religion includes a diverse array of perspectives that are critical of how religion has been studied, and of features of religion itself—including its institutions, interpretations, and ramifications for society. Feminist approaches are representative of cultural studies and postmodern critiques both of aspects of religion and its study. In this regard, feminists' criticisms of patriarchal institutions, texts, interpretations, and assumptions have been important voices in a wider critique of socially constructed relationships and concepts of power, status, and identity. In addition to greater awareness of gender, there are critical perspectives that focus attention on socio-economic disparities, environmental degradation, and ongoing biases linked to race, sexual orientation, or colonial exploitation. Voices from the margins continually emerge to represent themselves, audit past records, and criticize hegemonic powers. In the acts of reclaiming, rereading, and reforming religious traditions and religious studies, these voices often shift into a theological tone that sets norms for what religion must have been, how religion should be, and what it should become.

Another type of critical approach makes its own normative claims in more of an anti-theological direction. There have been critiques of religion throughout the Enlightenment, the modern era, and beyond—including assertions of the death of god and predictions of the death of religion. Religion has outlived these predictions as surely as the world has outlived many religions' predictions for the end of time. Not only has religion staved off death, it is very much alive, with surging numbers of evangelical converts and a central role in politics, culture, and the daily beliefs and practices of most people in the world. Although this resurgence refutes the prediction of religion's demise, there is a popular strain of criticism that accuses religion, religious beliefs, and religious practitioners of anti-rational and funda-mentalist outlooks that are detrimental to everything from science education to world peace. This genre of critique is not one of the classic approaches to the study of religion. Unlike feminist scholarship, the popular strain of criticism is not demonstrably becoming an increasingly established perspective within academic religious studies. It is, however, representative of an influential perspective on religion that continues to shape how religion is studied, explained, and understood.

Thus the popular discourse critical of religion can, and probably should, be described as an approach to the study of religion. Admittedly, its critiques are often reductionistic and at times simplistic as well as selective in picking and choosing what to analyze in a tradition or text. However, all approaches in the study of religion, including those deriving from the scholarly community of better-informed specialists, tend to be selective, and many of these are themselves criticized for being overly reductionistic in their attempts to "explain away" religion. Significantly, popular, anti-religion perspectives, and contrasting theological perspectives, are especially influential in shaping students' views about religion before they pursue any form of academic study of religion at university. Popular literature and the opinions of family members and friends from both extremes typically inform their attitudes and understandings about religion. These extremes vary in substance, rigor, and comprehensiveness, leaving the discipline of religious studies at the university to clarify its role as a study of religion that does not embrace believers' faith commitments, preferences for one tradition over others, or critics' dismissal of religion as a whole.

As with theological approaches at the other end of the spectrum, there can be overlap here with religious studies proper. However, normative assumptions in the anti-religion literature about what religion "really is" and what should be its fate and expression often push a political agenda or ideological commitment onto a collision course with the relatively objective ideals of religious studies in a secular, academic setting. There are also other works sympathetically disposed toward religion, and supportive of certain religious values and insights, or at least based upon a greater awareness of religion and its role in our lives and society. A number of these books are written for a more popular audience and straddle the fence between the academic study of religion and a more normative promotion of religion. In addition to discussing these popular genres, which take religion as their subject, in the final section we will also briefly examine ongoing critiques of and reflections on theoretical and methodological issues in religious studies from within academe. Religious studies scholars, such as Russell McCutcheon and J. Z. Smith, have criticized religious studies as poorly defined and insufficiently reflective and proactive in forging its own respectable academic identity. These and other scholars have attempted to shape the discipline with a more critical awareness of what it is and what it is not.

Feminist approaches

Postmodern critiques of scholarly works have heightened our awareness of potential weaknesses in many academic disciplines. Postmodernism refers to a recent intellectual movement characterized by scrutinizing and deconstructing modern assumptions, privileged positions, and dominant approaches. With accusations of being, at best, naïve and likely malicious, postmodern critics took to task academic studies in which the analysis and conclusions were portrayed as objective truths. We have noted throughout this book how such aspirations for scientific certainty, especially in the social sciences, derived from efforts to study history, society, culture, and so on with methodologies more appropriate to the pure sciences. Unfortunately, those "scientistic" (i.e. science-like) attempts were intrinsically flawed because they did not adequately recognize the limitations that are inherently present in the perspectives (worldviews, *darshanas*) of the researchers. While a scientist may examine and measure, with a high degree of objectivity, how the boiling point of water changes as different amounts of salt are dissolved in it, it is unreasonable to expect an anthropologist to measure with objectivity how social cohesion in a remote village is affected as members of neighboring tribes and other foreigners move into the village and mingle with the group under study. Not only are there no adequate instruments, like thermometers, to measure social cohesion, but the researcher has himself, as a foreign visitor, already affected the social cohesion of the group under study. Actually, the distinction between pure science and social science is much more complex, for certain social scientists, such as some anthropologists and sociologists, do attempt to find pervasive patterns and relationships within the cultures and societies they study. They are looking for systems and laws. Conversely, hard science is itself culturally situated, for there are variations in the kinds of instrumentation one chooses to use, the scales of measurement, the objects of study, and even the observations made and the conclusions obtained from them.

Nevertheless, the anthropological endeavor aptly illustrates the challenge to objectivity, for ethnographers go to their field sites, which typically are remote societies, fully aware that they will encounter people whose values and ways of understanding the world are different from their own. Thus the anthropologist affirms at the outset that there are differing worldviews, realities shaped by culture, and so on, and that the anthropologist's own perspective is just one of these types of perspectives. However, early ethnographies attempted to depict foreign cultures as if they were being described objectively, revealing the way these cultures actually were, because they were studied in a detached scientific manner. Postmodern sensitivities have transformed contemporary anthropology as it soon became obvious that the ethnographer's own cultural background significantly colored and shaped her "participant-observation." The researcher's own culture (as well as her age, experience, gender, appearance, social background, and so on) affected the degree to which she was able to participate in the activities of the studied culture, as well as what she chose to observe and how she reported on her discoveries. The realization that in the observation of any event there are multiple and often differing perspectives, which when taken together might provide a more complete picture of what actually took place, is known as the Rashomon effect. This is named after the film, *Rashomon,* by the influential Japanese director Akira Kurosawa, which recounts how four different witnesses to a crime all have their own versions about what happened. The Rashomon effect highlights the currently well-accepted position among scholars that each of us is situated culturally, historically, spatially, bodily, and so on, and can thus only provide a limited and partial picture of reality as we have perceived or experienced it. It is in relationship with the foregoing set of realizations that feminist perspectives in the study of religion derive.

What is feminism?

Of course, feminist approaches to the study of religion are also the outgrowth of the feminist movement, which began to gain momentum in the late nineteenth and early twentieth century, particularly with its victories in many countries to grant women the right to vote. In the United States, for instance, women's right to vote on the same terms as men was only achieved in 1928. In both World Wars I and II, the labor shortage caused by the large numbers of troops in battle drove women into occupations, such as industrial manufacturing, which were traditionally occupied by men. Socialist and communist ideologies also promoted the equality of women, and thus by the 1950s women in the West had mostly achieved legal equality with men. Women in the West had also begun to be accepted as capable of engaging in occupations and lifestyles beyond their traditional domestic roles as housewives and mothers. Their capacity to select different career options was boosted with the development of effective forms of contraception (e.g. the birth control pill in the 1960s), which gave women much more control over their fertility, empowering them with choices about when or even whether to have children. However, despite legal equality and new freedoms of choice, the social, economic, and cultural realities were quite different. For instance, women were (and still are in many instances) subtly (and overtly) discriminated against when seeking employment in a wide variety of professions (e.g. politics, law, business, higher education, science, religion), often also receiving less income when doing the same work as men. Second-wave feminism, as it is often called to distinguish it from the first wave which had succeeded in winning official equality, was concerned with rectifying the actual inequalities that still exist between men and women. In the struggles of second-wave feminism, it became evident that religion was a powerful force in shaping a society's perceptions of women and in generating attitudes toward them. In part, feminist approaches to the study of religion seek to explore what those features might be.

The term "feminism" is often mistakenly understood as referring to radical wings of the feminist movement, sometimes called "militant" or "radical feminism." Caricature images of this brand of feminism portray it as populated mainly by men-hating lesbian women, who look like men and want simply to invert the male-dominated (i.e. patriarchal) structures of authority and place themselves instead at the helm of social, political, and economic power. It is crucial to recognize that although women's issues naturally interest women, feminism actually refers to a (movement peopled by women and men who are interested in achieving a status for women that is genuinely egalitarian with men, not just legally, but culturally and in all relevant spheres of social life.)It is linked to a moral philosophy of liberation which views unequal social systems (e.g. master–slave, landowner–serf) as unjust since they depend on the domination of one segment of humanity, who should rightly be freed from their oppression into a state of independence, self-determination, and equal opportunity. At one end of the spectrum, the feminist movement may promote the liberation of women through extreme revolutionary measures. However, its more benign side involves educating both men and women about the structures, both explicit and implicit, through which women have been marginalized, subordinated, or simply oppressed throughout history and even today. The postmodern critiques and the women's movement approaches discussed above mesh with this educational dimension of the feminist agenda. For instance, a simple example of an implicit form of marginalization is embedded within the structure of the English language. In a sentence such as "A doctor (or nurse) should wash his hands regularly," the male pronoun "his" is used to refer to both male and female doctors (or nurses), but implicitly endorses or gives primacy to the masculine sex. Since language plays a huge role in shaping attitudes, many feminists have pressed to have people alerted to this problematic function of language and to make efforts to alter its usage (not an easy task). This book has utilized a variety of these approaches, both because it is sympathetic to this argument and to demonstrate how gender-sensitive or inclusive language may be used. For instance, one may use a plural (e.g. "Doctors should wash their hands regularly") to avoid the clumsier dual gender form (e.g. "A doctor should wash his/her hands regularly"). Another alternative is simply not to favor the male pronoun for the general case (e.g. A doctor should wash her hands). Of course, there are much more elaborate and ongoing applications of the postmodern feminist analysis of implicit and explicit social and cultural inequalities. These play significant roles in the feminist approach to the study of religion.

Feminist voices

Mary Daly and radical feminist activism

An influential feminist voice in the study of religion is that of Mary Daly (b. 1928). Although Daly is not a religious studies scholar, but a philosopher and theologian who would prefer to label herself as a radical lesbian feminist, her writings have influenced both religion and the study of religion. Daly sees the woes of the world, such as environmental degradation, constant warfare, racist and ethnocentric attitudes, and particularly the terrible plight of women, as a direct consequence of patriarchy. Patriarchy (Greek: *pater*—father + *arché*—rule) refers to the control and dominance of a society and its culture by men, who in Daly's terminology occupy the foreground and relegate women to the background through a variety of strategies, including the negative labeling of dissenting voices. After an in-depth study of Christian theology, its structures, and purveyors, Daly found Christianity to be a religion unsympathetic and even hostile to women, and in *Beyond God the Father: Toward a Philosophy of Women's Liberation* (1973) essentially promoted the view that women should not attempt to transform the religion from within, but instead should abandon it completely. Christianity is grounded in a male conception of supreme divinity (God the Father, Jesus the Son, and the Holy Spirit), its historical development and theological elaborations were mainly furthered by males (e.g. Paul of Tarsus, Augustine of Hippo, Thomas Aquinas), and its organizational structures are governed by exclusively male clergy (e.g. the Pope and the priesthood). Women may have had some substantial roles (e.g. as deaconesses) in the early Church, but are now completely marginalized from any influence in Christianity. To attempt to transform the religion from within, which in its very unlikely but best conceivable achievement would merely have women filling male roles as priests, and so on, would still be woefully inadequate, since the entire theological construction of the religion is patriarchal and toxic to women's self-actualization. Daly considers most of the mainstream religions (e.g. Christianity, Judaism, Islam, Hinduism, Buddhism, etc.), as well as political or secular ideologies (e.g. Marxism, Maoism), as embodying patriarchy. One cannot fully explore and thus understand what it is to be a woman within these frameworks. Renowned for creating and encouraging the creation of new words (i.e. neologisms) (e.g. hag-iography), investing words with new meanings (e.g. his-tory), or reinvesting them with lost meanings, all of which playfully evoke the serious concerns of feminism, Daly, in her later works, such as *Gyn/Ecology* (1978) and *Quintessence* (1998), continues to articulate a call for a meta-patriarchal society. Language, as discussed above, plays a crucial role in sustaining cultural norms, and Daly champions the endeavor to subvert patriarchal language structures through the metaphor of male castration, delivering disempowering surgical strikes at the symbolic phallus at the core of a patriarchal society's modes of communication.

By meta-patriarchy, Daly does not hope for a matriarchy that merely replicates the male style of dominance with women at the top, but for something that transcends the pernicious features of patriarchy altogether. She offers the idea that such a society may have existed in the remote past, a notion that certain feminists have attempted to uncover. There is now a stream of arguments that the world's existing patriarchies were pre-dated not by Daly's meta-patriarchy, but by primordial matriarchies. However, anthropological evidence reveals that there are only a few matrilineal societies (e.g. the Minangkabau of west Sumatra) in existence today. In typical matrilineal groups, one belongs to one's mother's lineage, as opposed to the currently more common patrilineal descent systems, where one traces one's lineage through one's fathers. It is harder to confirm the existence of any classically matriarchal society in existence anywhere in the world today, which makes the notion of widespread ancient matriarchies to be highly unlikely. The idea that matriarchal societies dominated world cultures in the remote past derived from speculative ideas about the evolution of societies and cultures. Archeological finds of ancient female figurines (e.g. the so-called Venus of Willendorf, dated at about 22,000 BCE) also led to hypotheses about the existence of widespread goddess worship cults, although there is no consensus about what those figures represented and how they were used. Others have proposed that a single Great Mother Goddess religion permeated most of Europe, and just as male god worship is often a mark of patriarchal societies, ancient goddess worship was likely a sign of a primordial matriarchy. Although the widespread existence of goddesses in antiquity, many of them mother goddesses with characteristics related to nurturing life and ensuring agricultural and human fertility, is undisputed, most scholars are nevertheless unconvinced that these were all representations of the same Great Mother Goddess. They are also unconvinced that the presence and worship of a high goddess confirms the existence of a matriarchal society. In contemporary India, for instance, where a Great Goddess and numerous other goddess cults flourish, and have done so for over a thousand years, these still exist within strongly patriarchal cultures. However, the proponents of a primordial matriarchy argue that these goddess-based strands are the vestige of once prominent matriarchal societies, which were overrun by male god worshippers, who subsequently suppressed both goddesses and women.

Certain groups of feminists applaud these efforts to argue for the existence of ancient examples of societies in which women were not oppressed, but dominant. Since in their view the stories of women's experiences throughout history have been marginalized, ignored, or suppressed by men, who unconsciously or purposefully chose to write women out of their narratives, a vital agenda for many feminists is to uncover and reconstruct these hidden voices ("her-story" as opposed to "his-tory"). This is a vibrant facet of feminist approaches to the study of religion, for women and their lives, concerns, and experiences have often been of peripheral interest to a male-dominated scholarly world, and thus largely unstudied. However, this is also one crucial area in which the feminist religious studies scholar might part ways with certain factions of the broader feminist agenda. For instance, many feminists support the idea that if one cannot adequately recover women's past (through rigorous archeological and historical methods), it is perfectly fine to invent it. The rationale for such constructions is as follows: history, origins, and ancient traditions can play important roles in rooting and supporting the growth of new traditions, and if a new women-centered spirituality is to flourish in the future, it is vital that women construct an idealized past, as history ought to have been, not how it actually was, in order to develop a meaningful vision for the future. Pre-patriarchal matriarchies, goddess-centered religions, highly regarded women mystics, seers, and saints, wizened but wise hags and crones, and powerful witches schooled in the arcane arts of healing and spell-casting, who are deeply in touch with the cycles of the natural world, know the potent secrets of herbal remedies, and so on, form part of this idealized, and often imaginarily concocted, continuum from the past, through the present, to the future. One sees resonances of these notions in contemporary New Age religious movements, such as Wicca.

Moderate feminist activism

The activist agendas that drive feminist approaches cause them to be viewed with suspicion within religious studies, which strives for a value-free orientation. Some religious studies scholars have suggested that all feminist approaches are akin to theology (since their analyses will never challenge basic assumptions about men and women, and are constantly engaged in a form of apologetics for and promotion of women), and distinguish feminist studies from women's studies, which is potentially more neutral, women being solely a category of focus, like myth, scripture, ritual, deity, and so on, without any activist agenda. Some have therefore suggested the use of the term "womanist" instead of "feminist." Actually, the term "womanist" derives from African-American women, such as the author Alice Walker and the theologian Delores Williams, but has been embraced by other groups of non-white women who have aligned themselves with the term. For instance, Ada Maria Isasi-Diaz is a voice for the Latin American wing of womanist theology, sometimes known as mujerista (*mujer* meaning woman in Spanish) theology. Womanists noted that the experience of oppression being articulated in the feminist movement was primarily by white women and focused on sexism (i.e. discrimination based on sex/gender). However, the experience of "women of color" was further complicated by issues of race and class, which intensified the nature of their oppression. In this sense, "womanism" may be regarded as a broader category than "feminism," seeking for women a freedom from oppression on a wide array of issues, including gender, sexual orientation, physical abilities, race, and social class. Such distinctions between "feminist" or "womanist" can, of course, ultimately only be terminological, for it would be rare to find feminists opposed to the broader womanist agenda. Thus both feminism and womanism are agenda-driven. It might be reasonable to assert that whatever one chooses to focus upon as an object of study (e.g. myth, ritual, women, priests, saints, salvation), that category is inevitably brought to the forefront, and our understanding of it potentially furthered. Thus there is an agenda in every piece of research, namely, to further our understanding of the category under examination. In feminist or womanist approaches to the study of religion, the feminine (e.g. women, female deities, and feminine categories and qualities, such as motherhood, nature, fertility) in some form or feature is the focus, and thereby our understanding of that category is inevitably enhanced.

The theological struggles of Mary Daly, the efforts to rework religious history, or the formulations of new feminine-embracing religions are thus certainly all commendable objects of study for the religious studies scholar. However, unlike Mary Daly and other feminist theologians, the religious studies scholar is not expected to be engaged in the practice of feminist theology (while occupied in the work of the discipline), but primarily in describing, analyzing, and critically reflecting upon it. For instance, Daly's theology (or thea-logy) envisions Ultimate Reality as a dynamic process, Be-ing, and best understood as a verb, rather than as a static essence connoted by the noun, Being. She speaks of patriarchal religions as necrophilic (lovers of the dead—in part because they venerate deceased figures, glorify the afterlife, and so on, while negating this-worldly realities), and idealized feminist religion as biophilic (lovers of life). One might note resonances in her theology with the process philosophy of Whitehead, and so on. Daly's theology is far more complex than the simplified version which has been presented here, offers a trenchant critique of many mainstream (or male-stream) religious theologies, and has been influential in the theological frameworks and theorizing of numerous other feminists, whether or not they agree with her ideas. Her thoughts and influence are thus certainly worthy of study, although her methods and objectives are not those of the disciple of religious studies. Other influential feminist theologians (all Christian) include Elisabeth Schüssler Fiorenza (b. 1938) and Rosemary Radford Ruether (b. 1936). While Daly has advocated that women leave the religious traditions to which they once belonged because they are sexist, androcentric, and misogynistic, Schüssler Fiorenza and Ruether, although mostly in agreement with those designations, do not consider most religious traditions to be incorrigible, and promote theological efforts to bring about their transformations from within.

Religious studies and feminism

Unlike those feminists who actively engage in reinventing history, the religious studies scholar is expected to attempt to work with as much rigor as possible to get at historical truth (even though postmodernism has alerted us to the challenges therein). Although there may be differing emphases and interpretations, these should still be grounded upon the factual data that is available. Feminist approaches in religious studies should not attempt to obfuscate or twist what is known of the past in order to promote a feminist goal, but may reasonably attempt to uncover features of the past that have been ignored or misinterpreted through the disproportionate lack of attention paid to women. An illustrative example of the feminist struggle with historical interpretation may be found in the work of Miranda Shaw, who studies the texts of Tantric Tibetan Buddhism. Tantric Buddhism, and Tantra in general, contrasts with traditional (i.e. non-Tantric) Buddhism or Hinduism, in that while these latter orthodox approaches are quite evidently male-centered, Tantra upholds the feminine, both in its divine and human forms. There are numerous female deities, *bodhisattvas*, and so on, in Tantric Buddhism, and women practitioners are held in high regard in these texts. A naïve interpretation of Tantric texts might lead one to suggest that during the period when Tantra flourished, women definitely were respected, held important roles as Tantric teachers, participated in rituals on equal terms with men, and so on. However, most scholars, judging from contemporary attitudes to women and from the mainstream, orthodox scriptural portrayals of women (mostly negative, as emotionally fickle, seducers of men, and so on) have argued that Tantra, too, despite what its texts say, was dominated by males and probably exploitative of women. Such an interpretation was clearly in resonance with second-wave feminism, for it sought to cut through the surface appearance of what the texts appeared to be saying, asserting that women were actually marginalized and oppressed by men even in the Tantric Buddhist tradition. In *Passionate Enlightenment* (1995), Miranda Shaw returns to the medieval Buddhist Tantric texts, reads them closely and on their own terms, and argues for a position that appears to parallel the naïve first-order interpretation. Since we have little compelling evidence about the status of women in Tantric Buddhist communities in the past, other than what the texts themselves tell us, Shaw argues that there is no compelling reason to impose the negative attitudes towards women found in orthodox texts of Buddhism of the period, onto the realities of medieval Tantric Buddhism. When the data is collated as she presents it, and she does so with due scholarly rigor, she makes a strong case for her interpretation, namely that women held roles of respect and power in the period when those texts were composed and among the Tantric Buddhist groups that composed and utilized them. Shaw's interpretations, although they may be disputed by other Buddhist scholars (feminists included), function within the parameters of acceptable scholarly analysis, and by providing an empowering past for women within the Buddhist tradition, offer a foundation for an empowering future. Her work represents a strand within what is sometimes called third-wave feminism.

Third-wave feminism coexists with and is sometimes in tension with second-wave feminism. Third-wave feminism is highly subscribed to by women within milieus where the successes of second-wave feminism have been evident. These are often younger, educated women who enjoy social status and success, and who wish to move beyond the male-female, oppressor-oppressed dichotomies and polemics that are crucial to the agenda of second-wave feminism. It is worth keeping in mind that such distinctions and labels have limited value and generate their own types of problems. The cutting edge in current feminism is not to advocate specific kinds of behaviors and attitudes for all women (e.g. sexually liberal, independent, career-oriented), but to uphold the freedom for each and every woman to choose her own lifestyle, even if this means choosing what would earlier have been considered a subservient or exploited position within the patriarchal order (e.g. sex-worker, exotic dancer, housewife). Its sweep has broadened to engage the concerns of women in subcultures (e.g. girls, the elderly, native women, women of color) within and beyond the West. Here, too, feminist approaches in the study of religion are particularly vibrant and complex. For instance, each of the world's major religious traditions (e.g. Islam) often extends across various societies and cultures (e.g. parts of Africa, the Middle East, India, China, Southeast Asia), and the norms and values of women (and men) in one area (e.g. American Muslim women) may be rather different from those halfway around the world (e.g. Saudi Arabian Muslim women) although they belong to and are influenced by the same religious cultural system. So a feminist Muslim woman in Saudi Arabia may, perhaps, choose to wear a headscarf, while an American Muslim woman may not, but the feminist agenda might be to allow each of these women the right to choose the reverse if they so desired (unless the headscarf was deemed an absolute religious requirement, and supported by the women of that religious group).

Recovering the place of women in religion

There is a rich body of exciting scholarly work emerging that examines women's rituals, domestic concerns, social organization, oral histories, and so on. Feminist scholars of religion interested in political science might examine power relations between men and women in religion, their differing modes of power and spheres of influence, and the forms of inequality that might exist between men's and women's access to these powers and their respective abilities to exercise them. Do women wield power in religious organizations, and if so, how? Does a specific religious ideology grant women power in public spaces, only in the home, or not at all? Feminist scholars might investigate questions such as: Why can a woman not be a Catholic priest/priestess or a Theravada Buddhist monk/nun? And they might then analyze the rationales behind the arguments provided by the religious traditions themselves, or study the historical processes and attitudes that have shaped these realities. Feminist psychologists of religion might investigate how concepts of masculinity and femininity are constructed by religious ideas. Are men associated with spirituality and women with materiality? Is spirituality then valued more than materiality? Are women regarded as spiritually inferior in some branches of Hinduism because of their association with menstrual blood and its ritually polluting effects? What effects do religiously sanctioned distinctions between men and women have on individuals and social groups?

This seems an opportune juncture to point out that the discipline of religious studies is not merely concerned with inquiry and description in its exploration of religious phenomena. Description primarily serves as a basis for the analysis and critical appraisal of the material that one has studied. While religious studies scholars should not attempt to change the religious traditions that are studied (while engaged in the work of the discipline), it is vital that they insist on articulating the truth of what has been examined, to the best degree possible, regardless of what implications those findings might have for the religious tradition being studied. This does not compromise ethical issues of confidentiality, in which a researcher may reasonably agree to keep the name of an informant anonymous, or agree not to divulge secret information provided in an interview or ceremony. However, it is a common error among novice religious studies students (and some mature scholars) to engage in a sort of apologetics of religious tolerance on one hand, or in some sort of anti-religious polemic on the other, in their work. However disturbing or disagreeable a religious belief or practice may personally seem to the researcher (e.g. genital mutilation of women or human sacrifice), it is as inappropriate to make personal negative moral judgments or criticisms about it within the framework of one's work, as it is to cloak the findings of one's research, compromise the rigor of one's analysis, and modify the language in which it is articulated, in order to justify or protect the religious tradition being studied. It is therefore simply good religious studies, and not intrinsically part of a feminist agenda, for a religious studies scholar who finds marked discrimination against women in a particular religion to document this and other such realities, even though such research may subsequently fuel feminist agendas and incur criticisms from adherents of those religious traditions being scrutinized. By striving for neutrality but accuracy, religious studies scholars implicitly side with a prime philosophical value (and agenda) in academia, namely, that the struggle to acquire and share "truth"—however contested this may be—is, in itself, a noble and precious endeavor. It would be naïve, however, to imagine that there are no consequences to sharing such knowledge, for there are multiple ways in which one's research may be received and utilized, and these do not always honor—and may even severely condemn—the scholar and/or her work. In this sense, the scholar's work is not value-free, and can indeed bring about change, but the philosophical ethos behind one's research is to illuminate and provide clarity on a subject, which in turn may result in its transformation.

A suitable example of these issues is evident in the portrayal of Mary Magdalene in the Christian tradition. It is commonly believed by many Christians that Mary Magdalene was a prostitute who repented of her sinful life and became a devout follower of Jesus of Nazareth, the founder of Christianity. However, scholarly studies of the Christian gospels indicate that although in the Gospel of Luke (8:2) Mary Magdalene is said to have had seven demons cast out of her, there is no definitive connection between her and a woman in the previous chapter of the Gospel of Luke (7:37–50), who is called a sinner and who washes Jesus's feet with her tears, wipes them with her hair, kisses and anoints them. There are historical processes through which the belief in Mary Magdalene as a prostitute arose, such as a sermon by Pope Gregory I (in 591 CE), in which he affirms a connection between Mary and the woman sinner who washes Jesus's feet. In the Gospel of John (7:53–8:11), Jesus protects a woman, said to be an adulterer, from being stoned to death. Later popular Christian traditions—as is evident in several Hollywood films on the life of Jesus—further identify Mary Magdalene with that woman, although this is nowhere stated in the text. Clearly, the close scholarly reading of Christian scriptures can reveal truths about Mary Magdalene that are at odds with the actual beliefs of many Christians. The example of Mary is further complicated when one begins to examine other sources, such as the Christian gospels found at Nag Hammadi in Egypt in 1945 and the Akhmim Codex collection (from Akhmim, Egypt, and only translated in the 1950s), which were not included in the Christian canon (the New Testament). Among these early, non-canonical (i.e. apocryphal) works is a Gospel of Mary, which was mentioned by Christian theologians as early as the third century CE, but which was not found and translated by scholars until recently. Most scholars believe this is a gospel attributed to Mary Magdalene (very few think that Mary may refer to Jesus's mother), who was a close disciple of Jesus. In this gospel, the teachings that Mary attributes to Jesus have parallels with Gnostic philosophical ideas, which themselves parallel the metaphysical notions found in many Eastern religions. The gospel relates how other disciples of Jesus, namely Andrew and Peter, doubt that Mary's presentations are the teachings of Jesus, apparently given privately to her, because Jesus gave her preferential treatment. The disciple Matthew (Levi) then speaks up on her behalf and points out that Jesus loved Mary more than the others and considered her worthy to preach his message. In the Gospel of Philip, another apocryphal gospel also with Gnostic metaphysical notions, Jesus is depicted as kissing Mary, who is his companion and whom he seems to love or cherish more than the others, causing them dismay. The Gospel of John (a canonical Christian gospel) refers to a tension between Peter and an unnamed "beloved disciple," which some scholars suggest might have been Mary Magdalene.

What is evident in this scholarly research is that Mary Magdalene appears to have been regarded, by many factions of the early Christian movement, as an important and worthy disciple, who held a respected leadership role. In fact, to the sects that followed her, it was Mary who held the authority of the Church after Jesus's death. Here, the scholarly work of translation and analysis is relatively neutral, and not intended to undermine Christianity. However, the information garnered by this research may serve the agendas of feminist Christian theologians, who, unlike Mary Daly, favor the transformation of the subordinate positions of women within the power structures of Christian organizations, such as the Catholic Church, while remaining within Catholicism. For certain orthodox Christian apologists, such information may be regarded as the unfortunate uncovering of material that was best left forgotten or suppressed, and which now needs to be discredited, marginalized, or refuted through all acceptable means at their disposal. The activities of both such groups, who are acting from within the context of the Christian religious tradition either to transform it or to maintain its traditional structures, are suitable objects of study by scholars of religion, who should themselves be disinterested in either agenda (when engaged in the work of the discipline).

Since women constitute half the human race, and it seems reasonable that their involvement should thus make up a substantial part of what we know about humanity's religious impulse, the study of women's religious experience has been woefully neglected. Thus feminist approaches to the study of religion seek to rectify this imbalance. They strive to shed light on, or give appropriate attention to, the feminine dimensions in all the various areas in which they may be relevant to the religious phenomena under investigation. Ignored or marginalized scriptures may be reexamined to discover what they might tell us about women's status and activities. Just as there is intellectual curiosity about Jesus's mother, and his possible female companion, Mary Magdalene, one wonders about the wives of Muhammad, the prophet and founder of Islam, and his daughters, or the women in the life of the Buddha, Siddhartha Gautama— his mother, Maya, his stepmother, Prajapati, and his wife, Yashodhara—all significant females in the lives of these religiously influential males. There were innumerable renowned women saints and mystics in all the world's religions, whose lives and teachings may be beneficially examined. Even the writings of male theologians, mystics, and philosophers may be scrutinized, with the methodologies of postmodern deconstruction, to discover what their attitudes might have been to the feminine, either through their explicit comments, or through their omissions. Myths may be studied to uncover how they depict women or female deities, and religious rituals (liturgies) examined for women's roles within them. Since men in many of the world's cultures had the exclusive privilege of learning to read and write, the study of written texts from those cultural communities inevitably privileges male concerns. Women's religious experiences may be unearthed through oral histories, songs, folktales, and myths. Anthropological approaches to the study of religion are thus particularly useful in these areas, and especially so in the study of women's religious rituals. When one considers that the mainstream religions of the world have been dominated by men, and have often excluded women, particularly in leadership roles, it is hardly unusual to note that women have found their own ways of exploring their spiritual yearnings, both within the traditional, male-constructed frameworks, and outside these structures, in their own forms and fashions. These may include forms of devotional worship, dietary regulations such as fasts, communal singing and dancing, trance and spirit possession, and healing ceremonies. Such religious forms are typical of most marginal groups, including women. While religious authorities have often denigrated such practices as "folk" or "popular" religion, or even dismissed them as "superstition," they are of no less value in our understanding of human religiosity, and are proving to be rich areas of research for religious studies scholars.

The feminist critique of religious studies

A crucial disjuncture between feminist approaches and the academic study of religion as it is often understood is sometimes evident in a particular feminist critique of the entire style and framework of the academic world. The pseudo-scientific and purportedly objective approach to the study of any subject (in this case, religion) is said to be, at the outset, structured according to male parameters of discourse. In its extreme form, this critique would claim that logic and rational arguments presented in a systematic, linear form (i.e. typically male ways of thinking and expressing) are antithetical to an intuitive and poetic articulation of ideas (i.e. typically female modes of thought and expression). However, many modern feminists reject this kind of critique, because it derives from an earlier period in contemporary feminism when strong dichotomies were drawn between males and females, beyond their visible physical differences. For instance, men were associated with the linear, rational, left-brain, objective, and analytic modes of thinking, while women were associated with relational, intuitive, right-brain, subjective, and synthesizing modes of thought. However, such typologies are now recognized as inherently restrictive, since they purportedly describe but actually prescribe, for both men and women, how they ought to be, think, and feel. It is not wrong, neither is it impossible, for women to think and write rationally, nor for men to be intuitive. Nevertheless, there is certainly more than a nugget of truth in the feminist (and indeed postmodern) critique of the structural styles of the academic enterprise, which has been populated for centuries mostly by men, and thus shaped by masculine cultures.

In this presentation of the discipline of religious studies, we have striven to articulate a vision for how the scholarly study of religion may be conducted in a fluid and ever-creative manner. It should adhere with rigor to the tenets of attempted neutrality in the quest for knowledge but be open to the stylistic transformations that its varied practitioners bring to the discipline, based on their personal and situated personas, shaped by such features as gender, social status, and cultural orientation.

Feminist voices

Leila Ahmed: well-known Egyptian-American professor of women's studies in religion who has focused on women and gender in Islam, Muslim feminism, Arab nationalism, and Islam in America, among other topics. Works: *Women and Gender in Islam: The Historical Roots of a Modern Debate* (1992).

Asma Barlas: Muslim scholar known for criticizing male-oriented exegesis of the Qur'an, offering alternative readings, and defending the right of Muslims to interpret the sacred texts for themselves; also one of the first women to be inducted into the Pakistani foreign service. Works: *"Believing Women" in Islam: Unreading Patriarchal Interpretations of the Qur'an* (2002).

Mary Daly: Radical lesbian feminist philosopher/theologian; rejected her Catholic roots after concluding that efforts to reform Christianity to be inclusive of women was futile; associated with post-Christian feminist theology; known for coining numerous words (sometimes known as Daly-isms) that emphasize feminist ideals (e.g. Gyn/Ecology) or critique patriarchal ideals (e.g. phallocracy). Works: *The Church and the Second Sex* (1968); *Beyond God the Father: Toward a Philosophy of Women's Liberation* (1973); *Gyn/Ecology: The Metaethics of Radical Feminism* (1976); *Quintessence: Realizing the Archaic Future* (1998).

Wendy Doniger: American historian of religions; known primarily for her work on comparative mythology, particularly from Hindu Sanskrit texts, she has often applied feminist interpretations to her analyses. Works: *Asceticism and Eroticism in the Mythology of Siva* (1973); *Hindu Myths: A Sourcebook* (1975); *Women, Androgynes, and other Mythical Beasts* (1980).

Rita M. Gross: American religious studies scholar; spearheaded feminist analyses of the Buddhist tradition, and then feminist approaches to religious studies in general. Works: *Buddhism After Patriarchy: A Feminist History, Analysis, and Reconstruction of Buddhism* (1993).

Judith Plaskow: Co-founder of *The Journal of Feminist Studies in Religion* and past President of the American Academy of Religion. Works: *Sex, Sin and Grace: Women's Experience and the Theologies of Reinhold Niebuhr and Paul Tillich* (1980); *Standing Again at Sinai: Judaism from a Feminist Perspective* (1990); *The Coming of Lilith: Essays on Feminism, Judaism, and Sexual Ethics* (2005).

Rosemary R. Ruether: Christian Church historian and feminist theologian; known for her feminist critique of Christianity, with efforts to reform the tradition from within. Works: *Sexism and God-Talk: Toward a Feminist Theology* (1983).

E. Schüssler Fiorenza: Catholic feminist theologian; associated with the application of a "hermeneutics of suspicion," an approach to the interpretation of Christian writings that were crafted from male-centered perspectives; offers models through which one might recover the lost voice or perspective of women. Works: *In Memory of Her: A Feminist Theological Reconstruction of Christian Origins* (1984).

Miranda Shaw: American religious studies scholar; known for feminist interpretations of Tantric Buddhism. Works: *Passionate Enlightenment: Women in Tantric Buddhism* (1995).

Amina Wadud: Muslim feminist scholar; founding member of Sisters in Islam; known also for the controversy surrounding her role leading Friday prayers to Muslim congregations of men and women on several occasions. Works: *Qur'an and Woman: Rereading the Sacred Text from a Woman's Perspective* (1999); *Inside the Gender Jihad: Women's Reform in Islam* (2006).

Popular literature: dispelling religion vs. emphasizing its relevance

This section looks within and beyond the walls of the academy to explore the relationship between religious studies and books that emphasize perceived dangers or benefits of religion. Some are best-sellers with extensive exposure to the public through television, radio, and newspaper interviews. Rather than cutting edge scholarship, they more typically emphasize the author's analysis—including controversial commentary and polemical, at times even vitriolic, views. While most of the authors considered below have academic credentials and affiliations, they are not necessarily religious studies scholars or may be "changing hats" as they write from the perspectives of a scholar, adherent, or concerned global citizen. In short, this literature represents some of the most visible conversations about religion including how it is being connected to politics, evolution, human potential, and terrorism. A survey of these books is one way to take the pulse of how religion is being critiqued, defended, explained, understood—and misunderstood—within and beyond the university in the early twenty-first century.

Some approaches are consistent with the academic study of religion, while others form religious discourses or discourses about religion that, although outside the secular academic study of religion, still connect to the discipline as an appropriate subject matter for religious studies. The more popular literature attempting to dispel the hold of religion on politics and people's beliefs is typically not addressed as part of religious studies proper, but represents an influential perspective on religion as well as a sort of approach to the study of religion. These works are at times woefully reductionistic, selective, and meant to serve purposes beyond understanding religion, but similar misgivings are also used to critique psychological and sociological approaches to the study of religion.

More to the point, our students and colleagues are reading one or more of these works, as are millions of others based on their best-seller status. For students attending a religious studies course for the first time, it is often polemical positions from both ends of the spectrum that have most formatively shaped their perspectives about religion. That is, they are often either adherents of one religion who have been exposed primarily to sermons and to believers speaking or writing confessionally to others in their tradition, or they come with an anti-religion bias informed by many factors, including the views shaped or at least articulated by best-selling authors such as Christopher Hitchens, Richard Dawkins, and Sam Harris, whose books are examined below. Unlike these critical perspectives—or the inverse forms of theological apologetics—the mandate for religious studies scholars is to advocate neither for a religious tradition nor against religion as a whole. However, to introduce the academic study of religion in a university setting, it can be useful to meet students where they are and explain both where these theological and critical perspectives intersect with academic religious studies and where they do not meet the standards for the secular study of religion in the academy.

Detractors: atheists unite

Recent works by Hitchens, Dawkins, and Harris are reaching a vastly larger audience than do traditional academic works. In fact, as of the end of July 2007, each could be found on the *New York Times* Best Sellers List. Hitchens's *god is not Great: How Religion Poisons Everything* (2007) and Dawkins's *The God Delusion* (2006) held the #3 and #28 spots respectively for hardcover nonfiction, and Harris's *The End of Faith: Religion, Terror, and the Future of Reason* (2004) was #32 in paperback nonfiction. Dawkins's book was more than one year old at that time and Harris's *The End of Faith* came out in paperback more than two years previously, which speaks to the books' enduring popularity. Each book is critical of religion, though for different reasons and from various perspectives. Dawkins is a well-established academic famous for *The Selfish Gene* (1976), which explains biological and cultural evolution in terms of the propagation of genes—rather than organisms—as the unit of evolutionary natural selection. In other words, he argues that many aspects of biology and culture that would otherwise be difficult to explain can be understood in terms of genes doing whatever is necessary to preserve, replicate, and pass on their DNA. His reputation has grown through many subsequent works that have moved from his area of evolutionary biology to more wide-ranging writings on science appropriate to his title at Oxford, Professor of the Public Understanding of Science. Hitchens is an erudite journalist, political commentator, and contrarian public intellectual who also held an academic position as a visiting professor at the New School in New York City in 2005. Harris, a Stanford graduate in philosophy, was a graduate student in neuroscience when he penned his anti-religion best-seller. He has since written a similarly no-holds-barred follow-up book, *Letter to a Christian Nation* (2006). After writing this section in the summer of 2007, the grouping of these three along with Daniel Dennett, who was featured in the cognitive psychology section earlier in this text, was reinforced with the occasion of a discussion among the four of them at the end of September 2007. Their conversation was recorded and made available online and by a DVD entitled *The Four Horsemen*.

Richard Dawkins: no more deference to religious beliefs, guidance, and identity

Dawkins's foundation convened this discussion. As the title suggests, in *The God Delusion*, Dawkins both debunks "spectacularly weak" arguments for the existence of God and even provides what he claims to be much more robust arguments to "almost certainly" rule out God's existence. He takes on a wide array of arguments that have been used to posit God's existence, including early theological formulations such as the five "proofs" offered by the great theologian Thomas Aquinas in the thirteenth century and St Anselm's famous—though less than convincing—ontological argument in the eleventh century, which boils down to his claim "And assuredly that, than which nothing greater can be conceived, cannot exist in the understanding alone." In other words, one can conceive of God as the most perfect being, and a God that actually exists is more perfect than a mere concept of God limited to our imagination, therefore an actually existing God *is* this most perfect being. Dawkins deconstructs this argument in his own way and cites famous refutations from Hume and Kant as well as the refutation by the philosopher Douglas Gasking, whose amusing inverted proof that God does not exist maintains that "an even more formidable and incredible creator" than the existing God posited by St Anselm "would be a God which did not exist." Dawkins's stroll through unconvincing proofs winds from bad science and personal experience to arguments from scripture and the religious allegiances of some admired scientists. Some examples are more spoof than proof—for example, the silly list from godlessgeeks.com, a website that includes the "Argument from Non-belief: The majority of the world's population are non-believers in Christianity. This is just what Satan intended. Therefore God exists." Others' arguments are well known, although sometimes less than heart-felt, such as Pascal's Wager, in which Blaise Pascal, with a mathematician's concern for odds, argued for at least paying lip service to belief in God or a deathbed conversion, for the entirely practical reason that there is little to lose in belief whereas the penalty of eternal damnation is unnecessarily risky on the off-chance that atheists are wrong.

Dawkins also tackles more current arguments that champion "intelligent design" to explain the "irreducible complexity" in nature. He asserts that this new guise of creationism disingenuously attempts to dispel evolution by claiming that such intricate "creations" could not be the mere product of chance. Dawkins retorts that this misses the point because natural selection with its many intermediate stages is the key, not random chance immediately hitting on the perfect design. Dawkins is understandably exasperated with the intentional misrepresentation of science. He attempts to insulate it from other indignities by explaining and differentiating both science and atheism from religion, in order to dissuade readers from redirecting his own critiques of religion back to either science or atheism as examples of modern, secular religions with their own dogmatism. His allegiance to and identification with atheism is as strong as, and related to, his identity as a scientist. In the preface to *The God Delusion*, Dawkins states that one of his consciousness-raising aims is to inform people that they can leave their religions and that "to be an atheist is a realistic aspiration, and a brave and splendid one" consistent with also being "happy, balanced, moral, and intellectually fulfilled." His call for atheist pride is joined by the goals that people will better understand the cosmos through natural selection and similar insights with great explanatory power, and that they will stop making reference to a "Muslim child" or "Catholic child" when such a religious designation merely refers to the beliefs of their parents and culture. He follows up on this latter concern in chapter 9, "Childhood, Abuse and the Escape from Religion," by indicting religion for a litany of abuses—physical, mental, and educational—against children. His concerns about the indoctrination of children dovetail with his larger agenda against ways in which religion and religious views can be used to distort views, identity, and knowledge—particularly evolution and science more generally—while remaining protected from intellectual scrutiny due to accommodations and polite respect that Dawkins believes to be undeserved.

His arguments draw from a wide array of sources and enlist personal anecdotes and other engaging, accessible examples to reinforce his assertions. Some of his critiques connect with earlier theorists. For example, Dawkins's statement that "the childhood phenomenon of the 'imaginary friend' . . . has affinities with religious belief" connects both to Freud's idea of religion as illusory and religion as only appropriate in the childhood of a person or civilization. While some claims will strike many scholars of religion as overly strident, simplistic, or hyperbolic, he is thought-provoking on key issues in the strained relationship between science and religion. For example, Dawkins aggressively resists the idea of NOMA, an acronym for "non-overlapping magisterial," which was coined by Stephen Jay Gould. Gould was a well-known evolutionary biologist, paleontologist, and intellectual sparring opponent of Dawkins—a well-matched opponent in terms of his own gift for making science engaging and accessible to a non-specialist audience. The idea, which is much older than the acronym, maintains that there are non-overlapping spheres of expertise where scientists, who understand facts and theories about the physical universe, are asked to politely recognize the limits of their inquiries and hand over to theologians the big "why" questions of "ultimate meaning and moral value." Dawkins neither wants scientists to refrain from commenting on God—or whether the universe might show signs of a divine, "creative superintendent"—nor does he see justification in ceding such questions to theologians. To Dawkins, those like Gould, who have been excessively accommodating to religion in this way, have done so only for reasons of polite co-existence. Dawkins does not believe that theologians actually have expertise or insight that outstrips scientists with regard to "deep cosmological" questions such as "Why does anything exist at all?" He acknowledges that science does not have the best record for advice on moral values, but he finds religion quite problematic as an arbiter of what is good and bad, and how to live one's life accordingly. To illustrate some of the problems associated with deferring to religion for such guidance, he asks, "Which religion?" and which reading of which religious text. He finds literal readings of the Bible, for example stoning to death as punishment for adultery, less than an ideal guide. Interestingly, he gives Buddhism and Confucianism a pass due to the common Western perception that such Asian philosophical "ways of life" are not real religions, which, in this case, is meant as a compliment.

Christopher Hitchens: defending civilization from religion

Hitchens is similarly disenchanted with religion. He articulates numerous intellectual, cultural, ethical, and philosophical objections to specific formulations of god and religion as well as to religion as a whole. Hitchens digs into sacred texts to argue with religious believers. Like Dawkins and Harris, Hitchens pulls no punches in his critique of religion. While the unusual lowercase "g" in the title *god is not Great* graphically represents his aim to diminish the status of the divine, it is the subtitle, *How Religion Poisons Everything*, which demonstrates the sweeping scope of his indictment of religion. Even a distracted reader, who somehow may have missed the subtitle or the negating "not" of the title, should be able to grasp the anti-religion orientation of the book by means of chapter titles such as "Religion Kills," "Religion's Corrupt Beginnings," "Religion as an Original Sin," and "Is Religion Child Abuse?" The chapter titles explicitly reveal that Hitchens is not a Christian apologist condemning a wrathful Old Testament while asserting love and redemption as the dominant characteristics of the New Testament. Instead, he moves from a chapter titled "The Nightmare of the 'Old' Testament" to "The 'New' Testament Exceeds the Evil of the 'Old' One."

Hitchens also brings personal recollections and anecdotes into the work to inform the reader of his own early journey to a perspective highly critical of religious explanations, and of subsequent observations throughout his life that reinforced and gave more scientific and scholarly support to what he felt intuitively from age nine. In all three works of popular criticism of religion surveyed here, the authors share their personal experiences and convictions as sources of authority for their arguments. Although it is increasingly common in cultural studies, anthropology, and other disciplines to situate oneself—including signaling to the reader one's perspective and identity politics—the blend of anecdote, and more importantly, deeply felt personal convictions, characterizes the types of arguments presented in this genre as opposed to most academic studies of religion. Like academic works, each appeals to primary sources or scientific studies and analysis; however, unlike the relative dispassion of many academic works, where the author might even fade into the background in favor of emphasizing the thesis and authoritative sources that support it, these authors insert themselves more directly and forcefully into the argument. In other words, their objections to religion are both personal and professional. While this differentiates these works from much of the academic study of religion, it can have the positive benefits of making their books more engaging and accessible.

The end of the first chapter in *god is not Great* builds from a nuanced view about the dangers of faith. Hitchens asserts that "all arguments about philosophy, science, history, and human nature" are rooted in arguments with faith. However, for Hitchens, religious faith will never die out, and should not, because we are "still-evolving creatures" with fears and uncertainty. Moreover, he states that he would be happy to be a good neighbor to religious individuals and groups if they would only be equally obliging by leaving him alone. However, he claims this modest request is naïve and impossible. Instead, "people of faith are in their different ways planning your and my destruction, and the destruction of all the hard-won human attainments that I have touched upon." Now the nuance has dissolved into the more black and white rhetoric of our current, explosive political and cultural circumstances. Hitchens's culminating sentence of the first chapter exclaims "*Religion poisons everything*" and one is led to believe that his motivation for exposing the ingredients and dangers of this poison stems from an attempt to defend, not just the atheist position, but civilization more broadly. At the very end of his book, Hitchens suggests that such a defense of civilization, which necessitates a fight against religion, could lead to a new Enlightenment. However, to get there, according to Hitchens, requires knowing the enemy and the need "to transcend our prehistory, and escape the gnarled hands which reach out to drag us back to the catacombs and the reeking altars and the guilty pleasures of subjection and abjection." It is not simply a matter of growing out of religion in the developmental models of Freud or

Erikson, but instead one must fight off religion to escape its grasp and attain something truly great.

Sam Harris: at war against the danger and irrationality of Western religion

Harris anticipated parts of both of these critiques in his 2004 best-seller. Reviews and comments about *The End of Faith* demonstrate that Harris struck a chord with people who already felt deeply troubled by what they perceived as the danger and irrationality of religion, from suicide bombers claiming that Islam provides religious justification for their actions to the political influence of right-wing Christians in the United States. Although some of the claims and analysis fail to go beyond a superficial reading of the interaction between politics and religious traditions, Harris's strident tone and the force and breadth of his critique have been appreciatively received by a wide range of readers who have found refreshing the direct style of his assault on religion as the enemy of reason. Praise and objections to this book are closely related. For example, the book begins with a scene of a suicide bomber who "succeeds" in his mission, for which his parents are rewarded with gifts along with their feelings of pride and confidence in the certainty of their son's salvation and his victims' damnation. Harris further asserts near the beginning of his chapter "The Problem with Islam" that "We are at war with Islam." He acknowledges the previous cultural flowering of Islam—it "has had its moments"—but asserts that the current danger must be acknowledged and is endemic to Islam itself, not just to extremists in the tradition.

This gets to the crux of appreciation, discomfort, or outrage felt in response to this book. Some applaud the book, taking the view that "Harris is unafraid to tell it like it is" in favorable comparison with religious moderates or even non-religious scholars and commentators, who they believe have been missing the critical point with their silence or arguments that Islam is at heart a religion of peace, or that current conflicts and circumstances have arisen more out of political than religious considerations. Harris rejects the idea that "an otherwise peaceful religion" has been "'hijacked' by extremists." Instead, he counters, "We are at war with precisely the vision of life that is prescribed to all Muslims in the Koran, and further elaborated in the literature of the hadith, which recounts the sayings and actions of the Prophet." This same sentiment, greeted as refreshing by some, is the source of discomfort or outrage for many others, including many Muslims and scholars of Islam, who reject the monolithic portrayal of the tradition as essentially fundamentalist and militant. Harris believes the militancy is foundational to the tradition, and getting away from it would require moving far away from fundamentalist and literalist interpretations. He claims that the transformation that would allow "a future in which Islam and the West do not stand on the brink of mutual annihilation" would require Muslims "to ignore most of their canon, just as most Christians have learned to do." For Harris, faith commitments lead to a different, destructive future. Throughout the book, he is critical of religion but takes particular aim at faith, which he describes as blind, irrational, and terribly dangerous in the contemporary world with weapons of mass destruction.

His section on the "Wisdom of the East" clarifies that he finds Eastern "spirituality" strikingly different from and superior to the limitations and dangers of Christian, Jewish, and Muslim faith. To illustrate this difference, he cites a passage on the nature of consciousness by the eighth-century Buddhist tantric master, Padmasambhava. His praise of this passage, selected at random "with closed eyes," is as extreme as the earlier critique. Harris argues: "One could live an eon as a Christian, a Muslim, or a Jew and never encounter any teachings like this about the nature of consciousness." Moreover he deems these Buddhist expressions of consciousness to be "precise, phenomenological studies" unmatched even by scientific, Western "contemporary literature on consciousness, which spans philosophy, cognitive science, psychology, and neuroscience . . .." Harris brings insights from these fields into his critique of religion, and he makes further references to Eastern spirituality, which he credits for some of his own ethical sensibilities and perspectives. For these sources, he avoids the word "religion"; and just before the epilogue, he states: "Mysticism is a rational enterprise. Religion is not." Mysticism is credited with direct experience of the world and religion is deemed to be denial, characterized by dangerous ignorance where "bad concepts" are "held in place of good ones for all time."

This passionate defense of reason at times reads more like an unreasonably venomous assault on certain religions and beliefs. There are more measured and persuasive sections in Harris's book, but these extreme positions give the work some of its emotional force and reveal a normative dimension that shares with theology an entitlement to determine what religion should be. Of course, in the case of Harris's *The End of Faith*, the normative working premise—that religion *should not be*—shapes the examples and arguments in a sort of anti-religious inversion of religious apologetics. This anti-religion normative stance holds for the other two best-sellers as well.

Comparison of critiques

Harris's book was the first of this best-selling group and overlaps with the other two from its attention to scientific critiques and explanations of religion's origins and function to particular criticisms of Jewish, Christian, and especially Muslim beliefs, politics, and violence. Furthermore, the later two books by Dawkins and Hitchens reference Harris's book positively, though Dawkins is more emphatic in his praise. There are certainly differences among their views. Hitchens, for example, criticizes Dawkins and Dennett for designating atheists as "brights." He also includes the chapter "There Is No 'Eastern' Solution" to clearly extend his critique to Asian religions. On the other hand, Harris and Dawkins both remove certain Asian religious traditions from the objectionable category of religion, and treat them as more rational philosophies, practices in empirical awareness, or ethical systems. Despite occasional differences of view, these and related books can be considered collectively as a sort of genre or even an approach to the study of religion. This is not simply because purchasing one from Amazon prompts you to consider the others with the message, "Customers who bought this item also bought," but relates to a recent rise in a long tradition of thinkers studying religion to debunk religion in favor of science or a political philosophy deemed by the author to be more modern, rational, humane, real, or desirable.

Of course, criticism of religion is not new. Enlightenment thinkers, such as Voltaire, skewered religion for what they perceived as its irrational superstitions, excesses, and ill effects on society. Friedrich Schleiermacher's *On Religion: Speeches to Its Cultured Despisers*, reacted against negative portrayals and dismissals of religion at the end of the eighteenth century, and many nineteeth-, twentieth- and twenty-first-century texts fall on either side of this divide. The works discussed above are especially influential representatives of the side critical of religion. There are innumerable other critiques of particular religions or religion as a whole. Some call for a separation of religion and politics. Others seek to remove religious faith positions from education—especially with regard to attempts to supplant the teaching of evolution with creationism or intelligent design. Some critics advocate adopting different expressions of religion or spirituality, while others call for an end to religion altogether or an embrace of atheism. For example, David Mills's *Atheist Universe: The Thinking Person's Answer to Christian Fundamentalism* (2004) presents for the lay reader a series of arguments for atheism and rebuttals to Christian claims and concerns. Numerous other examples of religion's detractors could be marshaled to make this point. Based on the enduring tensions between religion and faith—evident in our earliest examples from the traditional philosophical and theological approaches to the present—and the passions and politics of our times, not to mention the commercial success of the three best-sellers we have surveyed, it is safe to assume that many more are on their way.

Supporters: necessary benefits of religion

On the other side of this divide, there are many books directly refuting the claims of these detractors. Writings by Alister McGrath—*Dawkins' God: Genes, Memes and the Meaning of Life*—and Terry Eagleton—"Lunging, Flailing, Mispunching," his disparaging review of Dawkins's work in the 19 October 2006 *London Review of Books*—for example, take Dawkins's *The God Delusion* to task.

Books for the faithful

Moreover, there are, of course, many more books, in fact entire bookstores and institutions, devoted to promoting religious faith. Much of this literature relates to theology or promotes religion with particular emphasis on how a particular tradition or practice can guide, deepen, improve, enrich, or save the reader. Other books, including the popular *Left Behind* series, tap into a religious audience, at least in part, for entertainment and commercial purposes, but have little to do with the study of religion except as subject matter for academic analysis. In fact, the puzzling and intriguing popularity of the *Left Behind* series emphasizes the depth of the cultural divide between the chorus of voices critical of religion and the religious majority, including the rapidly growing evangelical Christian communities. The ostensibly final book in this series by Tim LaHaye and Jerry Jenkins, *Kingdom Come: The Final Victory*, came out in 2007, the same year as the widely anticipated final installment of the Harry Potter series. However, whereas the news and popularity of each release of J. K. Rowling's books about the boy wizard's adventures have been remarkably widespread, the *Left Behind* series is relatively unknown beyond some Christian communities despite sales of over 43 million books, seven of the first fifteen achieving #1 status on the *New York Times* Best Sellers List, and the ninth book, *Desecration*, outselling all other novels in 2001. As with market segmentation in other forms of media, such as television and films, these books have found an audience, as have the critiques of religion, but the overlap in readership is most likely negligible.

Books that emphasize religion's importance

There are other books, however, that attempt to straddle the divide between intellectual dismissal of religion and faith-based advocacy. For example, some books rooted in religious studies and written by academics who are sympathetic to religion attempt to shed light on the benefits of religion, or dangers that escalate in the absence of religious practices, sensibilities, experiences, virtues, perspectives, motivations, and even scholarship. Admittedly, these books generally do not enjoy the wide readership of either genre of best-sellers mentioned above, but they do seek to address and inspire a wider audience than do most academic works. Huston Smith's *Why Religion Matters: The Fate of the Human Spirit in an Age of Disbelief*, and Henry Rosemont Jr.'s *Rationality and Religious Experience: The Continuing Relevance of the World's Spiritual Traditions*, provide two examples from 2001 that assert a positive role for religion. There are links between these books beyond their shared date at the beginning of a new millennium. Smith, who also wrote a commentary in Rosemont's *Rationality and Religious Experience*, continues to enjoy a sixty-year influential career as a professor and author of world religions whose embrace of a wide array of religious practices and values demonstrates personal commitment as well as professional interest. He is best known to many for his book, *The World's Religions: Our Great Wisdom Traditions*. Originally published in 1958 as *The Religions of Man*, this text and his subsequent books, films, and public television series have introduced millions of readers and viewers to the core perspectives, beliefs, and practices of major religious traditions. *Why Religion Matters* extends his arguments from *Forgotten Truth: The Common Vision of the World's Religions* (1972), by critiquing materialism, science, modernity, consumerism, and postmodernism.

Huston Smith, like the authors of the popular anti-religion manifestos, draws from a wide variety of sources including stories, personal anecdotes, and examples from science, religion, and popular culture. He dismisses the "polemical bluster" of Dawkins and Dennett as "diehard" spokesmen for a "scientistic counterpart" to the now extinct "religious triumphalism." He asserts that despite various forecasts for the death of religion among educated people, it "seems clear that both science and religion are here to stay." He does not, however, consider them to be equal partners for plumbing the depths of truth and human potential. For Smith, religious insights can best inspire wisdom, nurture the human spirit, and enrich society. He objects to the way in which the new term "spirituality" has displaced "religion" to denote vague, "good" spiritual qualities in juxtaposition with the sullied reputation of institutional religion.

Smith addresses science throughout his book with particular reference to physics, biology, and cognitive science as the three strands with "the largest metaphysical implications," including their attention to the origins of the universe, life, and human beings respectively. Smith identifies neuroscience as a "mental materialism" at the heart of cognitive psychology, which we briefly addressed earlier in this work as one of the latest psychological approaches to the study of religion. He objects to much of the field's direction and hype—characterizing this relatively new field as "drunk with its dizzying growth and the prospect of limitless horizons." Smith prefers religion's horizon, the "happy ending" of an "abode of total purity" envisioned in different, but related, ways by various religions and religious dispositions. Smith writes here as a religious adherent whose vision and views are informed by his scholarship, but extend beyond the boundaries of the academic study of religion.

Smith explicitly states his position as an adversary of "dogmatic scientific materialists" who, he believes, "are as exceptional as dogmatic religious fanatics." He believes that most people on each side of the divide between science and religion are moderates who respect each other. However, he asserts that "militant scientists who make up in polemical zeal what they lack in numbers" are ill equipped to "join hands in the coming century" and to "try to understand where we believers are coming from." Clearly, Huston Smith's critique is aimed squarely at Dawkins, Dennett, and the genre of religion's detractors surveyed above. Moreover, Smith posits a "religious sense" that "recognizes instinctively that the ultimate questions human beings ask . . . are the defining essence of humanity." Furthermore, this religious spirit directs people to band together to pursue the answers to these questions even though "final answers are unattainable." His vision is religious. Although exceptionally well versed in and shaped by religious studies, his religious claims rely on authority outside the secular academic study of religion.

Rosemont's address is more securely situated within religious studies, and the related book exemplifies the overlap between scholarship and appreciation of religion. Rosemont is a highly acclaimed scholar of philosophy, linguistics, and religion, who specializes in Chinese religions and the comparative philosophy of religion. His book, *Rationality and Religious Experience*, includes the address Rosemont delivered for the first Hsuan Hua Memorial Lecture, which was sponsored by the Institute for World Religions, the Graduate Theological Union, and the Center for Chinese Studies at the University of California at Berkeley. The sponsorship suggests the overlapping contexts of secular academic studies of East Asia, theology (from an organization respected for its diversity and academic rigor), and interfaith dialogue—the Institute for World Religions was founded by the extraordinarily influential Ch'an (the school of Chinese Buddhism known as Zen in Japan) Patriarch Hsuan Hua and the Roman Catholic Cardinal Yu-Bin as an "open forum" to encourage a diverse array of participants "to examine the role of religion in a modern world." Even the publisher, Open Court, exemplifies this same overlap as its founder, Paul Carus, was a leading figure in religious dialogue and study as exemplified by his Open Court books on Buddhism, journals for comparative religion and philosophy, and his support of the 1893 World's Parliament of Religions in Chicago.

These contextual notes about *Rationality and Religious Experience* are offered to demonstrate that there is a well-established and continuing tradition of religious studies scholarship and cross-cultural religious and philosophical dialogue that has been supportive of religion, though not necessarily uncritically so. Such forums, from the famous 1893 Parliament to the twenty-first-century annual Hsuan Hua Memorial Lecture, can provide provocative discussions capable of advancing understanding about religion and philosophy. The relationship between these activities and religious studies is more complex. The World's Parliament of Religions intentionally chose to showcase representatives of religions rather than scholars, who may or may not also be adherents. The Hsuan Hua Memorial Lecture, on the other hand, selected a highly esteemed scholar for its inaugural address. Nonetheless, the lecture series' emphasis on ethics and spiritual values in combination with its interfaith context and the religious reputation of Hsuan Hua himself provokes the potential for blurring the lines between the academic study of religion and religious advocacy.

Rosemont's address brought his keen academic analysis of comparative religion and philosophy—including complementary links between less literal readings of Abrahamic traditions' sacred texts and the guidance offered by certain experiential and non-dualistic realizations in Asian traditions—to the fore, along with his own insights. Moreover, the academic credentials of *Rationality and Religious Experience* are further enhanced by the format, in which Rosemont's thought-provoking lecture is followed first by Huston Smith's commentary, then a lengthy response and discussion section, and finally an ensuing epilogue from Rosemont. This combination of a carefully researched and considered lecture stimulating a challenging back-and-forth discussion is characteristic of the academic enterprise.

Rosemont acknowledges the justifiable skepticism about whether the world's religions can and should "have a significant bearing on the lives of people living in a global, postmodern society." He concedes that claims from all religions, taken at face value, violate science and strain credibility past the breaking point. Literal readings of sacred texts simply cannot be accepted "as descriptions of how the world came to be, what is in it, how it functions, and what its future will be." However, Rosemont maintains that these accounts can still say "something that is true." In a similar response to the question concerning whether religion should shape society,

Rosemont supports the skeptics' hesitation over the role religion should play in the world given the grisly history of destruction wrought by religious fanatics. Even while attributing these failings to religion, he ultimately finds its potential benefit more persuasive than its possible harm. For evidence in favor of this conclusion he points to the unifying and peaceful religious heroes who have emerged from these same traditions, as well as the assumption that religious fanaticism will not go away, but it is more likely to be curbed by moderates from inside the tradition. He moves more fully into a position of advocating religion by positing that if they are read anew and in a comparative context, sacred texts reveal truths which are not in conflict with rationality, but which

> can guide us back from the abyss of meaninglessness that is becoming increasingly characteristic of contemporary life, an altogether material life in which many of us are obliged to take jobs we do not like or find satisfying in order to buy things that we do not need and that do not satisfy us either, all the while destroying our natural and social environments as we do so.

Rosemont's evidence, analysis, and arguments weave support characteristic of the academic study of religion with a purpose that is constructive beyond the typical permits of secular academic study. Although he straddles the fence between religious studies and advocacy, Rosemont's response to Huston Smith's question about his silence on metaphysics in sacred texts suggests that Rosemont's position lies between Smith's celebration of a sacred quality beyond science's grasp and those scholars of the scientific study of religion who strictly limit the scope of their study to religion as a natural phenomenon. Rosemont assures us that his silence on metaphysics was intentional for a variety of reasons, from the fact that Chinese religions—Buddhism, Daoism, and Confucianism—do not make the same claims of a transcendental or "wholly other" metaphysical realm, to linguistic concerns about the nature of language and problems of translation. Moreover, he asserts that appeals to an elusive metaphysics are not necessary to demonstrate religion's relevance. In this sense, he is more directly addressing the critics of religion—those on the other side who might dismiss religion as irrational and harmful. Rosemont asserts that

> even the most dyed-in-the-wool, empirically and logically oriented agnostic rationalist has good reason for attending to the sacred texts of the world's religions with great respect, in the fully rational belief that those texts can aid us measurably in leading productive and ultimately satisfying lives, enhancing the joys thereof, and mitigating their sorrows.

This requires depth of insight and additional readings and meaning beyond the simple, literal interpretation where the rationalist critic might discard the tradition when a statement appears to be in conflict with science or contemporary norms.

Calls for religious literacy

There are also several recent books arguing for greater religious literacy for atheists and believers alike, such as Jacques Berlinerblau's *The Secular Bible: Why Nonbelievers Must Take Religion Seriously* (2005) and Stephen Prothero's *Religious Literacy: What Every American Needs to Know—And Doesn't* (2007). The titles are reasonably self-explanatory and simultaneously address religion's importance and how deeply it is embedded in society while decrying the widespread ignorance of religion. These various more popular works—whether critiquing religion, supporting it, or advocating greater understanding and awareness regardless of pro or con orientation—form a relevant, contemporary discourse on the study of religion, even if most of them are not fully religious studies scholarship. The majority of these books have been written by academics, though not necessarily religious studies scholars. Importantly, they are directed to a wider audience and demonstrate attempts by public intellectuals to shape the study and understanding of religion beyond the university setting. It is too soon to assess the lasting effects of the *New York Times* best-sellers and their authors' appearances on radio and television programs—including increasingly influential new media forums such as Jon Stewart's *The Daily Show*—but these trends provide revealing glimpses into the wider discourse about religion and its study.

Assorted quotations on religion

Ralph Waldo Emerson: "The religion of one age is the literary entertainment of the next."

Sigmund Freud: "An illusion it would be to suppose that what science cannot give us we can get elsewhere."

Galileo Galilei: "I do not think it is necessary to believe that the same God who has given us our senses, reason, and intelligence wished us to abandon their use, giving us by some other means the information that we could gain through them."

Mohandas K. Gandhi: "The most heinous and the most cruel crimes of which history has record have been committed under the cover of religion or equally noble motives."

Sam Harris: "Everything of value that people get from religion can be had more honestly, without presuming anything on insufficient evidence. The rest is self-deception, set to music."

Abraham Joshua Heschel: "The tragedy of religion is partly due to its isolation from life, as if God could be segregated."

William James: "Although all the special manifestations of religion may have been absurd (I mean its creeds and theories), yet the life of it as a whole is mankind's most important function."

Thomas Jefferson: "A professorship of theology should have no place in our institution."

D. H. Lawrence: "A person has no religion who has not slowly and painfully gathered one together, adding to it, shaping it, and one's religion is never complete and final, it seems, but must always be undergoing modification."

Abraham Lincoln: "When I do good, I feel good; when I do bad, I feel bad. That's my religion."

Martin Luther: "A religion that gives nothing, costs nothing, and suffers nothing, is worth nothing."

Ferdinand Magellan: "The church says the earth is flat, but I know that it is round, for I have seen the shadow on the moon, and I have more faith in a shadow than in the church."

Kiyozawa Manshi: "Religious conviction is the inner peace gained by relying on that which transcends man . . . Religion is not a path to follow to become a good man in this world. It is a path reaching beyond man."

Karl Marx: "Religion is the sigh of the oppressed creature, the heart of a heartless world, and the soul of soulless conditions. It is the opium of the people."

H. L. Mencken: "The scientist who yields anything to theology, however slight, is yielding to ignorance and false pretenses, and as certainly as if he granted that a horse-hair put into a bottle of water will turn into a snake."

Max Müller: "To know one religion is to know none."

Friedrich Schleiermacher: "The essence of religion consists in the feeling of an absolute dependence."

Seneca the Younger: "Religion is regarded by the common people as true, by the wise as false, and by the rulers as useful."

Huston Smith: "If we take the world's enduring religions at their best, we discover the distilled wisdom of the human race."

Mark Twain: "In religion and politics people's beliefs and convictions are in almost every case gotten at second-hand, and without examination, from authorities who have not themselves examined the questions at issue but have taken them at second-hand from other non-examiners, whose opinions about them were not worth a brass farthing."

Gene Edward Veith: "Those who think all religions are the same look at the wrappings instead of the content."

6

Studying religion in context

Perspectives and conclusions

Historical approaches
Comparative approaches
Some concluding theoretical and methodological issues
in the study of religion

Historical and comparative approaches to the study of religion were formative to the origins of religious studies and remain important today despite a withering critique of both by postmodern theorists. The two are linked together in our survey for various reasons. Each can refer to methods in the study of religion, but both the "history of religion" and "comparative religion" have been used as more general terms synonymous with the relatively new discipline of religious studies. These terms were used to distinguish the academic study of religion from traditional theological and philosophical studies. Comparative religion highlighted how this academic study of religion encompasses traditions, texts, myths, and rituals beyond Christianity, and uses comparison to categorize, abstract, and distill religious types, recurrent themes, and the diverse expressions of what may be more unified, or at least meaningfully related, religious modes. Similarly, the history of religion called for examining each religion's history and the relationship among religions and between religion and other aspects of society aided by the historian's questions, research methods, insights, and standards.

Historical approaches

History is generally a narrative account—typically written, although there are oral histories—of the past, drawn from a variety of relatively reliable sources. History strives for neutrality in its presentation of facts about the past. Historians also attempt to analyze events to illustrate relationships, particularly cause and effect, between processes or events to demonstrate how a certain situation resulted from previous factors. Although historians have not always agreed with each other on their analyses of past events (e.g. on what was the real cause of the war against the former ruler of

Iraq, Saddam Hussein), there has often been a generally naïve acceptance, particularly by non-specialist readers of history, that even though analyses and interpretations may vary, historical "facts" are unquestionable. However, postmodern sensibilities have dramatically affected the discipline of history, where even certain items once accepted as "facts"—such as whether Christopher Columbus really did "discover" the New World in 1492—are now placed under scrutiny.

The sweeping historical meta-narratives of the rise and fall of civilizations have fallen out of favor and been replaced by studies more deep than broad—that is, more attentive to unique qualities of specific historical context and wary of periodization, which characterizes a vast span of time as an essentially unified whole, or of similar generalizations that do not sufficiently differentiate between the experiences and context of different places, times, classes, cultures, genders, societies, institutions, and individual agents. The same movements can be detected in historical approaches to religious studies. Some earlier works had more pronounced comparative dimensions and could suggest not just a progression of an individual tradition but of religion as a whole. This idea of progress invoked social evolutionary notions of religion developing from its infancy—primitive religions characterized by animism or a lack of texts or central authority—to its maturity, which, not coincidentally, closely resembled the forms of Christianity typical of the theorists discussing religion in this way. Distortions from theories of progress, social evolution, history, and civilization that culminate in Western Christianity—as well as related bias in some comparative studies—have inspired postmodern critiques and attacks on the excesses and problems of both historical and comparative approaches.

However, each approach, done conscientiously, is still valuable and necessary for the study of religion. Religion is one of many subjects of study within the discipline of history. There is no essential difference between a historical study of religion conducted by a scholar in a history department or a colleague in religious studies who employs this approach. Moreover, academic studies that do not explicitly identify themselves with this approach nonetheless typically require some attention to historical context. Some approaches pay close attention to history and others feel free to uproot data from historical context, but the latter are usually criticized if they attempt to escape it altogether. Even the notion of "postmodern" presumes historical progression from pre-modern to modern to postmodern as well as time-bound notions of modernity and the modern project.

Comparative and historical approaches are also linked by their relative freedom to employ a wide variety of theoretical tools. Neither approach is particularly aligned with or determined by any one theory or ideological commitment. The subject matter, emphasis, and theoretical stance can differ considerably among historians in general and even among historical studies of religion in particular. The most useful training and sources needed to study early Christian communities are quite different from the resources necessary to understand the entry and development of Buddhism in China. However, there may be considerable overlap in the types of questions asked and the theoretical tools used to better understand and explain the historical dynamics involved. Then again, the theoretical tools may be significantly different between these studies or even among studies that focus on the same tradition, place, and time period. Some historians have a strongly determined theoretical stance and ideological commitment. For example, some Marxist historians not only focus on social class and economic influences on history; they also agree with, and may even attempt to foster, the teleological view of Karl Marx that history is moving in a particular direction toward a classless society. However, such a strong ideological commitment is the exception rather than the norm. There is still greater variety in the commitment to and orientation of theoretical stances. Many historians would not be troubled by a relatively weak, or loose, correlation between historical approach and theoretical perspective. For them, an overly determined ideological or theoretical perspective can distort analysis of history by reading into the historical record the very conclusions with which such an historian began his or her study. In short, most would not strive to be known as theoreticians. Moreover, some historians of religion who are well known for their sociological or phenomenological perspectives have been placed in those categories already rather than discussed in this brief overview.

Comparative approaches

Even in these introductory preceding sections, we have already drawn attention to shared elements among religions. Such similarities can be as obvious as the observation that most religions consist of sets of beliefs and assortments of practices, or more particularly, that they may possess sacred specialists, revere scriptures, or utilize symbols. The comparative perspective and approach in the discipline of religious studies differs from the kind of comparison that an evangelical (i.e. missionary) tradition might take. Missionaries may seek to compare religions, pointing out how one religion's values are misguided in order to present their own tradition more favorably. In religious studies, the trend has been to try to understand religions more effectively through comparison, but not to assert the hierarchical superiority of one religion over the other.

Any of the above approaches to the study of religion, or the study of anything else for that matter, can and do make use of comparison. Comparison is inevitable for any study that includes categories. In fact, it is apparent in any study that uses language. If language were to disavow comparison and categories in favor of absolute uniqueness, the explosion of vocabulary would be matched by the implosion of our ability to communicate. The variance along a spectrum can be summarized in a simplistic way by noting that sometimes comparison in studies of religion is at the forefront, and at other times it is not.

Scholars such as Eric Sharpe and William Paden have contributed histories and studies of this approach, and seminal figures such as Max Müller, James Frazer, Mircea Eliade, Joseph Campbell, and Wendy Doniger have helped shape the academic study of religion through their use of comparative approaches. Müller, Frazer, and Doniger all appear in our section on anthropological approaches. Müller also appears under phenomenological approaches along with Eliade and Campbell. Eliade, in turn, championed the use of the term "history of religion" for his discipline, further linking these contextual approaches. Joseph Campbell, who also appears in the section exploring psychological approaches to religion due to his link with Jung, is one of the most widely read comparativists, whose popular books and television series study myths from all over the world and reveal similarities among the themes encountered there. The discovery of such themes as the quest of the hero against seemingly insurmountable odds (e.g. Jason and the Golden Fleece and the search for the Holy Grail), for instance, can lead us to insights into the shared concerns of human beings throughout time and in widely dispersed places. Other scholars have, however, pointed out that the comparative perspective may tend to gloss over unique differentiating features within individual myths as one attempts to search for similarities. J. Z. Smith has been one such effective critic of comparison that is insufficiently attuned to difference. This tension between focusing on particulars, that is, on regional specifics within their cultural contexts, and the search for universals, on shared meanings, symbols, and such, is intrinsic to the comparative perspective. Kimberley Patton and Benjamin Ray's *A Magic Still Dwells: Comparative Religion in the Postmodern Age* (2000) provides a series of insightful essays from influential scholars addressing the problems and promise of this approach.

Some concluding theoretical and methodological issues in the study of religion

When considering the historical development of the discipline of religious studies, two major trends emerge. These derive from one of the discipline's classic dichotomies, namely, "insider" versus "outsider" approaches. The developments of insider approaches move from what were once thick theological and apologetic studies of one's own traditions, to thin, or thickly veiled, theological or apologetic studies of one's own traditions. One also finds within this orientation scholarship that accepts (sometimes with great subtlety) the notion of supernatural realities within the framework of studying other people's religions, or religion in general (e.g. certain phenomenological approaches might fit into this category). One might suggest that these approaches are generically theological, or apologetic, not because they espouse any particular religious notion, but because they accept the existence of some sort of spiritual reality to which human beings have related in various ways, at various times, and within various cultures. In contrast, the outsider approaches might be regarded as philosophical, insofar as they attempt to examine religious beliefs and practices and analyze these intellectually. In early expressions of these approaches, the religions studied were not typically those of the scholar, who might also have expressed various degrees of disdain or even hostility towards the subject matter. This is because religious beliefs and practices were, and still are, often seen as irrational or emotional, going against fundamental orientations of the outsider approach, which is grounded in the application of rational thought to the object of study. However, in recent decades, the trajectory of outsider approaches has been to try to understand the human propensity for religion in less pejorative terms, to seek within religion an expression of rational behaviour, and so on. A key criterion in outsider approaches is the non-belief by the scholar in any of the supernatural categories of the religious tradition being studied.

To some extent, the theological and philosophical perspectives in religious studies, which we have categorized as "traditional" in this text, have matured with the discipline over the last century so as to be not so far apart as they once were. Until a few decades ago, it was incumbent on scholars to conceal their personal religious orientations and present their studies with a semblance of objectivity (i.e. the outsider philosophical orientation) mixed with sensitivity (i.e. the insider apologetic orientation). No one should have been able to tell whether the approach was insider or outsider. Thus both the Muslim and the atheist might conduct scholarly studies of Islam, but the former should guard against any hint of an apologetics that distorts objectivity and reason in the data gathering and analysis, and the latter should guard against any taint of aloofness or disdain that might jeopardize a sympathetic engagement with the experiential reality of believers. This secrecy of religious orientation ("don't ask, don't tell") continues to the present day, although postmodern sensibilities have led some religious studies scholars to think it valuable to make one's personal orientation (insider or outsider) evident to the reader at the outset. It would not be incorrect to suggest that in the current culture of the discipline of religious studies one is more likely to forgive the work of an undeclared scholar who errs on the side of the outsider perspective than on the insider. Nevertheless, it is also possible to hear scathing rebukes of purportedly sensitive objective scholarship from factions in the discipline who seek full disclosure of a scholar's social, cultural, religious, and other statuses. It would also perhaps be correct to suggest that in reality there is more work that errs on the side of insider perspectives. The simple fact is that there are more insiders working on their own religious traditions, albeit making efforts to do so within their understanding of the constraining parameters of the discipline of religious studies.

One of the most intriguing theoretical implications in religious studies derives from ruminations by scholars such as J. Z. Smith. Smith and others have argued that although people through much of history and virtually everywhere engage in practices and entertain thoughts through which they relate to deities or other supernatural entities, these ideas and acts are deeply interwoven with other features of their existence. They are not typically being consciously religious here and non-religious there. The notion of "religion" is thus a creation of academics, who separate it from other thoughts and actions, and then engage in the study of what they designate as "religion." Smith, for instance, argues that scholars should thus not restrict themselves exclusively to the phenomena that religious insiders would designate as features of "their religion" (e.g. canonical scriptures), but should be willing to look at virtually anything which can be justified as further elucidating the realities of human religiosity.

Studying religion

Jonathan Z. Smith: "Religion is solely the creation of the scholar's study. It is created for the scholar's analytic purposes by his imaginative acts of comparision and generalization. Religion has no independent existence apart from the academy. For this reason, the student of religion, and most particularly the historian of religion, must be relentlessly selfconscious."

A provocative implication of these observations and prescriptions is that they recognize the religious studies scholar as engaged in an enterprise that elevates the discipline over its conventional, narrowly defined subject matter. Additionally, when engaged in the exercise of one's scholarly activities, the discipline of religious studies is more important to the scholar than any religion being studied. This notion is not at all unusual if we apply it to some other discipline: for example, we might say that when engaged in research in chemistry, the proper exercise of the scientific methods of chemistry is more important than the polymers being studied. Just as polymers are useful entities but are not intrinsically sacrosanct, so too are religions for the scholar engaged in her disciplinary research. Religions need not be handled with overly reserved politeness. Just because a suicide bomber believes that his act of mass murder will guarantee him a place in paradise does not make that belief and behaviour sacrosanct for the scholar. Just because the followers of a religious tradition believe that its founder is divine, and his teachings will enable them to attain liberation, does not give this belief a status that elevates it beyond disciplinary analysis. Just because a martyr believes that her crucifixion absolves all humanity of its sins does not make the belief and practice beyond scrutiny, doubt, or analysis. In other words, the taboos of religious believers need to be understood and appreciated, but need not (or even should not) be embraced by religious studies scholars in the exercise of their discipline. Furthermore, it is not necessary or even sufficient to study exclusively what others tell us are their religions and their defining parameters. It is necessary for the scholar to look beyond these insider-defined features and categories to social, political, economic, and cultural traits, and so on. These may be so intrinsically interconnected with each other and with the insider-defined religious categories as to make them all arguably "religious."

One might suggest that the exploratory terrain of religious studies is everything within the purview of humanity's conceptions of and relationship to reality as perceived, conceived, and imagined. This conception of religion as intrinsically connected to virtually all features of existence and defined by the scholar's choice is different from the notion of religion as being difficult to define because of fuzzy boundaries. It is also different from the notion that "religion" is simply a commonly used term, like most other terms, such as music or matter, which are relatively easily grasped and adequately applied by most people. Instead, the implication here is that it is the scholar who can and does define the object of her study as "religion," provided she can make a convincing case for why this is so. It raises intriguing and provocative questions as to whether religious studies scholars are then themselves engaged in religious activities when occupied with the interest of their discipline. Is the discipline of religious studies religious? Perhaps it is, if one understands the question through the framework of this all-encompassing scope of religion, the scholar's role in creating the category, and the imaginative activities employed by scholars to participate in the practice of religious studies. However, this question—in the way it would most likely be initially read and understood—could, and probably should, also be answered "no," in the sense that one need not be religious to do religious studies, and that the doing of religious studies is not a religious type of practice. This is because while engaged in the academic study of religion at a secular university, one should neither be setting the norms of a religious tradition nor should the scholar be restricting his or her analysis of that tradition in deference to the tradition's own taboos and ultimate claims. Moreover, although the practice of religious studies may require scholars to develop and exemplify such qualities as sensitivity, patience, judgment, and critical analysis, as well as a passion for understanding, which are traits shared and promoted by certain religious traditions, the scholars' quest in the practice of their discipline is a fully human undertaking.

Select websites

www.sastor.com—Scholarly Approaches to the Study and Teaching of Religion
More links are available at this, our own, site along with a more extensive glossary and chronology. We are developing an expanded collection of resources—audio, visual, articles, news, reviews—to better understand and pursue the academic study of religion.

www.as.ua.edu/rel/studyingreligion.html—Studying Religion
A well-developed site by Russell T. McCutcheon, who is one of the leading scholars and theorists on the academic study of religion. It includes biographies, definitions, and resources as well as essays that explore the essentials, functions, and classifications of religion.

www.aarweb.org—American Academy of Religion (AAR)
"The world's largest association of academics who research or teach topics related to religion." Parts of this site, such as job listings, are for members only; however, it is filled with useful information, links from related organizations, and unique features, such as its Syllabus Project and the Religionsource database of 5,000 religious studies experts who are willing to answer media inquiries.

www.as.ua.edu/naasr—North American Association for the Study of Religion
This organization emphasizes theory and method as exemplified by its journal, *Method and Theory in the Study of Religion*, its monograph series, *Key Thinkers in the Study of Religion*, and even the "selection of recent books" featured on this site.

www.sacred-texts.com—Internet Sacred Text Archive
This site includes an astounding array of primary texts available online or through their CDs and DVDs. The "largest freely available archive of online books about religion, mythology, folklore and the esoteric on the Internet. The site is dedicated to religious tolerance and scholarship, and has the largest readership of any similar site on the web."

http://vos.ucsb.edu/browse.asp?id=2730—Voice of the Shuttle: Religious Studies
This page—the religious studies section of the massive VoS directory for humanities research—includes impressively comprehensive links to a wide variety of resources.

www.pluralism.org—Pluralism Project at Harvard
This website includes engaging multimedia resources organized by tradition, place, and other means to survey America's religious diversity.

Chronology of select significant persons and seminal texts

Conventions

Circa (Latin for "around" or "about"), here abbreviated as c., is used to indicate approximate dates.

Books are given with their original date of publication (where known) and their title in English (on its own or following the original), even for cases where an English translation was not published until later.

Before the Common/Christian Era (BCE)

c. 1100s	Zarathustra	Also Zoroaster; Iranian prophet considered the founder of Zoroastrianism, to whom the composition of ancient hymns (*gatha*) are attributed.
c. 700s	Homer	Mythic Greek poet to whom the major Western epics, the *Odyssey* and the *Iliad*, are attributed.
c. 700s	Hesiod	Greek poet to whom the authorship of *Works and Days* and the *Theogony* are attributed.
c. 610–546	Anaximander	Pre-Socratic Greek philosopher known for his contributions in science and geometry.
c. 500s	Laozi	Also Lao-tzu; Mythic Chinese philosopher; credited with the formulation of Daoist (Taoist) teachings; attributed with the authorship of the *Daodejing* (*Tao Te Ching*).
c. 580–490	Xenophanes	Greek philosopher and poet known for his critique of polytheism.
551–479	Kongzi	Also K'ung Fu-tzu or Confucius; enormously influential Chinese teacher of social and ethical values; teachings contained in the *Analects*.
c. 549–477	Vardhamana	Indian teacher; known as Mahavira; associated with conveying the teachings of the Jains.

c. 540–480	Heraclitus	Metaphysical philosopher known for his philosophy of constant change, and considered one of the patriarchs of process philosophies.
c. 400s	Valmiki	Indian poet to whom the composition of the Indian epic, the *Ramayana*, is attributed.
c. 490–410	Siddhartha Gautama	Indian teacher; known as the Buddha (Awakened One); associated with teachings for the ending of suffering and the attainment of spiritual liberation (*nirvana*).
c. 484–425	Herodotus	Author of the *Histories*, an account of Greek struggles with the Persian invasions, and sometimes regarded as the father of history.
c. 469–399	Socrates	Greek philosopher known for his teaching method of questioning students; teacher of Plato.
c. 427–347	Plato	Tremendously influential Greek philosopher; student of Socrates; thought contained in various texts known as dialogues, such as the *Republic* and the *Timaeus*.
384–322	Aristotle	Enormously influential Greek philosopher; student of Plato and teacher of Alexander the Great; made contributions in numerous areas, particularly logic, psychology, natural science, ethics, and poetics.
c. 365–290	Zhuangzi	Also Chuang-tzu; Chinese Daoist (Taoist) philosopher whose unique genius accounts for the "inner chapters" of the text that bears his name.
c. 325–270	Euclid	Greek mathematician, whose influential work *Elements* forms the basis of classical (Euclidean) geometry.

Common/Christian Era (CE)

20 BCE–50 CE	Philo Judeaus	Hellenic Jewish philosopher known for promoting the notion of interpreting scriptural accounts as allegories.
c. 7 BCE–26 CE	Jesus of Nazareth	Jewish teacher (rabbi), designated by his followers as the Messiah or Christ; pivotal figure in Christian beliefs.
c. 150–250	Nagarjuna	Indian-born philosopher; founder of the Madhyamaka school of Mahayana Buddhism; author of the *Mulamadhyamakakarika* (*Fundamental Verses on the Middle Way*).
354–430	Augustine of Hippo	Influential Christian Church father; known for his doctrine of original sin; author of *City of God, On Christian Doctrine*, and the *Confessions*.

538–597	Zhiyi (Chih-i)	Chinese founder of Tiantai (T'ien-T'ai) School of Buddhism; known for harmonizing and systematizing the vast corpus of Indian Buddhist literature into a unified vehicle, with the *Lotus Sutra* as the dominant text.
570–632	Muhammad	Arabian prophet and founder of Islam; believed by Muslims to have received the instructions of Allah (God), contained in the Qur'an.
774–835	Kûkai	Towering figure in Japanese religion and culture, also known as Kobo Daishi; founded the Shingon school of Vajrayana Buddhism; as a young man, wrote an early work of comparative religion, *Ten Stages of Religious Consciousness*, which describes and ranks various Asian religious traditions.
c. 788–820	Shankara	Hindu philosopher, known for his doctrine of extreme non-dualism; wrote influential commentaries on the Upanishads, and the *Bhagavad Gita*.
980–1037	Ibn Sina (Avicenna)	Influential Muslim philosopher and physician from Persia.
1014–20		*Kitab al-Shifa (Book of Healing)*
1033–1109	Anselm of Canterbury	Italian theologian; influential early scholastic known for his ontological argument for the existence of God.
1058–1111	Al-Ghazali (Algazel)	Persian Muslim theologian known for his contributions to the legitimacy of Islamic mysticism (Sufism); author of *Tahafut al-Falasifa* (*Incoherence of the Philosophers*).
c. 1100– 1160	Peter Lombard	French-Italian scholastic theologian.
c. 1150		*Four Books of Sentences*
1126–1198	Ibn Rushd (Averroes)	Spanish-born, influential Muslim philosopher/ theologian, whose commentaries on Aristotle's works contributed to the revival of secular thought in Christian Europe; author of *Tahafut al-Tahafut* (*Incoherence of the Incoherence*), a critique of a work by Al-Ghazali.
1135–1204	Moses Maimonides	Jewish theologian and philosopher; known for his formulation of a creed for Jews and for authoring the *Mishneh Torah*, a comprehensive study of Jewish law, as well as the more philosophical *Guide for the Perplexed*, which harmonized faith with reason and marked the apex of Medieval Jewish theology and philosophy.

1222–1282	Nichiren	Japanese Buddhist monk; known for advocating reverence of the *Lotus Sutra* with exceptional polemical and proselytizing zeal.
1225–1274	Thomas Aquinas	Italian Dominican friar; exponent of Aristotelian philosophy; possibly the most influential of Catholic theologians.
1265–74		*Summa Theologica*
1266–1308	John Duns Scotus	Influential Scottish theologian, known for his support of the Catholic doctrine of the immaculate conception of Mary, mother of Jesus, and for divorcing faith from reason.
c. 1288– 1347	William of Ockham	English scholastic philosopher, known for the doctrine of parsimony in the formulation of explanations and theories (Occam's Razor).
1357–1419	Tsong Khapa	Tibetan Buddhist systematizer, reformer, and theologian who instituted rigorous standards of virtue, practice, textual study, interpretation, and debate. His *Great Exposition of the Path* integrated diverse teachings and offering guidance for Buddhists' daily life, philosophical perspective, and ultimate religious aims.
1469–1538	Nanak	Founder of the Sikh religious tradition, whose writings are contained within the Sikh holy book, the *Guru Granth Sahib.*
1596–1650	René Descartes	French thinker; regarded as the father of modern Western philosophy.
1637		*Discourse on the Method*
1641		*Meditations on First Philosophy*
1643–1727	Isaac Newton	English physicist; known for his laws of motion and gravitation.
1687		*Philosophiae Naturalis Principia Mathematica*
1704		*Opticks*
1711–1776	David Hume	Scottish philosopher; known for his criticism of the argument for the existence of God based on the notion of intelligent design.
1779		*Dialogues Concerning Natural Religion*
1724–1804	Immanuel Kant	German philosopher; known for contributions in metaphysics and epistemology.
1781		*Critique of Pure Reason*
1749–1832	J. W. von Goethe	German intellectual who made major contributions to many fields including philosophy and literature.
1806		*Faust* (Part I)
1832		*Faust* (Part II)

1768–1834	Friedrich Schleiermacher	German Protestant theologian who conceived of religion as founded upon inner sentiments, such as the feeling of utter dependence.
1799		*On Religion: Speeches to Its Cultured Despisers*
1805–1844	Joseph Smith	American preacher and prophet; founder of the Mormon religious tradition or the Church of Jesus Christ of Latter-day Saints.
1809–1882	Charles Darwin	English naturalist known for his theory of biological evolution.
1859		*On the Origin of Species*
1813–1855	Søren Kierkegaard	Danish philosopher/theologian; known for his contributions to the notion of faith and to the philosophy of existentialism.
1818–1874	P. D. Chantepie de la Saussaye	Dutch scholar who like Cornelius Petrus Tiele (1830–1902) advocated phenomenological approaches that categorized and compared religious phenomena beyond Christianity.
1818–1883	Karl Marx	Prussian-born, influential social, political, and economic theorist; considered the father of communist political philosophy.
1848		*Communist Manifesto* (coauthored with Friedrich Engels)
1867–94		*Das Kapital* (*Capital*) (three volumes)
1820–1903	Herbert Spencer	English philosopher; coined the term "survival of the fittest" to explain Charles Darwin's theory of evolution; promoted the notion of the evolution of societies.
1823–1900	F. Max Müller	German-born philologist, comparativist, and "father of the scientific study of religion (*Religionswissenschaft*)"; specialized in Sanskrit; theorized on the origins of myths.
1879		*Sacred Books of the East* (beginning of this massive, multi-volume project)
1832–1917	E. B. Tylor	English anthropologist; pioneer in the anthropological study of religion.
1871		*Primitive Culture*
1842–1910	William James	American psychologist and philosopher who emphasized the value of immediate, personal, religious experience.
1891		*The Principles of Psychology*
1902		*The Varieties of Religious Experience*
1844–1900	Friedrich Nietzsche	German philosopher known for his critique of religious morality.
1883–5		*Thus Spoke Zarathustra*

1886		*Beyond Good and Evil*
1887		*On the Genealogy of Morals*
1844–1912	Andrew Lang	Scottish folklorist who contributed to the development of the anthropology of religion.
1854–1941	J. G. Frazer	Scottish mythologist; known for his contributions to the study of magic in various cultures.
1890		*The Golden Bough*
1856–1939	Sigmund Freud	Founding father of psychoanalysis; indicated that religion provides benefits to civilization but ultimately is illusory, is akin to a childhood neurosis, and lacks scientific rigor.
1912–13		*Totem and Taboo*
1927		*The Future of an Illusion*
1939		*Moses and Monotheism*
1858–1917	Émile Durkheim	French founder of the modern discipline of sociology; theorized on totemism as the earliest form of religion.
1912		*The Elementary Forms of the Religious Life*
1858–1942	Franz Boas	German-born American; considered the father of American cultural anthropology.
1859–1919	Shaku Sōen	Japanese Zen monk and abbot; known for his reforms, lay students, and influence at the 1893 World's Parliament of Religions in Chicago.
1861–1947	Alfred N. Whitehead	English mathematician and philosopher; associated-with the development of process philosophy.
1929		*Process and Reality*
1864–1920	Max Weber	German sociologist and political theorist on religion; especially well known for *The Protestant Ethic and the Spirit of Capitalism*, which emerged from publications in 1904–5; also wrote *The Religion of China* and *The Religion of India*.
1868–1954	Wilhelm Schmidt	Catholic priest and anthropologist; known for his theory of original monotheism.
1869–1937	Rudolf Otto	German scholar of religion; used "numinous" to designate religious dimensions—including feelings of awe and terror— beyond the grasp of reason and scientific explanation.
1923		*The Idea of the Holy*
1870–1966	D. T. Suzuki	Japanese scholar, and lay student of Shaku Sōen, who most influentially introduced Zen and related religious and artistic traditions from Japan to the West; wrote more than 100 books and lectured extensively in North America and Europe.
1938		*Zen Buddhism and Its Influence on Japanese Culture*

1872–1970	Bertrand Russell	British mathematician and philosopher; major contributor to the development of analytic philosophy.
1910–13		*Principia Mathematica* (in three volumes, coauthored with A. N. Whitehead)
1875–1961	Carl Gustav Jung	Swiss founder of analytic (Jungian) psychology; evaluated religion more positively than Freud; notion of universal archetypes that emerge from a collective unconscious and the importance of individuation.
1938		*Psychology of Religion*
1956		*Answer to Job*
1958		*Psychology and Religion: West and East*
1878–1965	Martin Buber	Austrian-born, Jewish philosopher, known for his insights concerning divine and human relationships, interpretations of Jewish scripture, and revival of Jewish consciousness and community.
1923		*Ich und Du* (*I and Thou*)
1879–1955	Albert Einstein	German-born theoretical physicist known for his theory of relativity and contributions to quantum theory.
1881–1955	A. R. Radcliffe-Brown	British social anthropologist, associated with structural functionalism as an approach to the study of societies and culture.
1952		*Structure and Function in Primitive Society*
1884–1942	B. Malinowski	Polish-born anthropologist; known for his emphasis on fieldwork in the study of societies and their cultures.
1922		*Argonauts of the Western Pacific*
1948		*Magic, Science, and Religion*
1884–1964	Gerald B. Gardner	British civil servant, who together with Doreen Valiente (1922–1999), laid the foundation for the neo-Pagan movement known as Wicca.
1884–1976	Rudolf Bultmann	German Lutheran theologian, known for his influential work in biblical studies.
1921		*History of the Synoptic Tradition*
1886–1965	Paul Tillich	German-American Protestant theologian, known for his emphasis on religion as that which is founded upon a human being's ultimate concern.
1951–63		*Systematic Theology* (in three volumes)
1886–1968	Karl Barth	Influential Swiss-born Protestant Reformed theologian; known for his break from liberal theology and return to scripture as fundamental authority.
1932–68		*Church Dogmatics*

1889–1951	Ludwig Wittgenstein	Austrian philosopher; known for his contrbutions on the philosophy of language and on mind.
1921		*Tractatus Logico-Philosophicus*
1953		*Philosophical Investigations*
1890–1950	Gerardus van der Leeuw	Dutch theologian and phenomenologist who studied many religious traditions while setting aside, or bracketing, specific truth claims of a particular religion or about the sacred.
1933		*Phenomenology of Religion*
1901–1976	Werner Heisenberg	German physicist; known for the Heisenberg Uncertainty Principle; awarded the Nobel Prize in 1932.
1902–1973	E. E. Evans-Pritchard	British social anthropologist; contributed to functionalism linked to the interpretive approach.
1937		*Witchcraft, Oracles and Magic among the Azande*
1956		*Nuer Religion*
1965		*Theories of Primitive Religion*
1902–1994	Erik Erikson	German psychoanalyst and developmental psychologist; applied model of eight stages of a human's life cycle to key religious figures; asserted that religion could assist in adapting to each stage.
1958		*Young Man Luther: A Study in Psychoanalysis and History*
1969		*Gandhi's Truth: On the Origins of Militant Nonviolence*
1904–1987	Joseph Campbell	American intellectual; known for his work on comparative mythology.
1949		*The Hero with a Thousand Faces*
1959–68		*The Masks of the Gods* (in four volumes)
1988		*The Power of Myth* (with Bill Moyers)
1907–1986	Mircea Eliade	Romanian scholar of the "history of religion" at the University of Chicago; comparativist and phenomenologist who sought out manifestations of the sacred throughout the world's religions and myths.
1959		*Sacred and the Profane: The Nature of Religion*
1967		*From Primitives to Zen*
1986		*Encyclopedia of Religion* (ed., sixteen volumes)
1908–1970	Abraham Maslow	American humanistic psychologist; argued that basic needs must first be met before motivation and opportunity for higher values can be realized; religious "peak experiences" and "self-actualization" possible with development of higher needs.
1964		*Religions, Values, and Peak-Experiences*
1908–	Claude Lévi-Strauss	French anthropologist; pioneer of structuralism as an approach to study human social and cultural creations, such as myth and ritual.

1958		*Anthropologie Structurale* (*Structural Anthropology*)
1962		*La Pensée Sauvage* (*The Savage Mind*)
1964		*Cru et le Cuit* (*The Raw and the Cooked*)
1979		*Myth and Meaning*
1915–2006	Abe Masao (written Masao Abe in Western convention)	Japanese Zen Buddhist philosopher (member of the Kyoto School of Philosophy) and influential contributor to interfaith dialogue.
1985		*Zen and Western Thought* (ed. William LaFleur)
1995		*Buddhism and Interfaith Dialogue* (ed. Steven Heine)
2003		*Zen and the Modern World* (ed. Steven Heine)
1917–1992	David Bohm	American physicist and philosopher associated with concepts such as the "implicate order" of reality, which is seen as a "holomovement."
1980		*Wholeness and the Implicate Order*
1991		*The Undivided Universe: An Ontological Interpretation of Quantum Thoery*
1920–1983	Victor Turner	Scottish-born American anthropologist; known for his theoretical contributions on rites of passage.
1967		*The Forest of Symbols*
1969		*The Ritual Process: Structure and Anti-structure*
1921–2007	Mary Douglas	British social anthropologist; known for her contributions on the interpretation of symbols and values through category analysis.
1966		*Purity and Danger: An Analysis of Concepts of Pollution and Taboo*
1970		*Natural Symbols: Explorations in Cosmology*
1922	John Hick	American theologian; known for his writings on the philosophy of religion.
1980		*God Has Many Names*
1923–	René Girard	French scholar; asserted that violence and the sacred are inseparable: both originate in mimetic desire and the power and function of sacrificing a scapegoat to unite the group and stave off uncontrolled violence, which could otherwise tear society apart.
1977		*Violence and the Sacred*
1926–2006	Clifford Geertz	American anthropologist; regarded as the father of interpretive anthropology.
1960		*The Religion of Java*
1973		*The Interpretation of Cultures: Selected Essays*
1927–2001	Ninian Smart	Scottish scholar of religion; encouraged imaginative empathy in the exploration of religion, which is identifiable through multiple dimensions:

		perspectives, rituals, beliefs, myths, ethics, institutions and experiences.
1969		*The Religious Experience of Mankind*
1989		*The World's Religions*
1928–	Mary Daly	Feminist theologian and philosopher; prefers the self-descriptive terms "radical" and "lesbian"; known for her criticism of Christianity as a religion that cannot be adequately reformed to make it suitably egalitarian and inclusive for women.
1968		*The Church and the Second Sex*
1973		*Beyond God the Father: Toward a Philosophy of Women's Liberation*
1976		*Gyn/Ecology: The Metaethics of Radical Feminism*
1998		*Quintessence: Realizing the Archaic Future*
1929–	Peter Berger	American sociologist and theologian associated with the notions of social reality as a creation within the consciousness of individuals, and his analyses of secularization processes.
1967		*The Sacred Canopy: Elements of a Sociological Theory of Religion*
1932–	Alvin Plantinga	American philosopher/theologian; Christian apologist.
1977		*God, Freedom, and Evil*
2000		*Warranted Christian Belief*
1935–2003	Edward W. Saïd	Palestinian-American scholar; known for theory of orientalism; regarded as the founding figure of postcolonial theory.
1978		*Orientalism*
1981		*Covering Islam: How the Media and the Experts Determine How We See the Rest of the World*
c. 1935–	Rodney Stark	American sociologist of religion, known for his work on religious cults and the development of early Christianity.
1985		*The Future of Religion* (coauthored with W. Bainbridge)
1996		*The Rise of Christianity*
c. 1935–	Jonathan Z. Smith	American historian of religion; known for his theorizing on ritual, and the discipline of religious studies.
1978		*Map is not Territory: Studies in the History of Religion*
1982		*Imagining Religion*
1987		*To Take Place: Toward Theory in Ritual*
1936–	Rosemary R. Ruether	Christian feminist theologian.

1983		*Sexism and God-Talk: Toward a Feminist Theology*
1938–	E. Schüssler Fiorenza	Catholic feminist theologian.
1984		*In Memory of Her: A Feminist Theological Reconstruction of Christian Origins*
1939–	Fritjof Capra	Austrian-born physicist and philosopher, known for his speculations on the similarities between modern physics and ancient Eastern religious worldviews.
1975		*Tao of Physics*
1940–	Wendy Doniger	American historian of religions; known for her work on comparative mythology, particularly from Hindu Sanskrit texts.
1973		*Asceticism and Eroticism in the Mythology of Siva*
1975		*Hindu Myths: A Sourcebook*
1980		*Women, Androgynes, and other Mythical Beasts*
1942–	Stephen Hawking	British scientist and leading theoretical physicist renowned for his work on black holes.
1988		*A Brief History of Time*

Glossary

ablution: ritual washing typically related to purification.

aboriginal: original or early inhabitant; indigenous; native groups, animals, or plants.

aesthetics: the study of beauty; sometimes used for the formal study of artistic judgment.

agnostic: one who neither believes in god nor claims that god does not exist, but instead emphasizes that the existence and nature of god are unknown.

allegory: typically a symbolic tale or image, the meanings of which are hidden behind the literal, face-value interpretation.

altruism: possessing a concern for other beings over and above one's personal welfare.

ancestor worship: religious actions that are concerned with venerating or appeasing spirits of dead relatives.

animism: belief that features of the natural world, such as particular plants, lakes, mountains, animals, persons, and such, are abodes of spirits or souls.

anthropology: (*anthropos*—human being + *logos*—study); social science that concerns itself with the study of human beings; now primarily focussed on social organization and culture.

anthropomorphic: representation of gods with human characteristics or form.

anthropotheism: belief that gods are merely humans who have been elevated to divine status.

apeiron: Greek term for a single, undifferentiated, and subtle essence, which is the source of all things, and to which all things return.

apocalyptic: concerning the end of the world, including prophesies of catastrophic destruction; sometimes also concerns final judgment.

apocrypha: mostly texts, whose authenticity is in doubt.

apologetics: a branch of theology that seeks to justify the doctrines of a particular faith through formal arguments.

apologist: defender or advocate for a particular religious tradition, belief, or view.

apostasy: rejection of the faith that one once held.

appease: to pacify, propitiate, relieve, or satisfy; often refers to sacrifice, offerings, praise, and rituals designed to pacify a god or spirit in order to avoid harm.

archetype: in Jungian psychology, a mental image and universal prototype inherited from ancient humans and found in the collective unconscious.

asceticism: the practice of self-denial and austerity; often a feature of disciplines concerned with the purification of one's spirit or soul.

atheist: one who does not believe in the existence of any supernatural divine entity.

autochthonous: see indigenous.

avatar: manifestation or incarnation of a deity, especially in Hinduism.

biological evolution: well-documented scientific theory that life differentiates through time, based in part on principles of adaptation to the environment and success in reproduction.

blasphemy: irreverent or contemptuous act or statement directed toward a deity or sacred space or rite.

bracketing: see *epoché.*

Buddhism: ethical and philosophical system developed from the teachings of Siddhartha Gautama, known as the Buddha (Awakened One); based on moral and contemplative practices.

canon: core collection of scriptures designated by a religious group as legitimate or authoritative.

capitalism: economic and social system based on the private ownership of wealth, property, material goods, and other capital, as well as the means of its production and distribution, which is related to the free market, competition, and the profit motive.

Cartesianism: philosophical doctrine of René Descartes, according to which reason is the source and test of knowledge, in contrast to the focus on experience in empiricism.

Catholic: literally "universal"; typically used for the Roman branch of Christianity, in distinction from the Greek or Eastern Orthodox and Protestant branches that separated from it.

celibacy: principle of abstaining from sexual intercourse or even any sexual activity, generally motivated by spiritual concerns.

charisma: power, charm, talent, appeal that inspires devotion in others; can be understood as divinely given.

Christianity: beliefs and practices of followers of Jesus of Nazareth, who hold him to be the sole son of God; grounded in the principle of love.

cognitive science: study of the mind's processes; cognitive studies of religion draw from a wide range of psychological, anthropological, and other approaches, including focus on the evolutionary interplay among biological, social, and cultural components that shape and perpetuate mental processes.

communism: typically applied to a political philosophy of more extreme than moderate sharing of resources by a society for the welfare of all.

communitas: word popularized by American anthropologist Victor Turner to refer to feelings of connection and solidarity with a group.

comparativist: a person or approach that seeks to analyze similarities (and differences) between two objects of study; in religious studies, it often applies to approaches that seek out common themes across different religious traditions.

Confucianism: moral and ethical approach to life based on the teachings of the Chinese scholar Confucius (also known as Kongzi/K'ungFu-tzu); grounded in maintaining orderly relationships through the cultivation of human virtues.

contemporary: living at the same time, e.g. Karl Barth was a contemporary of Paul Tillich; occurring in the present, e.g. contemporary attitudes.

cosmology: a branch of philosophy and subset of metaphysics that deals with the origin (cosmogony) and nature of the cosmos; now mostly under the disciplines of science in the West.

creationism: belief that the universe, earth, humans, and other living organisms were created by divine act rather than natural processes; typically refers to the literal truth of a biblical account of creation in opposition to evolution.

creed: formal statement of belief, e.g. Nicene Creed in Christianity.

cult: sect; veneration directed at a person or object; commonly used as a pejorative term for someone else's religious group, which is seen to be strange or sinister.

culture: the collectively shared beliefs, activities, and values of a social group.

damnation: the notion of being condemned to some terrible punishment, often for a religious failing, and often for eternity.

dao: term in East Asian religions for "way" or "path" with reference to a religious and philosophical worldview and guide to a meaningful and harmonious life; in Daoism, it can be understood as a generative source as well as an ongoing natural pattern; also written as *tao.*

Daoism: philosophy, beliefs, and rites grounded on a profound relationship to the mysterious workings of nature; also written as Taoism.

darshana: Sanskrit term for viewpoint, perspective, or worldview; typically applied to religious/philosophical systems, such as Buddhism, Jainism, Vedanta, or Yoga.

deism: belief in a supreme being, typically a creator deity, who no longer intervenes in the functions of the universe; the movement arose in the seventeenth century with an emphasis on reason as opposed to beliefs in supernatural events and relationships with divine entities.

didactic: instructive; intended to teach a moral lesson; can be used in a pejorative sense to imply a patronizing tone.

discipline: any branch of knowledge or body of teachings.

discursive: related to reasoning and rational argumentation, as opposed to intuition.

divination: seeking guidance from supernatural sources (e.g. gods or spirits), often with the aid of some material medium (e.g. person or instrument).

dogma: religious doctrine or other principles that authorities insist is incontrovertibly true.

dogmatism: assertion that only one's own views, including religious doctrine, are true.

dualism: division into two opposite aspects, such as good and evil; also applied to worldviews that are not monistic and thus see reality as made up of more than one fundamental component (e.g. God and the creation).

Eastern religions: term applied primarily to Hinduism, Jainism, Sikhism, Buddhism, Confucianism, Daoism, and Shinto.

eclectic: bringing together various ideas, practices, styles, or aesthetics from diverse sources.

empirical: dealing with evidence gathered by the senses, as through experimental observation; often set in contrast with knowledge obtained through theorizing.

enlightenment: term used as equivalent to the Hindu concept of *moksha*, or the Buddhist notion of *nirvana*, and referring to freedom from ignorance or illusions concerning the nature of the self and reality.

Enlightenment, the: eighteenth-century intellectual movement in the West that emphasized the use of reason in the pursuit of truth, as it critiqued irrational beliefs and practices.

epiphany: sudden revelation or understanding; originates with the sense of the sudden appearance of a god (see theophany) or muse, which is both startling and inspiring; now used more for any sudden insight or comprehension; there is also a Christian festival of this name.

epistemology: branch of philosophy and subset of metaphysics concerning the source and nature of knowledge.

epoché: phenomenological "bracketing" in which suspension of one's own beliefs and an openness that neither confirms nor denies truth claims assist one in empathetically engaging with another's worldview.

eschatology: the study of conceptions of end-times (*eschaton*); also used in particular religious traditions to refer to the end-time doctrines.

esoteric: used to describe inner or secret religious knowledge or rites reserved for initiated groups, which require guidance from a master; hidden from or dangerous to the non-initiate; counter to exoteric.

ethics: branch of philosophy dealing with evaluating behaviour on a scale based on conceptions of right and wrong and the application of ethical theories to moral problems.

evangelical: pertaining to the spreading of the Christian gospel; often characterized by fervent zeal.

evolution: development and diversification through time; used especially for living organisms—see biological evolution—but also applied to societies, etc.

excommunication: a punishment in which a member is excluded from a religious community and some of its privileges.

exegesis: explanation and interpretation of a text; especially the scholarly and critical explication of scripture.

existentialism: philosophical approach that is grounded in the experience of the individual human being's encounter with reality, which is ultimately governed by personally meaningful choices made in the face of a fundamentally meaningless or irrational world.

exorcism: religious ritual to expel demons or spirits from a person or place.

exoteric: outer religious rites, readings, and knowledge accessible to all.

extant: still in existence, surviving; remaining (e.g. most monks argue that there is no extant lineage of fully ordained Theravada nuns).

fatalism: belief that one's fate is predetermined or predestined and that humans are powerless to change their fate.

feminism: primarily social and intellectual movement that strives for equality of the sexes, typically through the removal of women's oppression.

fieldwork: term generally used to indicate work conducted away from one's home-base; for anthropologists, this usually involves the method of "participant observation."

functionalism: theoretical approach in the social sciences which is centered on revealing the interdependent roles played by facets within a society or culture and how these operate (i.e. their function) in maintaining the character of the whole.

fundamentalism: religious orientation grounded in an attempt to return to fundamental or core beliefs and practices in a tradition; often associated with rigid, literal, and narrow interpretations based on readings of primary scriptures.

Gnosticism: Western religious and philosophical movement during the pre- and early Christian period that emphasized the need to attain a special knowledge (*gnosis*) for salvation from ignorance and mortality.

grace: a spiritual essence, typically conveyed by a divine power.

guru: advanced spiritual teacher, often capable of granting initiations; associated with Asian traditions, especially Hinduism, but now used more generically for a sage or expert.

henotheism: worship of one god without denying the existence of other deities.

heresy: beliefs or practices judged by authorities to be against orthodoxy.

hermeneutics: interpretation.

hierophany: appearance of the sacred; broader than theophany (appearance of a god); used by Eliade for his emphasis on manifestations of the sacred as distinct from the profane.

Hinduism: constellation of beliefs and practices that includes acceptance of the scriptural authority of the Vedas and the class/caste system; religion of the majority of the populace in South Asia.

humanism: a philosophical movement or doctrine holding that humans can resolve their problems, build societies, and establish values and morals without reference to god.

humanities: disciplines concerned with the self-expression of human beings; typically includes language and literature, history, philosophy, and the arts.

icon: image or likeness; painting, statue, or other visual representation of the sacred.

iconoclasm: opposition to the use of religious images; Islam, for example, is iconoclastic with regard to depicting Allah or Muhammad.

immediate: experience or knowledge received directly or intuitively without the mediating role of rational, discursive thought.

imminent: about to happen; near; of this world as opposed to transcendent.

indigenous: native; already existing locally rather than imported from abroad.

individuation: for Jung, the important coming together of the complementary conscious and unconscious aspects of the self.

ineffable: beyond words and description; inexpressible because words are inadequate or because uttering a name or description is forbidden.

insider: term used in religious studies to refer to adherents of a particular religious tradition.

intelligent design: a revamped form of creationism that argues the universe provides evidence of a guiding intelligent entity more consistent with a divine designer than with the natural selection of evolution.

irreducibility: refers to a reluctance or inability to simplify something out of concern for losing an essential quality, or distorting it beyond meaningful recognition in order to fit a model.

Islam: beliefs and practices based on the message transmitted by the prophet Muhammad and preserved in the Qur'an; characterized by strict monotheism.

Jainism: ethical and philosophical system grounded in the teachings of Vardhamana Mahavira, known as the Jina (Conqueror); based on moral and contemplative practices.

Judaism: beliefs and practices of the Jews, a people who follow the teachings contained in the Hebrew Bible (Tanakh); monotheistic; centred on maintaining a contractual agreement (covenant) with God.

laity/lay person: ordinary person; non-ordained religious adherent (i.e. not a monk, nun, renunciant, or religious specialist).

lama: honorific title of an accomplished Tibetan Buddhist spiritual leader; some lamas known as *tulkus* are thought to be able to control their rebirth and continue to occupy high religious office, such as the Dalai Lama.

liminal: (*limen*—threshold); term popularized by the American anthropologist Victor Turner, which refers to a transition period or state, often characterized by the absence of structures that sandwich it.

literalist: one who interprets the content of texts at their face value, rather than discerning other meanings (e.g. symbolic, metaphoric, allegorical, hyperbolic) within them.

liturgy: formal prescriptions typically for the performance of religious rituals.

logical positivism: rejects metaphysics and restricts philosophical problems to those that can be solved through logical analysis.

logos: Greek for "word"; in Christianity it is described as a principle of absolute, divine reason and order that is embodied in Jesus Christ.

magic: activities involving the manipulation of features of reality that are hidden to the non-practitioner, and which thus appear mysterious or miraculous.

mandala: geometrical cosmic map, especially in Tantric Buddhism and Hinduism.

martyrdom: condition of willingness to suffer or die for one's religious beliefs; derived from the Greek term for "witness."

Marxism: political and economic philosophy based on the teachings of Karl Marx with an emphasis on class struggle and economic constraints on history and culture; typically socialist or communist, as opposed to capitalist.

matriarchy: a society dominated by women.

mediate: to intervene, link, or convey; as opposed to "immediate."

medium: person who claims to communicate with spirits or through whom spirits communicate and are consulted.

messianic: relating to a messiah, or savior; especially the Messiah prophesied in the Old Testament to deliver the Jewish nation, or Jesus, who is understood by Christians to be the promised Messiah and savior of humankind.

metanoetic: "beyond noetic"; mystical experience, for example, is often described as a deep insight into truth and reality beyond the reach of rational, discursive, mental activity and intellect to which "noetic" is related.

metaphysics: "beyond physics"; branch of philosophy that typically includes cosmology, ontology, and epistemology; it probes into questions concerning the ultimate nature of existence.

methodology: system of methods used within a given discipline or area of study.

milieu: the social environment, context, setting, or backdrop.

millenarianism: believing in a coming golden age of peace—often with a sense that this age is imminent or, at least, inevitable; sometimes used for a group seeking radical change to solve current societal problems; often used for the Christian notion of a future 1,000-year period of Christ's reign.

mimetic desire: the motive force that concerns desiring that which others desire; for René Girard, the origins of violence and the sacred are linked to this desire.

mind-brain: refers to the multiple neuro-cognitive systems responsible for how we understand reality, and act in various settings and situations.

missionary: one who typically leaves home for a distant place with the intention of converting others to a particular set of beliefs, often through teachings and charitable deeds.

modernism: primarily intellectual and aesthetic movement of the late nineteenth to early twentieth century that reacted against tradition by promoting change and novelty.

moksha: Sanskrit term primarily found in Hinduism to refer to release from the bondage of ignorance, illusion, and the cycles of rebirth.

monastic: a monk or nun living in solitude or religious community; relating to these renunciants, their monastery, or way of life.

monism: belief in "oneness"; notion that there is ultimately only one substance or essence, and no distinction between god and the world or matter and mind.

monk: male monastic; often living under religious vows along with other men.

monotheism: belief in the existence of a single god (i.e. God); Islam is a monotheistic religion.

morality: a code of virtuous conduct based on accepted notions of right and wrong.

mysticism: generally applied to a religious approach entailing a direct (i.e. unmediated) personal engagement with a supernatural principle or deity.

myth: typically ancient story involving supernatural events and beings, such as deities and heroes, believed to be true by particular communities.

mythology: collection of traditional stories believed by some to be true and pertaining to past events that involve supernatural deeds, events, or persons, such as deities, spirits, or heroic human beings.

neurotheology: term designating the seemingly unlikely pairing of brain science and theology in Andrew Newberg's neuroimaging studies that correlate brain activity with intense prayer, meditation, or visualization.

New Age: idealized conception of an emerging contemporary period, characterized by a disparate set of beliefs and practices arising from the counter-culture movement of the 1960s; concerned with body, mind, and spirit development and self-realization through an eclectic fusion of ideas and activities drawn from both contemporary and traditional (often Eastern) spiritual teachings.

nirvana: Sanskrit term primarily found in Buddhism (and Jainism) that refers to the extinguishing of sorrow derived from illusions and ignorance.

noetic: relating to mental activity or the intellect.

NOMA: acronym for "non-overlapping magisterial," which maintains that there are non-overlapping spheres of expertise separating the domain of scientists from that of theologians.

non-duality: neither dualism nor monism; typical of East Asian religious ideas of complementariness, such as yin and yang, but resists seeing true opposition or separateness between these or any other pairings (e.g. imminent-transcendent, earth-heaven, ordinary world-enlightenment).

numinous: referring to the divine, spiritual, mysterious, transcendent, or sacred power.

nun: female monastic; often living under religious vows with other women.

Occam's Razor: principle in philosophy and science that when choosing among suitable explanations for an unknown phenomenon, the one with the least assumptions is to be preferred; also known as Ockham's Razor.

omnipotent: having all powers; a commonly assigned attribute of God.

omniscience: having all knowledge; a commonly assigned attribute of God.

ontology: a branch of philosophy and subset of metaphysics that deals with the nature of existence or being.

oracle: religious specialist functioning as a medium communicating with gods or spirits, or the message derived from this or other forms of divination.

ordination: ceremony or ritual act that confers special religious status on someone who has left lay life for a more full commitment to religious vows and pursuits.

orthodoxy: "correct belief"; essential beliefs and practices; opposite of heresy.

orthopraxy: "correct action/practice"; emphasized in traditions where practice is more central than belief; e.g. Hinduism and many other Asian traditions.

outsider: term used in religious studies to refer to one who does not belong to a religious tradition under examination.

pagan: pejorative term for an adherent of polytheism, animism, or any religion other than Christianity—or other than Western monotheistic traditions more generally; now increasingly value-neutral label for an adherent of neo-paganism or other nature religion.

panentheism: doctrine that God permeates every aspect of the entire creation but is simultaneously beyond it.

pantheism: doctrine that the entire universe collectively is divine, or is God; thus there is no God distinct from the creation.

pantheon: full assembly of deities in a religion, e.g. the many Greek gods and goddesses or the Daoist pantheon.

parable: story designed to teach a lesson or reinforce a moral; similar to allegory, but the characters are not symbols as with an allegory.

paradigm: overarching set of values, principles, and perspectives through which a cultural group approaches or understands reality; it serves as a sort of template that shapes or defines their understanding.

patriarchy: a society dominated by men.

Patristic Era: period dominated by the Church fathers, patriarchs (i.e. influential male figures) whose theological ideas shaped Christian doctrine for several centuries after the death of Jesus; typically extends until about the eighth century, but certain Christian groups regard it as longer, or even ongoing.

pejorative: having a negative connotation; expressing contempt or disapproval.

periodization: categorization scheme to characterize a relatively large block of time by some overly simplified unifying feature (e.g. Jurassic Age, medieval period, the Renaissance).

phenomena: the objects of a person's perceptions or items of reality as they are perceived by a person's senses or mind.

phenomenology: twentieth-century philosophical movement, spearheaded by Edmund Husserl, which emphasizes the study of human consciousness through the subjective experience of its interaction with items (i.e. phenomena) of reality.

philology: (*philos*—love + *logos*—word); the formal study of language, including its origins, grammatical structures, and intended meanings; often narrowly applied to the study of texts in ancient languages.

philosophy: (*philia*— love + *sophia*—wisdom); systematic pursuit of wisdom; in the West, it is routinely applied to approaches that primarily use reason in this endeavour.

pilgrimage: a religious journey, entailing some ordeal, to one or more sacred sites.

polemics: the practice of argumentation and refutation of an opponent's opinions, particularly in theological and philosophical writings.

polytheism: belief in the existence of more than one deity (gods or goddesses).

postmodernism: primarily intellectual and aesthetic movement of the late twentieth and early twenty-first centuries that developed from modernism; fundamentally characterized by the uncovering of implicit assumptions and hidden structures in human creations for the sake of scrutiny; rejects notions of an objective reality or single, dominant perspective.

predestination: religious concept that disallows free will and asserts that events are fixed to happen in a certain way; for John Calvin this refers to the idea that God determined the destiny of the entire universe and everything in it even before creation.

priest: religious official; typically sanctioned to perform rituals.

profane: not sacred; worldly; everyday or ordinary.

prophet: person who makes proclamations about the will, disposition, or plans of the divine; these can include predictions of what will happen or forecasts of what may happen unless people change their errant ways (e.g. the prophets of the Old Testament).

propitiate: sacrifice or other means to pacify or please gods and spirits; see appease.

proselyte: a convert from another religious tradition.

proselytize: active attempt to convert others to a particular belief.

Protestant: one of many branches of Christianity that developed in protest against the Western Roman Catholic Church during the Reformation.

purity: religiously clean state not in danger of polluting the sacred.

quantum mechanics: branch of physics that uses statistical mathematics to explain the nature and behaviour of reality at the atomic and sub-atomic levels.

quietism: refers to religious traditions and practices that emphasize meditation, mental tranquility, devotional contemplation, and some forms of mysticism.

redemption: concept prevalent in Christian doctrines, that the death of Jesus of Nazareth paid the ransom necessary to deliver (i.e. redeem) humanity from the penalties of its sinful condition.

reductionism: the intellectual tendency to explain away the complexities of a phenomenon being examined, by oversimplifying its causes or nature.

reincarnation: term for a soul being reborn into another body after death; in Buddhism "rebirth" is a more accurate term due to its doctrine of *anatman*, no soul; see also transmigration.

religion: a person or group's collective of beliefs, values, and activities concerning their relationship with their conceptions of ultimate reality.

religionist: students or scholars of the discipline of religious studies; in older usage someone deeply committed to a particular faith.

Religionswissenschaft: German term for "science of religion."

Renaissance: "rebirth"; post-medieval (c. fourteenth- to early seventeenth-century) movement in the West that ushered in a revival of creativity, especially in the arts, music, and literature, inspired by access to classical Greek and Roman literature.

renunciant: a religious practitioner who renounces ordinary, secular, lay life in the pursuit of religion; could be living a solitary ascetic existence or in a religious community.

revelation: disclosure of truth or knowledge from a divine source.

rites of passage: rituals that mark a change in status, e.g. birth, puberty, marriage, and death.

ritual: series of traditional actions deemed to be necessary, meaningful, or appropriate in particular situational contexts.

sacrament: term typically used in Christian traditions to refer to rites that serve as an outward and visible sign of an invisible process deemed to be sacred, such as the receipt of grace.

sacred: set apart and regarded as worthy of special attention or veneration.

sacrifice: ritual offering (e.g. slaughtered animal, food or drink, valued possession) directed to gods or spirits to thank, propitiate, or exchange for guidance or blessing.

sacrilege: intentional violation of a sacred site or object.

saint: one of the terms for a revered and highly accomplished religious person.

sanctuary: protected or sacred space, such as a church or temple.

salvation: the state of being saved; varying notion in many religions that human beings need to be safely delivered from the perils they face now or in an after-life.

scholasticism: movement of philosophical theology in the West, originating as early as the ninth century CE and enduring until the seventeenth century CE; attempted to validate religious teachings with rational philosophical methods.

science: any organized body of knowledge gained through experience; in modern usage it refers to knowledge derived through the application of the "scientific method."

scientific method: orderly approach to confronting a question concerning the functioning of the natural world: involving formulating hypothetical solutions, devising experiments to test the hypotheses, observing the experimental tests, and reaching conclusions based on rational analyses of the data collected.

scientism: generally a pejorative term referring to the inappropriate application of the methods and values of the scientific method to areas of human activity, often in an attempt to grant these the status that accompanies science, or alternatively, to demean their value as unscientific.

scripture: religious literature of a particular community, generally deemed sacred and originating from some supernatural source; often originally orally transmitted before being committed to writing.

sect: term used for a religious group or school within the larger tradition: for example, Zen is a sect of Buddhism and Rinzai is a sect within Zen; can also have pejorative connotations of a heretical or dangerous subgroup.

sectarian: refers to the views or identity of a particular sect and reinforces the differentiation between groups; can include a sense of narrow-minded adherence to one group or actions taken on behalf of that group.

secular: term used to indicate anything that is of a worldly, rather than spiritual, nature.

secularization: sociological term for a process through which something loses its spiritual value and becomes more worldly.

seminal: person, text, event, or idea that significantly influenced later developments.

semiotics: systematic study of signs and symbols.

shaman: specialist in supernatural affairs who typically mediates between the worldly and otherworldly realms; often found in small-scale societies.

Shinto: ritual-based tradition, with political overtones, indigenous to the islands of Japan, centered on the appeasement of spirits known as *kami.*

Sikhism: tradition primarily based on the moral and religious instructions contained within a revered book, the *Guru Granth Sahib*, which includes the teachings of ten teachers (*gurus*), the first of whom was the founder, Guru Nanak.

skeptic: a person who doubts and questions accepted opinions, religious beliefs, or even the possibility of knowledge in some sphere.

socialism: typically a political philosophy in which resources are moderately shared by members of a society for the welfare of all.

society: any group of people who share some cohesive feature.

somatic: relating to the body.

soteriology: the study of conceptions of salvation (being saved); often used to refer to the doctrines of salvation in particular religious traditions.

soul: the essential, life-giving principle within living beings, often believed to endure after death of the physical body; frequently thought of as immortal and linked to the moral imperatives of a religion.

spirit: a generally incorporeal supernatural being; one's essential being or animating, life-giving principle.

spiritualism: beliefs and practices consistent with the notion that spirits of the dead can communicate with the living.

structuralism: theoretical approach in the social sciences concerned with uncovering the fundamental structures within an object of study, such as a myth; these structures often involve embedded binary oppositions, such as good/evil, nature/culture, or sacred/profane.

sui generis: of its own kind; unique; irreducible to other categories.

supernatural: something that seems beyond the natural order of reality.

syncretism: merging of different religions or elements of different religious traditions.

taboo: from Polynesian *tapu* or *tabu;* refers to a strong social prohibition, the breaking of which generally entails being susceptible to punishment, delivered either by the social group, or from some divine agency.

tao/**Taoism:**   see *dao* and Daoism.

Tantra: typically secret body of beliefs and practices of Eastern origin, concerned with self-realization mostly through body–mind ritual activities centred on the transcendence of dualities, symbolically understood as male and female principles.

teleology: the study of the purposes, goals, or ends (Greek: *telos*); also used to refer to the mediate and ultimate objectives in religious systems and practices.

thaumaturge: wonder worker; performer of miracles or magic.

theism: belief in the existence of a deity or god.

theocracy: "god + rule": government where religious officials rule in god's name.

theodicy: (*theos*—god + *dike*—justice): branch of theology that seeks to justify the existence of evil and injustice in a world presided over by a good and just deity.

theology: (*theos*—god + *logos*—study): intellectual reflections on the nature of the divine; typically done within the framework of a religious tradition's accepted beliefs.

theophany: appearance or manifestation of a god, see also the broader term, hierophany.

totemism: a cluster of beliefs and activities centered upon a perceived relationship between a person or group (often kin) and an entity, such as a plant or animal.

transcendent: beyond or above the ordinary; apart from and beyond the limitations of the material world, such as the power or realm of the divine.

transmigration: see reincarnation; this term is slightly more broad in its sense of a soul or spirit of some type moving from one existence to the next; includes movement up and down a hierarchy of beings (e.g. levels of hell dwellers, ghosts, animals, humans, and gods common to many Asian cosmologies).

triumphalism: attitude that one's religion is superior to other beliefs and traditions.

utilitarianism: theory in which ethics are defined by the effects of actions; actions are deemed right if they are useful or beneficial to the happiness and well-being of a majority.

Verstehen: German for "understanding"; coined by the sociologist Max Weber to point to the need to interpret social actions and explanations.

vitalism: belief in a vital force upon which all life depends.

Western religions: term applied primarily to Judaism, Christianity, and Islam; also known as the Abrahamic religious traditions, since they all hold Abraham as a founding father.

Wicca: modern, nature-based religious movement loosely linked to pre-Christian pagan traditions of Western Europe.

worldview: the overarching perspective through which one understands reality; derived from the German term *Weltanschauung.*

yuga: Sanskrit term for long cycles of cosmic time, particularly in Hindu, Jain, and Buddhist worldviews.

Index

The Routledge Companion to the Study of Religion
Edited by Professor John R. Hinnells

'The editor should be congratulated for bringing together such connoisseurs and seasoned observers to guide us . . . the lack of triumphalism only adds to the lustre of the book.' – *Times Higher Education Suppliment*

'A companion in the very best sense of the word: it provides the reader with excellent guides and mentors to walk alongside on the path to understanding . . . The result is an intelligent, fair-minded, thorough, and cutting-edge exploration of the field of religious studies.' – *Wendy Doniger, Mircea Eliade Distinguished Service Professor of the History of Religions, University of Chicago USA*

The effective study of religion involves many disciplines and methods, from psychology to sociology, and from textual analysis to case studies in the field. It also requires an awareness of key thematic issues such as gender, science, fundamentalism, ritual, mysticism, and new religious movements.

Containing everything needed for a full understanding of theory and methods in religious studies, *The Routledge Companion to the Study of Religion*:

- surveys the history of religious studies and the key disciplinary approaches
- shows how to apply theories and methods to practical study
- highlights contemporary issues such as globalization, diaspora and politics
- explains why the study of religion is relevant in today's world

Beginning by explaining the most important methodological approaches to religion, including psychology, philosophy, anthropology and comparative study, the text then moves on to explore a wide variety of critical issues. Written entirely by renowned international specialists, and using clear and accessible language throughout, it is the perfect guide to the problems and questions found in exams and on courses.

ISBN13: 978–0–415–33310–8 (hbk)
ISBN13: 978–0–415–33311–5 (pbk)
ISBN13: 978–0–203–41269–5 (ebk)